Please renew/return this item by the last date shown.

So that your telephone call is charged at local rate,
please call the numbers as set out below:

	From Area codes 01923 or 0208:	From the rest of Herts:
Renewals:	01923 471373	01438 737373
Enquiries:	01923 471333	01438 737333
Minicom:	01923 471599	01438 737599

L32b

D1610113

KG
200
THE TRUE STORY

P. W. Stahl

KG 200

THE TRUE STORY

JANE'S

LONDON · NEW YORK · SYDNEY

First published in 1979 by Motorbuch-Verlag, Stuttgart, as *Geheimgeschwader KG 200: die Wahrheit nach über 30 Jahren* © Motorbuch-Verlag, Stuttgart.

This English translation copyright © 1981 Jane's Publishing Company Limited. All rights reserved.

First published in the United Kingdom in 1981 by
Jane's Publishing Company Limited
238 City Road, London EC1V 2PU

ISBN 0 7106 0096 8

First published in the United States of America in 1981 by
Jane's Publishing Incorporated
730 Fifth Avenue
New York
N.Y. 10019

ISBN 0 531 03729 0

Computer typesetting by Method Limited
Woodford Green, Essex

Printed in the United Kingdom by
Biddles Ltd, Guildford, Surrey

Contents

Translated and edited by Alex Vanags-Baginskis
with the help of his colleagues at Jane's Publishing Company.

Author's note:

My book *Bomber Pilot from the Polar Sea to Sahara** ended with the words: 'And so, all of a sudden, I belonged to KG 200. But that is another story'.
This is that other story.

*P.W. Stahl *Kampfflieger zwischen Eismeer und Sahara* (Motorbuch Verlag Stuttgart, 1972).

1. Transfer to *Olga*

The war was already in its sixth year. The Luftwaffe bomber arm in which I had long served had reached a very low point, and its units had been grounded one by one – in so far as they had not already simply been broken up and disbanded altogether.

The massed Anglo-American air raids now meant that precious aviation fuel was only available for the air defence of the Reich. The supply of aircraft, spare parts, and fuel had succumbed to these raids, and everywhere surplus Luftwaffe personnel were being incorporated into the front-line troops of the Army. Experienced, highly decorated aircrews found themselves overnight fighting as infantry on the Eastern Front.

At this time, early in October 1944, an order arrived at my unit KG 30 ordering all *Kommodore, Gruppenkomandeure und Staffel-kapitäne* to report to Rosenborn in Silesia for retraining as fighter pilots. There we met other officers from KG 6, KG 27 and KG 55 who had been earmarked for the same tasks as we were. (See facsimile reproduction of this reorganisation order in Appendix 1). Then, near the end of training we were suddenly ordered to Berlin where the *Reichsmarschall* wanted to see us personally.

What happened there throws some light on the background of this strange story. The fighter pilots had completely lost their standing in Göring's eyes and now we ex-bomber men were supposed to accomplish what 'those cowards' had been unable to do, to prevent the British and Americans carrying out their devastating raids as they pleased on targets in the Reich. It was really disgraceful to see how Göring laid into and insulted the fighter pilots in front of us, in the same breath expressing his expectation that we would 'sweep the skies over Germany clear again'.

We returned to Rosenborn in a fairly uneasy frame of mind. A few days later General Peltz, the General of Bombers, appeared to inform us that we would shortly be discharged from his sphere of authority. I knew him from the early days of the war when he was still a *Staffelkapitän* in a bomber *Geschwader*, and asked him frankly what he thought of the whole business. Peltz replied without hesitation:

'Nothing, absolutely nothing!'

It was then that I heard clearly for the first time from someone in high authority that the Luftwaffe was in a hopeless situation and that it was foolish even to think of a 'new aerial superiority'. Oh yes, in southern Germany hundreds of brand new Me 262 jet fighters were standing about in the forests, the very 'wonder birds' that were destined for us. In actual fact however, nearly all of these machines were unserviceable because they lacked important parts produced in factories around Germany that simply could not be delivered because of the collapsed transport network. According to Peltz there was no longer any possibility of making these aircraft fit for operational service.

He then asked me if I would wish to serve in a different capacity, and I replied frankly that I had an uneasy feeling just thinking about having to play a fighter role after so many years of service as a bomber and Stuka pilot even before hearing what he had to say. To give us, bomber pilots without any fighter experience, the revolutionary Me 262 was against every tenet of reason. As far as I was concerned, if there was something else going, I was prepared to give up all this last-minute jet fighter nonsense.

And then Peltz put the cards on the table: Werner Baumbach, who in the meantime had become *Kommodore* of KG 200, had asked him to sound me out whether I would be willing to lead a special detachment within his *Geschwader*. Peltz himself could not tell me any details; all he knew was that it involved large aircraft on special long-range flights under difficult navigational conditions. That kind of task was right up my street and without further ado I said yes. My only request was that I would be allowed to take my own crew and a few more proven men from my *Staffel* with me, to which the general agreed at once.

The very next day, 3 November 1944, I found myself on a train to Berlin and after the usual difficulties and delays caused by Allied air raids, I finally arrived at Gatow airfield where the *Geschwader* HQ was based. An official report to the *Kommodore* was followed by a friendly greeting and a prolonged exchange of reminiscences with questions and counterquestions about mutual acquaintances. We had known each other for quite some time now and had a lot of things to talk about, but my new appointment came first. Baumbach thought that there would be time enough next day to go into the details about the organisation and tasks of the *Geschwader*. For the time being I was told only that I was intended as a successor to a commander of an operational detachment based at Frankfurt/Main that had the task of carrying out supply flights over the enemy-occupied parts of western Europe and into the North African area. It was essential apparently to drop agents by parachute into these areas.

Baumbach also wanted to leave my introduction to the other officers of his staff until the following day, in so far as I would not have met them already in the officers' mess the same evening. In any case, there would be some old acquaintances among them.

I left Baumbach's office in a thoughtful frame of mind.

That evening in the officers' mess was marked by that almost euphoric fatalism that was typical of the situation at that time. As if nothing untoward had happened, the officers sat around in small groups in the elegant tranquility of the mess as if it was peacetime. They talked about trivia and matters of no consequence, while others played cards. I could hardly believe my eyes; the war and all its horrors could have been far away. Only Baumbach alone in this make-believe world seemed concerned about the critical situation and its possible consequences for KG 200, and brought it up in his conversation.

The *Geschwader* still disposed of a considerable and intact transport capacity – he mentioned two BV 222s, the largest flying boats in the world at that time, and then a whole list of aircraft types such as the Ju 252, Ju 90, Ju 290, Ju 188, He 111, various cargo gliders and some captured and rebuilt B-24 Liberator and B-17 Flying Fortress four-engined bombers. However, the only operations still under consideration were measures to be taken following the probable total collapse. Thus for instance the task of agents dropped into enemy territory was now to be to a lesser extent the gathering of military information but rather preparing for activities following an armistice. Of course, all details were highly secret. Nobody talked about these operations, not even among the aircrews in the mess. Baumbach mentioned all this in such a matter-of-fact voice that one was hard put to realize the stark implications of what he was saying. It was the first time I had heard someone in authority talk about 'total collapse' and of planning for postwar activities. Could the situation really be so bad?

Looking around the mess I noticed a group of young officers who seemed to hold themselves apart from the others. When I mentioned this to Baumbach he replied briefly that these were the so-called 'self-sacrificers'. It was only later that I found out more details about these men, members of KG 200.

3

The evening in the officers' mess gradually became louder and progressively livelier. I stayed on only a short while longer and then I made my excuses and left. After all, it takes some time to feel at home among mostly strange people, especially under these circumstances.

Before I left, Baumbach asked me to be ready for my introduction to duties and instructions the following day.

My new task was officially explained to me next morning: I was to take over command of Detachment *Olga* at Frankfurt/Main. The *Geschwader* had a number of such independent units operating on the Western and Eastern Fronts, all of them engaged in depositing people and material behind the enemy lines. The operational area allocated to Detachment *Olga* was western Europe and included England, Ireland and Iceland. It was intended shortly to disband Detachment *Carmen*, then still operating from northern Italy, with *Olga* also taking over its present tasks, which included operations over southern Italy and the North African area.

I was given only a superficial, rough summary regarding the organisation in general and the activities of the *Geschwader* in particular; in fact, there was hardly enough time to explain in detail all the tasks awaiting me at *Olga*.

I received all these instructions in the *Geschwader* liaison officer's room, and it soon became clear to me that this man really had a job on his hands. He was empowered to receive orders from such places as the RSHA (*Reichssicherheitshauptamt der SS*, the State Main Security Office of the SS), the *Abwehr* and other authorities, and was responsible for their subsequent actions. Although after the 'Canaris case'* Military Intelligence had been integrated into the RSHA, it still led an individual existence to some degree that was reflected in the different orders and methods used by the *Abwehr* people and the SD. And this *Oberstleutnant* had to decide if any given task could be carried out and which detachment should be commissioned to do so.

It was an unenviable task. On the one hand he was snowed under with requests for various transport operations, and on the other the available transport capacity was constantly sinking due to the heavy losses of crews and aircraft. But the biggest problem of all was that the powers-that-be seemed to have hardly any idea about the possibilities and limitations of such flying operations. How else could one explain

---

*Admiral Canaris, Chief of the *Abwehr*, had been implicated in the July 1944 plot against Hitler. He was shot in April 1945.

4

for example an order passed on to the *Geschwader* requesting that three agents should be landed by parachute at night on a grassy patch not bigger than a football field in the centre of Paris! The originators of this order were really under the impression that this would entail less danger of discovery than landing by parachute in an open field far away from inhabited places – and, apart from that, it would of course save the agents a long and difficult march. . . .

However, things became clear to me very soon afterwards. In this case the intention was to make a night landing in southern France, north of Montpelier. The selected field was big enough for landing a big transport aircraft and a nocturnal take-off after discharging its cargo. This operation was of the highest priority, of the most secret nature, and everything had already been settled, except the matter of considering the feasibility of its execution. I was asked straight out what I thought about it and if, in case of any doubts, I would be ready to carry out the flight myself.

Without knowing more details – at least as far as the flight itself was concerned – I had to decline. But it needed only one telephone call for two men in civilian clothes to appear on our doorstep half an hour later. One of them introduced himself as a German *Hauptmann* and the other a French Air Force lieutenant, and still a German POW at that. Apparently the *Hauptmann* had been an interpreter attached to the staff of General de Gaulle until a short while ago, where he had clandestinely set up an operation in southern France. He could not tell me more, only that it was urgently needed to supply the already existing and still developing organisation with people, material and money. The French Air Force lieutenant was supposed to become an important figure of this 'resistance' movement.

The course of this operation was planned as follows: the French lieutenant would be dropped by parachute over a site which he had proposed as a landing field for future supply flights. In addition to provisions he would be supplied with equipment to build up his own hideout, as well as a radio set with spare batteries. This load was to be dropped, attached to another parachute, simultaneously with the French officer.

The selected hideout was ostensibly quite safe from discovery if the dropping point was not missed by more than one kilometre and the transport aircraft did not behave suspiciously, such as giving itself away by a change in engine noise. After the successful execution of this first step the French lieutenant was to contact his political friends and

5

then report by radio after a predetermined period of time. His own base was only intended to fulfil the functions of a liaison and supply post but his tasks also included fixing and preparation of the landing field for supply aircraft.

Judging by the map the selected landing place seemed big enough and in the right position to serve as such without any special preparations. It was said to have been used in pre-war days by the *Armée de l'Air* as a training field for non-airfield landings, a place that was known as an *E-Hafen* in Luftwaffe service. Wide stretches of the surrounding countryside were only thinly inhabited or without any settlements, and it seemed quite possible to make a landing unnoticed. For navigation and 'homing' on the field the crew would have to make do with a couple of pocket torches on the ground. Yes, it could be done. But what if reality was quite different to that depicted on the map?

This is where the expert help of the French Air Force lieutenant came in: he would be set down in advance to check out the feasibility of the whole operation once more on the spot and make the final preparations. For my part, I listed the absolutely minimal essential requirements regarding the length of the landing field, freedom of obstacles and distances from the nearest inhabited places, roads, railway lines and so on.

Having done all this I could scarcely refrain from asking why was it so essential to actually land at all? After all, it was just as possible to carry out regular supply by parachute drops and this would minimize the danger of discovery. It was then explained to me then that it might also become necessary to fly people out, but it was mainly because the small ground organisation simply would not be able to quickly and carefully secure regular large-scale parachute drops. I could see their point.

Our conference was over and both mysterious guests took their leave.

'What do you think of it?' the *Oberstleutnant* liaison officer asked me. I told him about similar operations I had flown in northern Finland in September, October and November 1942. At that time our task was to supply a Finnish long-range reconnaissance unit that operated in Karelia, deep in the Soviet territory. The distances involved and the navigational problems were very similar to those of the planned operation in southern France, with the difference that the Finnish operation could be flown in daytime and no landings in the enemy hinterland were required.

'Apart from that nobody had to worry about a thing,' I continued, 'while in this case one has to consider how much one can trust the whole story at all, including the people involved. What guarantee is there that the aircraft won't be captured immediately after landing? After all, such things have happened before!'

Of course, the KG 200 liaison officer had expected these objections – in fact, he had considered the same possibilities himself. But he knew the source of these orders well enough to know that they could be trusted completely. Naturally, precautions had been taken to ensure the safety of the participants, but he did not go into any details. As he pointed out to me, 'It is still a long way before all the necessary preparations for this operation will have been completed. In the meantime, I should not lose any sleep over the whole business.'

Then he showed me a document listing all the operations to be carried out by *Olga* within the next month. It was a single sheet of size A4 paper with about 30 cryptic lines. Unless one knew the context nobody could make much sense out of such sentences as, for example: 'Armagnac; *3 Mann 3 + 20 kg ca 780 km zw. 20 u. 25. 10*'. Translated, it meant in this case that Operation *Armagnac* involved three men (each of whom would take 20 kg additional equipment), and that the flight would take place to some not yet defined area approximately 780 km from Frankfurt before the parachute drop. This particular operation had to be flown between 20 and 25 October.

The other entries on the list were in similar abbreviated code. In some cases the range figures quoted for penetration depth were such that I wondered what kind of aircraft type could achieve them. Women too were to be among our flying guests. There were also some entries listing only one man accompanied by 1000 kg and more load. Other operations were mere supply flights involving various droppable cargoes ranging from a few kilogrammes to half a lorry load.

Already a rough calculation made it clear that all this called for a considerable formation with a corresponding number of aircraft and personnel. Apart from that nobody seemed to have taken into account that weather could change from day to day and could easily upset all these plans. Otherwise how could they have simply ordered that the Armagnac operation must be carried out within a few days between 20 and 25 October? A lot of things could happen to affect a flight of some 800 km penetration depth! Surely, all the people concerned should have been aware by then that there was hardly a weather situation in

7

central Europe that could be guaranteed to remain uniform over such a large area – not to mention the difficulties of reliable weather forecasting and evaluation under wartime conditions.

The success or otherwise of such an operation depended on setting down people and other loads at night and in available ground visibility at an accurately fixed point. The target area had to be approached at low altitude and with engines throttled-back. And not only that: the drop zone had to be found right away, during the first approach flight, because experience had shown that prolonged searching turns in enemy hinterland immediately caused suspicion and endangered the whole operation.

I was also given to understand that *Olga* was months behind in fulfilling the allocated tasks. The main reason was of course that the detachment simply did not have sufficient aircraft and personnel, but the weather too had caused many delays lately. For one thing, all weather forecasts were rather sketchy due to the loss of forward stations beyond the Rhine and lack of regular weather reconnaissance flights.

Nevertheless, despite taking into consideration all these conditions, as well as the fact that in many cases the demands were far beyond the actual capabilities of the aircraft, one could clearly feel a certain reproach towards the operational command of *Olga*. As far as that was concerned I naturally could not and would not comment. After all, I had experienced myself throughout the war years that staffs would often issue peculiar and even senseless orders that were impossible to carry out. In this case too I had the impression that obviously impossible tasks had not been emphatically enough rejected but simply pushed further down the list. I was certain that this had nothing to do with the operational command of KG 200 but was rather a necessary 'tactic' adopted to cope with the RSHA.

However, I was determined to form my own opinion of the whole business, and was on my way the very next day. By train, this time.

For years now I had become used to moving about by aircraft, and I was dreading the prospect of a long journey by train. Originally, I was supposed to have collected a Ju 188 that had been earmarked for *Olga* from Berlin but the workshops at Finow could not supply the aircraft because of a lack of spare parts. This state of affairs was now an everyday occurence.

And so there was nothing for it but to take the train and my worst expectations were confirmed: it turned out to be a terrible night journey in an unheated carriage where the missing window panes had been crudely replaced by cardboard. Of course, timetables had lost their meaning a long time ago, ever since Allied bombing raids had been directed against the German transport system. I have no idea how many times the train stopped somewhere along the line, or how many stations we went through without stopping because there was an air raid on, but it was a journey to remember.

Fortunately I had left all my luggage in Berlin. I had been strongly advised to do so by all concerned, and assured that all my stuff would be sent after me by the next plane. 'What could you do with all that clutter in the middle of an air raid?' Well, they were right.

Many things did not function as they used to including telephones: communications had to be attempted in a round-about way by telegraphy. I was told that my expected arrival at *Olga* would be reported by radio 'so that somebody can collect you from the station'. Under normal circumstances that should have been that, but it was not.

I can still recall my arrival in Frankfurt/Main as if it happened only yesterday. I left the train and stood on the platform in the main station, looking around in vain for somebody who could have been sent to collect me. Instead, a strapping *Feldwebel* marched up to me and demanded to see my papers. He also wanted to know where I came from and where I was going. The tone of his voice did not go down all that well with me and I pulled him up short by replying that he should not ask so many questions but read the official travel documents instead. Perhaps I was treating the man unjustly. After all, the railway station guards had in addition to security duties also the unenviable task of checking if all travelling soldiers had the right to do so, and if they really were travelling 'on urgent missions that could be justified against our desperate defence on all fronts'. The front-line soldiers had coined a fitting nickname for these railway guard troops – *Heldenklau* (Hero Pilferers). And with justification – whoever did not satisfy the strict regulations was abruptly 'netted' and incorporated into some hastily organised unit and was guaranteed to find himself the very next day on one of the shortest ways to meeting a hero's death. These strict measures were a reflection of the grim situation; times had indeed changed.

The *Feldwebel's* voice interrupted my contemplation: '*Olga* – whatever is that?' I could not help him; I did not know about it all that much myself. The *Feldwebel* shrugged his shoulders and returned my

9

documents. He was only doing his duty, unthankful as it was.

As I could not see any military vehicle that could take me to the airfield the obvious solution was to telephone from the station guard office. But I had no luck there either. The officer in charge, an old *Hauptmann* with a War Service Cross on his chest, shook his head: telephoning – particularly to the airfield – was out of the question. The lines damaged by yesterday's air raid had still not been put in order. That being so, I wanted to know the best way to get there, to which the greying warrior replied in a somewhat sour tone: 'It could not do much harm to the gentlemen pilots if once in a while they had to struggle on foot!'

So be it. On the station forecourt I found a tram that despite the terrible destruction all over the town was apparently still going somewhere. I was lucky: after a short while the tramcar rattled and jangled its way south. The line went on over the Main bridge and my tram journey finally came to an end with a creak in a quiet and peaceful suburb. With my small overnight pack over the shoulder I made my way in a general southerly direction. It was a beautiful sunny late autumn day and I began to enjoy the walk through the forest. Then, after a while I could hear the sound of aircraft engines. Ours or theirs? Not that it would have mattered a great deal there, between the trees, but I was curious just the same. And there it was! Over a forest clearing I suddenly spotted a Ju 188 floating past at low altitude with its wheels down – obviously coming in to land. The engines too changed to higher revs, and after the machine had disappeared from sight I still had an audible signpost, so to speak. I reached the end of the forest and was facing the *Autobahn* that formed the eastern boundary of the airfield. This was it! In the southern end of the field I could just make out a few aircraft, carefully camouflaged between the trees. The airfield itself was empty, but there was some movement between the camouflaged aircraft and soon I could see a few men in dark overalls. A short while later my hunch was confirmed: they turned out to be technical personnel detailed to *Olga*.

The *Oberwerkmeister* (workshop chief) had a small van that had been converted to run on producer gas and he immediately offered me a lift to the command post. I had again caught up with motorisation.

Our journey took us a long way outside the airfield, whenever possible using the cover of the trees. I found this a bit exaggerated, but my driver shook his head 'Let a day or two go by, Sir, and then you will understand the caution in all our movements here!'

10

The command post of *Olga* consisted of two barracks well hidden in a wood. I had arrived.

When someone turns up as replacement for another formation commander as I had done, one can as a rule expect a somewhat reserved reception. But not here: my predecessor seemed overjoyed that I had finally appeared and he could 'take off'. In fact, if he had had his way he would have handed everything over there and then.

In any case, he reckoned I should be present that same night during the preparation and execution of current operations to get the hang of it. This did seem a bit rushed to me, but there was not much I could say. However, the Operations Officer, a *Leutnant* with an almost unrecognisable face disfigured by terrible burns, made my decision easier by suggesting that he would first take me to my assigned quarters at Schwanheim where I was to share a house with a dentist and his wife. After all, he said, I had been travelling right through the previous night and had done quite a bit of legwork, not to mention that I had arrived there without sleep, a wash or a shave – or a meal, for that matter.

And so I was on the move again, this time as a passenger in a somewhat dented Mercedes 170 V belonging to the detachment commander. On the way the Operations Officer told me some details of what I could expect at *Olga* and what I must know before officially taking over command. The *Leutnant* did not mince his words, and I was very grateful to him for being so frank with me, a total stranger.

The picture was not very encouraging. In fact, the whole situation regarding *Olga* was in hopeless confusion. What with the orders and requests piling up, and the shortage of available technical provisions, things were getting worse from day to day. The technical personnel under the *Oberwerkmeister* were the only bright spot in an otherwise gloomy scene: they were really a fine body of men, devoted to their job, and willingly worked round the clock to keep things going. As for the rest: the flying crews were a mixed bunch, from various units, and their qualifications and operational willingness were generally below par. Also, despite the fact that tasks assigned to this detachment were classified under 'special priority' no support was forthcoming from anyone to get things going.

The *Leutnant* added that he had wanted to tell me all this before I took over the business tomorrow because this change-over to a different commander was the best opportunity to draw attention to the various shortcomings and to request urgent redress of the whole

11

situation. Apparently my predecessor had long since resigned himself to the situation, and only wanted to get away as quickly as possible.

All this was hardly encouraging news, and gradually I began to question just what I had let myself in for.

2. Agents and VIPs

The official handing-over took place on the following day, and I soon realized that there was a large gap between the establishment on paper and the actual effective strength in both available aircraft and personnel.

There were six serviceable Ju 188s on hand, plus two captured and renovated B-17 Flying Fortresses, giving a total of only eight operational aircraft. It was also clear to me that the unit's effectiveness obviously suffered from the fact that both the flying crews and technical personnel had to be accommodated in private quarters outside the airfield. This was something I just had to take into account; the billets and workshops on the airfield could no longer be used due to the frequent bombing raids. All one could do was to improvise.

Naturally enough, all this also had a corresponding effect on the troops. Discipline left much to be desired because those who had no specific duties or tasks to do were able to evade all supervision. An added factor was that practically all flying – except for a few workshop test flights – was confined to nights, leaving the crews largely to their own devices in daytime. Under these circumstances morale was bound to deteriorate within a few weeks. As the unit was based effectively at home, anybody who had time to spare could go his own way – and did. I don't have to spell out here what the men would get up to on these trips; the opportunities were there. In short, what I found there was what in Prussian military parlance was fittingly described as a *Sauhaufen*, a rabble.

Things did not look much brighter on the operational side either. It was obvious to me that, considering the available transport capacity, far too much was expected of *Olga*. This was another hard fact of life I had to live with for the time being. According to official notes, of the thirty or so operations on order for this month, the *Olga* crews had flown just five or six, and it was already nearly mid-November. And not only that: these flights were without exception those that had required the least effort. All other operations stood on the 'waiting list'. I had an opportunity of finding out how this affected everything the same day.

About half way to Wiesbaden there was a large estate with big, roomy castle-like buildings in the grounds. In one of these 'castles' were accommodated some 60 agents belonging to various German secret services. In addition to that there were 40 'attendants', those people responsible for the training, preparation and execution of operations, as well as for controlling the individual agents or groups by radio after landing.

I had already been warned by my two guides (the present commander and the Operations Officer of *Olga*) that this part of my introduction would be fraught with even more difficulties.

There was a standing instruction for *Olga* that persons belonging to different operational groups, no matter if they were German 'attendants' or the agents themselves (known in the 'trade' jargon as *V-Leute = Vertrauensleute*, or 'trusted people') should never meet and get to know each other personally. This was easy enough at the beginning, when one simply had to see that they did not meet each other on the airfield. Apart from that one had to ensure that neither the *V-Leute* nor their 'attendants' got to know from which airfield they would start their journey into the unknown.

For this reason, care was taken to transport this 'human cargo' to the airfield only in darkness, in closed vehicles, arriving on the runway via some side entrance. Once there, each group was led to its own quarters for preparations and final instructions by parachute experts from *Olga*. This included fitting the parachutes to suit each individual person, and packing all equipment (except whatever the agent carried on his own body) into an additional load with its own parachute. This was dropped from the aircraft simultaneously with the agent and connected to him (or her) by a line so that it would not get lost on the ground.

As a precaution, all weapons were always packed into these separate loads. After all, it was not exactly to everyone's liking to have armed and utterly strange people, evidently able and capable of everything, aboard one's aircraft!

The problem was that intended operational flights had to be postponed more and more frequently, finally resulting in 'crowding', so that some groups had to be temporarily accommodated near the airfield until they could be flown out. This of course had nothing to do with the flying command, being the responsibility of the respective leader of the *V-Leute* or agents, but he nevertheless required help and support from the locally-sited Luftwaffe unit. Due to the highly secret nature of these activities he simply could not turn for help to the local military authorities when in need of billets and provisions for his people. Thus it had to be the KG 200 detachment in the know.

Suitable accommodation that ensured security and reasonable comfort, was thus a necessity. The place chosen was the 'castle' on the way to Wiesbaden which, suitably converted, also proved quite satisfactory to begin with. For one thing, if several groups happened to be present it was large enough to keep the people separate. However, as the number of those awaiting departure began to grow, it led to a situation that seemed full of dangers even to me, a complete novice in this field.

We parked our car out of sight from the 'castle' and walked the rest of the way. The grounds were protected from the outside world by a wall, but the entrance gate stood wide open. In the big park-like garden in front of the house I could see groups of civilians standing around or walking under the trees in the still warm November sun. Naturally they were talking to each other like people do when meeting others, but at the same time I was reminded by my 'guides' once more not to mention or expect any names. An official introduction was not desirable nor would be forthcoming.

As we walked towards the house all movement stopped and all eyes were fixed on us. Apparently everybody assumed we had arrived to collect those who would be flying out tonight. One could almost feel the tension in the air.

A small corner had already been selected for our discussion and we were immediately surrounded by a dozen or so men of various ages. They all seemed at ease with each other and it was impossible to tell who pulled more weight among them, who were the leaders and who were the agents.

From the following conversation, most of it in an impatient and reproachful tone, I could gather that even the most basic rules of security had long since been thrown to the winds. It could not have been otherwise under the given circumstances. Some of the people were understandably put out by the delays, and did not mince their words. There were even threats: 'If my operation is not carried out right away I will be forced to make a report to my superiors!'

Others were pleading: 'You will have to act. I am no longer able to keep up the mood of my people if we have to wait here any longer!'

And then there were almost violent remonstrations but these just showed how little idea these people had about flying operations. There was one man who said almost despairingly; 'Look, I have three Frenchmen here who have to be transported for an important mission over there as quickly as possible. They are people from very influential French circles. I have carefully selected and trained them myself, and they are expected in France right now. If they do not arrive as announced, all this work has been wasted – not to mention the lost opportunities that may never occur again!'

Although he was not supposed to know, our Operations Officer whispered to me that these Frenchmen actually belonged to influential political circles 'over there' which intended to persuade the Allied military command to hold back operations in the West so that the German command could repulse the Soviets in the East.

That just about described the last hopes that the German leadership held out for the German people. In fact, these hopes, and the allusions to 'wonder weapons' really still gave some a belief that the tide of the war could yet be turned.

My predecessor had evolved his own tactics when dealing with such impatient characters. He calmed them by pointing out that it was not he who had sent the individual groups here long before their time, and that he did not 'make the weather' either. For these reasons would the gentlemen please be so kind and apply to those authorities who were in fact responsible for all this. In all other respects the gentlemen should turn to me, his successor, when he pointed to me, without of course mentioning my name. So that was that. But what worried me was that the controllers of the *V-Leute* had obviously known about each other's tasks for quite some time. And it was also evident that their protégés too had got to know each other and more likely than not had discussed things among themselves. All it needed was just one double-agent among these sixty people and the betrayal would be complete – they could all expect a 'reception committee' on landing.

However, my worries in this respect were allayed by the people on the spot: everything here was so tightly secured that there could be no question of any of our *V-Leute* running a risk on landing. Well, it was not my problem – but I could not help recalling the 'keep them apart at all costs' rule and the open gates.

According to the weather forecast flying was 'on' the following night, although it was still impossible to say who should hold himself ready for departure. Also, we still did not know as yet exactly how many aircraft and crews would be available. Apart from that we had to wait and see in which part of our enormous operational area the

16

required minimal weather conditions could be confirmed. After all, our destinations included the North Sea and the Channel coasts, England, Holland, Belgium, France, the Biscay and the Mediterranean coastline.

During the drive back to the airfield I realised that I was caught between two irreconcilable problems. Initially, I had been excited by the challenge of the special flying tasks required of this detachment; now it was becoming clear that flying was going to be only a minor part of what I had to expect here.

First and foremost, it was a matter of commanding a military unit that had gone downhill in a big way. Then, I had to cope with great technical difficulties which, considering the rapidly deteriorating situation in the Reich were beyond a solution. And last but not least, I had to take care of the men and women who were waiting daily and hourly to be called and whose nerves after weeks of waiting in suspense were naturally strained.

But more was to come. When we arrived back at the command post we were greeted by a man who declared that he was the leader of an operational group for which he had managed to find provisional accommodation in Frankfurt itself. He had instructions to report at *Olga* today because his group had to be flown out tonight or, at the very latest, tomorrow night.

We immediately checked our list of operations and found their cover designation. The group consisted of two men and a woman, all Dutchmen who were supposed to be set down by parachute on an open field near a village not far from Utrecht.

With the help of a sketch map the group leader then explained the landing place in more detail: there was a railway bridge, a road fork, a small wood and, right behind it, the open field. That was where the three had to land. The farmhouse close by belonged to the girl's uncle; they were all expected there and would find a safe hiding place. Surely, this could be accomplished quite easily; after all, it was only a short hop from Frankfurt to Utrecht.

Naturally, the good fellow was completely taken aback when we explained that he just had to wait his turn; we had more urgent tasks to see to first. We advised him to be prepared to wait for several weeks, on hearing which he of course promptly asked for our assistance in obtaining a billet, provisions and other necessities for his group. However, in the expectation that the following night would make a bit more space in the 'castle' we consoled him to hang on until tomorrow.

17

'It goes like this from day to day and from hour to hour!', the other *Olga* officers told me. Something just had to be done!

As far as the meteorological stations could tell in the early afternoon, the weather did not look too bad, although it was still too early to select possible destinations. Our command post became busy, and then at my request, my predecessor agreed to plan and execute the coming operation so that I would at least have an idea of the kind of war that was being led from here.

The *Oberwerkmeister* reported four aircraft serviceable for the coming night, three Ju 188s and one B-17.

Slowly, the situation began to take shape and it was clear that no flights could be made to south and south-west France; the weather was unsuitable. On the other hand, things were looking promising over the Dutch-Belgian area, the Channel coast and over the Paris region and Brittany. Thanks to the current phase of the moon we could also expect good visibility on the ground for the second part of the night and in addition to that, the reported winds were also favourable for accurate dropping of live and inanimate cargoes.

We studied the maps. The intended operations with their cover designations, number of *V-Leute* and loads had been marked on them long since. It was breaking the security regulations but just had to be done under the circumstances to provide the necessary overall view of the situation. Apart from that, it was no longer possible to use separate aircraft for each task as it should have been done according to rules. We had to attempt to carry out several operations with one aircraft on the same flight.

This meant of course that agents of several separate groups would meet, but the danger of betrayal was no greater than when living together in one building.

The carrying capacity of the available aircraft was estimated as 22-25 people, made up of four to five for each Ju 188 and ten for the B-17. This puzzled me as I knew the Ju 188 to be a development of the Ju 88; with a full crew aboard there was only room for another one, or at the most two people with any personal equipment – but four to five? It was then that something new was revealed to me. Due to the lack of larger transport aircraft they had evolved a novel and quite amazing means of transport that was kept under thick secrecy wraps. It was like a giant 'bomb' but made of plywood and could be attached on underwing bomb racks like a normal bomb and also released in flight like one, simply by thumb pressure on the bomb release button on the

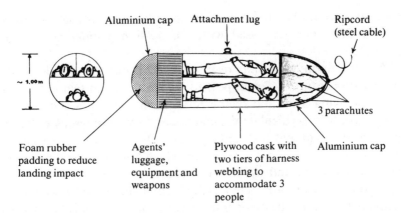

Aluminium cap   Attachment lug   Ripcord (steel cable)

~ 1.00 m

Foam rubber padding to reduce landing impact   Agents' luggage, equipment and weapons   Plywood cask with two tiers of harness webbing to accommodate 3 people   Aluminium cap   3 parachutes

control column. This plywood container was known as PAG (*Personen-Abwurf-Gerät*, or Personnel Drop Device). The double-walled plywood container was one metre in diameter and could carry three persons in prone position on two tiers. This 'human cargo' was stretched out and strapped down on strong harness webbing that accommodated two people side by side on the upper and one on the lower tier. In the upper part of the PAG were three parachutes under a streamlined aluminium cover. On releasing the container from the aircraft this cover was pulled off by a strong ripcord that simultaneously activated the parachutes. In the lower part of the device was space for a barrel-shaped container that carried the complete equipment of the group. The bottom consisted of a semi-spherical aluminium sheet cap that was filled with foam rubber to minimize the landing impact. As long as the PAG was attached underwing the agents could communicate with the crew via an R/T connection, which was of especial importance just before the release.

The use of the PAG simplified an operation in several ways. For one thing, it was possible to fix the landing point more accurately than when the agents would leave the aircraft separately with their own individual parachutes: on the ground, and especially in a 'blind' terrain, they now did not have to search for each other. Secondly, all their additional equipment was on the spot. But the main reason that led to the development and operational use of these streamlined containers was to lessen the danger of injuries during parachute jumps at night in an unknown area.

The only drawback that had to be taken into consideration was the fact that the container itself could hardly be disposed of quickly. The discovery of this unique device would result in an immediate search of

19

the area, and this had to be carefully considered before each operation with a PAG and discussed with the mission planner and people involved.

All afternoon we pored over our maps and the details of the intended operations. To support us we had roped in two *Feldwebeln* from the flying crews and an able fellow from the technical personnel. Their task was to calculate the courses and flying times, as well as to prepare the load and fuel tankage plans. We all had our hands full because we were still not sure exactly which 'targets' would be on our agenda that night and we had to prepare for all eventualities.

A courier on a motorcycle was then sent to the 'castle' to warn those who might possibly be on operations tonight. They would be collected in vehicles sent from *Olga* at dusk.

We had also included in our plans for the coming night two supply flights, one to a group in Holland and one in Paris, who had urgently requested supplies by radio. These consisted of replacement batteries for their radio sets, money and weapons, and were only two of similar postponed operations. 'Our' men had already been waiting for several nights at the previously agreed spots in the area, hoping to hear the sound of low-flying aircraft approaching from the right direction, pocket torches at the ready to give the agreed signal.

These supply consignments were packed into tough elongated boxes covered by rolls of red and white ribbons. The boxes were dropped without parachute, whereby the ribbons would unroll and ease the finding of these supplies at night.

The detachment really came to life only after dusk. The crews of the four available aircraft arrived and gathered in our operations room for their pre-flight briefing. From around the airfield one could hear the sound of engines starting up as the mechanics carried out the final checks on the parked aircraft. A fuel bowser struggled along the bumpy road alongside the runway – the usual activities on an airfield before operations, only this time in the gathering dusk and not at first light in the morning.

The *Oberwerkmeister* came in, reported the aircraft cleared for flight, and then mentioned certain points the crews had to watch out for. This taken care of, he again left the room with instructions regarding the tanking up of each aircraft depending on the expected depth of penetration. Then came the weather expert with the final summary of the expected meteorological conditions. His discourse took place in the large pre-flight briefing room in presence of all detailed aircrews. It was only at this stage that the final decisions were made regarding which operations – or better, combinations of operations – should be carried out.

Of course, apart from the wind, weather, the position of the moon and ease or otherwise of finding the target we also had to consider the enemy. If at all possible, our flights had to be carried out in such a way that they did not arouse immediate suspicion on the other side as to their real purpose. For that reason targets where the danger of identification was greatest were usually left to the very end of the flight. Moonlight was late that particular night and the first take-off was not scheduled until the second part of the night. This gave us sufficient time for detailed preparations.

In between appeared our *Spiess* (the detachment sergeant-major), a grey-haired *Feldwebel* who organised the distribution of coffee and sandwiches. Judging by the rich and plentiful choice he must have had some very good connections somewhere! Be as it may, it provided a most welcome break.

While we were enjoying a bite the irregular engine sounds indicated that the aircraft had started to roll from their various covers. The Ju 188s and the B-17 were moving without their navigation lights, carefully 'feeling' their way forward in the darkness. This was the only way to prevent their discovery by enemy night fighters.

Now my most important man became the parachute specialist. He was in charge of a large store of various parachutes and it was his responsibility to select the right kind and size of parachute for every occasion. Our *V-Leute* were using the so-called 'automatic parachutes' that were opened by a ripcord attached to the aircraft. In this way they had nothing to do themselves – and could not make any mistakes, as might happen with the normal manual parachute.

The 'dead loads' were dropped by special cargo parachutes of various types. Normally, every effort was made to set down a man with his pack in such a way that he would immediately have it handy to help find a safe hiding place. Only seldom were there 'reception committees' on hand that could gather up and move away all dropped loads in their own time. Such actions were possible in the wide open spaces in the East but hardly in the densely populated West.

We used quite a simple trick to unload our 'live' cargoes. The agent would sit or stand at the exit hatch and, at the signal of the 'despatcher' – usually a specially trained air gunner – the man just had to jump. If it did happen that the agent would suddenly 'freeze' at the vital moment, then the despatcher had to react in a split second by giving him a more or less gentle push.

The agent would hold his pack with both hands pressed to his chest. At the jerk caused by the opening of the parachute the pack would be whipped out of his grip and fall, pulling a ripcord that activated the cargo parachute. This opened under the agent and both together would now float down to the ground. The man and his pack were connected by another line which ensured that the vital operational equipment was not lost. And this is where the skill of the parachute specialist paid dividends: the sinking speed of both parachutes had to be balanced in such a way that the cargo parachute would fall slightly faster. This prevented them overtaking each other in descent which of course could lead to the danger of the parachutes twisting around each other.

In the meantime we had finally decided which operations could be flown that night. Two lorries with closed tarpaulin covers were sent to the 'castle'; their drivers had a list with cover-names they had to call out. The wheels of the mission had begun to turn.

Two hours before midnight both lorries were back with their human cargoes. Separated according to their task groups the men were led into various rooms where they met the aircrews that would fly them to their destinations. During this meeting they discussed together the expected situation and everything was planned down to the last metre: the direction of approach, and altitude and speed at the release point.

A standing rule was not to overfly inhabited areas or roads shortly before the target, to avoid arousing suspicion. The procedure was to fix a characteristic point on the ground some distance from the target that could be recognized even in moderate moonlight. On reaching this landmark, the pilot throttled back the engines, pressed his stopwatch and began the final approach at reduced speed in a gliding flight. This final gliding approach was calculated to pass over the target area at about 800 ft altitude, and it had to be right the first time; banking and searching around was to be avoided at all costs. The return flight too was to be carried out in such a way as not to make anybody suspicious on the ground.

While planning the final navigational preparations it could well happen that the release point had to be moved elsewhere. This of course created immediate problems with the *V-Leute* and their controller who, as a rule, were not airmen. They were under the impression that at the present state of technology it should be quite possible to fly accurately to any point on earth at night, over long distances, and even in enemy territory. Thus convinced, they quite naturally expected that whatever target areas they had chosen as the best and safest from their point of view would also be the right ones from the airmen's point of view. And when it was not the case, their whole world seemed to collapse because all their plans had been set on that. After all, the first steps on the ground after landing by parachute in enemy territory were the most dangerous.

That evening for the first time I got to know the people who were prepared to work for the enemy of their own nation and risk their lives doing so. One thing I noticed right away: they were not adventurers, as one perhaps would have expected, but quite the opposite. Also they looked and behaved literally like the proverbial 'man in the street'. Their clothing had been carefully chosen to suit their respective action areas and cover names, as well as the whole personality of the man they were supposed to be.

Visibly uneasy and nervous, they crowded around their respective controllers now acting as interpreters between their agents and the aircrew.

Soon it was the turn of the parachute specialist and his assistants who then got to work fitting parachutes and preparing the jettisonable loads. Then followed instructions regarding the functioning of this equipment and behaviour during the actual jump and descent. Over a period of time these parachute people had evolved this part of their work to a fine art that contributed a great deal in allaying anxiety and fear.

If it was intended to use the PAG containers, these were prepared in one of the few hangars that American bombs had left intact on the airfield. The activities there were even more secretive than in other preparation rooms.

The participants did not know until the last minute how they would be transported to their operational areas. It was quite understandable that there was a certain apprehension when they found out they would not be falling freely to the ground under a parachute, as they had imagined during the months of training. (There were no training or practical tests in parachute jumping for the *V-Leute*). Usually, it was then a matter of longer explanations regarding the advantages of the PAG method compared to individual parachutes, but even that did not help to still the frequently sceptical comments and often even outright refusal. After all, it was no small matter to let yourself be strapped inside a tight plywood tube together with two other people! Their torsoes and legs were lashed down tightly so as not to move around in bumpy flying weather or under sudden more violent manoeuvres, the PAG inmates could only move their arms freely. The only illumination was their own pocket torches – a dark and claustrophobic world indeed, without being able to do anything themselves if things went wrong.

When finally the men and their equipment had been stowed away, the ground crew fitted and secured the big capsule with three parachutes. From this moment on, the three agents were cut off from the outside world and their fate was in other hands.

The PAG was then transported to the airfield apron on the same special vehicle it had rested on for loading. A Ju 188 was already waiting. Now came the much more difficult procedure of attaching the large plywood container under the aircraft.

The loaded PAG weighed about 750 kg (1650 lb) and to lift it use was made of a simple if time-consuming method: two large inflatable rubber sacks of the type used to salvage belly-landed aircraft were pushed under the vehicle and slowly filled with compressed air. The vehicle with its PAG rose only inch by inch, being carefully manipulated to eventually connect its carrying lug with the bomb rack. This by no means easy task seemed to take an endlessly long time and I could not help feeling sorry for the three fellows inside that sealed plywood container, especially as the whole procedure could not be accomplished without quite a lot of pushing and jostling.

The relative size of the PAG was particularly noticeable once it was in position under the Ju 188: in normal tail-down attitude its rear end was only about eight inches off the ground.

During my years of combat service with a bomber unit I had grown used to the activities involved in preparing for and carrying out operational flights. I had known it as a matter of routine to have a whole formation of thirty or more aircraft bombed up, refuelled and up in the air again within the shortest possible time. The basic requirements here were not much different, the aircraft types were virtually the same, as were the penetration depths, and even the other prerequisites – weather data, navigation aids, and estimated enemy situation – did not seem to differ a great deal from a conventional mission. However, I was to learn during my first day with *Olga* that appearances can be deceptive.

Here, it needed a whole series of other preliminaries before an aircraft carrying out a special task ordered by the Intelligence authorities could become airborne. Apart from everything else, the fact that from the flying point of view the employer and executor came from two different worlds was especially aggravating.

For one thing, the aircrews here had the additional responsibility of ensuring that their passengers were set down in the correct place. If they made a mistake this could result not only in the loss of the agents and an uncompleted task, but even endanger an already existing organisation or create other unforeseen problems. For these reasons the supreme rule of conduct for all aircrews was the strict order to turn back if the drop point could not be clearly identified. The same applied if something suspicious was observed in the target area – even if this resulted in the Intelligence authorities expressing their disappointment in such a way as if to imply the airmen's own incompetence was the real reason.

But let's get back to the take-off preparations that night. –

At long last everything was checked and ready. The moon appeared like a broad sickle over the eastern horizon. Its pale light was quite sufficient for the aircraft to taxi to the take-off point without using their landing lights. Once there, the crew would give an agreed light signal to the flight control when they were ready, and only then would the runway illuminations be switched on. The aircraft would take off without navigation lights and disappear into the darkness. Immediately it had passed over the airfield boundary the runway illuminations were switched off again until the next machine was ready to go.

The crews were experienced men and the take-offs went off without any problems. Nevertheless we were delighted that there had been no last minute hitches and our *Olga* couriers were on their way. From our command post we were in contact with the various air defence and air observation posts who would keep us informed on the progress of our aircraft. Another reason for this close collaboration was to avoid our machines being identified in error as 'enemy' and getting shot at. Such mistakes by our air defences were practically an everyday occurence at that time and quite understandably because, apart from high-flying night fighters, hardly any other German aircraft were in the air.

Then came the long wait in the command post until the machines were back again. They had to keep complete radio silence on the way out and over the target, although this rule was somewhat relaxed on the way back.

In between regularly questioning our weather experts about possible developments in the target area and expected weather on landing at base, we had a lot of time for lively discussions with some of the agents' controllers. These men were by no means 'everyday' types. One could sense that at least right away, even if none of them would reveal what military or civil rank they actually held. All of them knew 'their' target areas in detail and spoke the local language. As we were now all part of the same confidential team our conversations were quite frank – and revealing. One of the first things I wanted to know was that, considering the generally hopeless situation in November 1944, were they still convinced of the successful outcome of their operations? Their affirmative answers came without hesitation: of course they were, otherwise they would not gamble with the lives of their *V-Leute*! True enough, they themselves were only carrying out orders, but the sources of these orders were ministries or high military or Party authorities, and they of all people should know enough of the situation to judge all these efforts to be justified.

Our *Leutnant* with the fire-scarred face was doubtful: – 'Isn't one or another of these foreigners just making this up to be flown home by us, thus hoping to avoid capture as a spy?'

I must admit I could not get rid of similar thoughts at the beginning either, although these doubts were resolutely disputed. Somehow though, the arguments were no more convincing than before.

It was obvious that my predecessor as commander of *Olga* until today already had other things on his mind before his expected departure on the morrow, but he nevertheless told us of an event that had taken place a while back.

"There was this most urgent order to fly a B-17 to a spot somewhere in the extreme south-western end of Europe. This order came to us from some mysterious Party authority that kept itself secret. But it certainly pulled some weight, because the preparations were carried out with an effort never seen before. Although I was the commander of this flying unit, they behaved towards me as if I were a mere chauffeur who just had to carry out orders and not ask any questions.

The Party big-shots in charge of that do were swarming around here in their dozens, in their 'Golden pheasant'* uniforms. It was a sight not to be missed!

Goldfasanen, a popular derogatory term for Nazi Party officials in their brown uniforms with golden braid.

Anyway, our task was to transport and drop by parachute ten people and half a lorry load of various supplies. And they were quite something I can tell you, made up of 'goodies' that normal mortals could only dream about in wartime: crates of selected provisions, hams, choice hard salami, chocolate, smoked foods, a complete photo laboratory, a whole series of the most expensive cameras, films, drawing materials, a complete copying outfit – you name it, they've had it! And of course weapons and ammunition. In addition there were sackfuls of money, boxes of jewelry, gold and other valuables. Then a whole collection of clothing of various kinds and for the most varied occasions.

Although they tried, our Party customers could not prevent us from having a look into their crates and boxes; after all, we were loading the aircraft and had to sort out these supplies in handy parachute loads. And not only that: we also had to know if certain items were a fire danger, susceptible to gunfire, and of course the physical size and weight.

(Our 'customers' could never understand these – to us – vital questions; quite understandably they did not want anybody else to know anything that would give a clue to the nature of any given operation. But there was a limit how far this secrecy could be kept in respect to the men who had to carry out these deliveries.)

In the case of that B-17 operation it was immediately obvious that only a part of this varied load could be taken up together with ten people over that distance. The rest of the stuff just had to be left here to be flown out and dropped there on several later flights.

What took place before the take-off on this first flight was fit for a film script. At the predetermined time a whole column of vehicles appeared at our gates and a group of 'Golden pheasants' stormed into the command post to convince themselves that everything had actually been prepared as requested. They became most indignant when it was pointed out they were in the way and disturbed our loading and take-off preparations. Somewhat annoyed, they then insisted that we handle their passengers, members of the highest foreign political circles, with the reverence they deserved. I still wonder what they expected us to do: bow and scrape?

Anyway, next moment, five men and five women walked into the room. Imagine the scene! The men dressed in elegant suits, the ladies wearing expensive fur coats, with fashionable shoes on their feet.

Our objections that these were not exactly the most suitable outfits for parachute jumps at night were rejected 'because these ladies and gentlemen would be met by a committee on landing, and shortly thereafter they had to appear in appropriate clothes to avoid any suspicions they had arrived there in an unusual way!'

Now, in some cases a plan like this had something going for it, and was at least theoretically quite good. But what if one landed in a puddle or on a bramble bush? I made another effort to point out that, in my modest opinion, at least the light and elegant dresses and shoes worn by the ladies were absolutely useless for a parachute jump, but to no avail.

You wouldn't believe it, but I was actually told that there were no objections to how these people were dressed – after all, the whole operational plan was based on their appearance and behaviour immediately after the landing!

I had to give up; there was no point in trying to convince people who 'knew better'.

I then noticed that our 'guests' seemed to be in rather high spirits, even while being fitted with their parachutes and equipment, something that struck me as most unusual. I realised then that they were 'under the influence', well on the way in fact. – 'Well, yes. A few drinks before the trip was quite in order – quite deliberate, in fact,' I was told by their uniformed assistants. After all, it is well known that alcohol could banish fear and loosen restraint.

I had not come across so much nonsense and ignorance in one place before, and the whole affair became an increasing embarrassment to us all.

Oh yes, we did fly that operation, and the ten figures were dropped over the required place on time. As far as *Olga* was concerned, that was it – we have not heard anything since. And all that large stock of additional equipment and supplies have also remained stored here, nobody has ever enquired about it.' – My predecessor grinned – 'Now you know where our sergeant-major got all those titbits we've had tonight!"

My first operational night with *Olga* was nearing its conclusion. Before very long the first of our machines was due back at the base.

As usual when expecting our own crews returning from operations, we became noticeably nervous and started calling our air observation posts more frequently, enquiring if they had any reports of incoming flights from the west.

Under the circumstances our aircraft were out of danger only after safely landing at their home base and tucked away in their hide-outs among the trees, an unenviable situation. It could happen that our air observer posts mistook one of our machines for the enemy and alerted the defences. Once that had happened, it was almost impossible to stop the Flak batteries and night fighters from going into action – and that was in the days when the air defences were still relatively intact on our side. Now, late in 1944, with essential communications constantly jammed or otherwise interfered with, one could no longer rely on the teamwork of individual command posts.

The radio operators in our radio room sat tense at their sets and listened attentively on the allocated frequencies. Although it was against the strict radio silence order our crews were advised to send a previously agreed short signal on the return flight on crossing the front line at the very latest. This would give us a clue when to expect the machine to land at the base.

We breathed a sigh of relief when the first brief signal came through; it was from one of our Ju 188s. From the reported estimated time of arrival we could calculate that it must be somewhere near Strasbourg, still over enemy territory. Immediately, we notified the Flak and night fighters command centres to prevent possible mistaken identity problems, and asked to be kept informed as soon as the machine was located by our own air defences.

While similar brief signals were coming in in short sequence from the other three machines, preparations were already being carried out for the landing: the flight control was notified to stand by to light up the obstacle and runway illuminations as agreed, and one of our pilots was on his way over to assist as an expert go-between. At the same time our airfield defence Flak were informed that our own aircraft would soon appear from the west. The Flak crews also had to have their searchlights and signal flare ammunition in readiness in case an aircraft would miss the airfield in this total darkness.

Final checks were also carried out on the airfield navigational radio beam as well as the VHF landing approach transmitter.

All this was really the responsibility of the local ground organisation, but some bad experience had shown that it was far better to look after these devices ourselves.

Outside, near the hidden parking places, ground crew and technical personnel were already waiting, ready to guide the aircraft now safely landed into their hide-outs with pocket torches.

The medical centre too was notified, in case there were wounded aboard. And finally, there was also our sergeant-major with his assistants, bringing up a large thermos container with hot milk soup for the returning aircrews.

Things ran according to plan that night. We received regular reports from our Flak sites, informing us on the position of our aircraft, and then it was time to go outside to watch the first approach and landing.

Soon we could hear the sound of aircraft engines from the westerly direction – at first indistinct but then clearer, and getting nearer rapidly. A searchlight stabbed a short vertical beam into the dark night sky, and a minute later a Ju 188 hushed low over the field. It was the time to switch on the airfield lighting. The engine noise grew quieter, almost fading, and we knew that a landing would take place very soon, although we could not see anything.

Despite the close watch kept by our Flak crews with their ground control radars it had long since been inadvisable to fly with navigation lights on over German territory. An enemy night fighter could appear on the scene very suddenly and an aircraft lit up like a Christmas tree would be a most welcome prize.

In fact, experienced pilots would often forego even using their landing searchlights. Thus it could happen that an aircraft that had landed would not be noticed until its pilot had to gun the engines to taxi in some corner of the field. And so it was this time.

A producer-gas powered lorry with blacked-out headlights lumbered across the airfield to the various parking places to collect the aircrews. The place began to quieten down again.

The post-flight reports by pilots, observers and jump masters were immediately set down in abbreviated form containing only the essentials, then encoded and transmitted to the *Geschwader* HQ in Berlin.

These reports were of special interest to me as the new detachment commander. They told me of the progress of each flight, conditions in the target area, provided a description of the cargo drop procedure, including observations of parachute landings as far as possible in each individual case, and so on, Of equal significance for me were the aircrew observations of ground conditions in the enemy territory. Was the aircraft spotted and attacked in any way? Where and how did that happen? How was the flight over the front lines on the way out and back? Could they see anything of the combat activity on the ground? Were they shot at by Flak? Could they tell if it was ours or theirs? Were there any observations about the weather, air activity, searchlights, light signals on the ground? Was the choice of the dropping point good or bad? How did the *V-Leute* behave at the time of their departure?

When all this was completed it was long since daylight and time to have breakfast. The first reports of enemy air penetrations were also already on hand, the war did not take any breaks.

At least we had the satisfaction of knowing that our aircraft had been hidden well camouflaged among the trees some distance from the airfield perimeter – a real but deadly game of hide and seek. It was advisable to evacuate the field in any case, and all soldiers who were not absolutely necessary were ordered to disperse to their quarters away from the base and hold themselves ready for possible recall to duty. The command post was locked, and the field seemed deserted. And so it was – but only to the unwelcome visitors from the 'other side'. That was our intention.

Quite some time previously *Olga* had established a second command post in a small tavern in a village some distance away from the airfield. There we had the necessary office space with all the equipment, radio and teleprinter sets, as well as the telephone extensions although these functioned only intermittently.

While the aircrews were being driven to their quarters to rest, our work went on until we too could call it a day and try to catch up on lost sleep.

3. Furtive Flights

The command of Detachment *Olga* was now in my hands, and the first thing I had to do was to familiarize myself with the Ju 188.

I asked our *Oberwerkmeister* to have a Ju 188 ready for me at dusk the same day. I had chosen this late hour for two reasons: firstly, one could be reasonably sure that the sky would be free of the American Mustangs and Thunderbolts that roamed around at low level throughout the daylight hours. From sheer boredom they would shoot at anything that moved on the ground, no matter if it was a farmer working with his horses in a field or a child on the way home from school.

A solitary Ju 188 would soon have been spotted and picked off. However, in the evening twilight things became more peaceful in the German skies. The enemy fighters had already made tracks for home to avoid landing in the darkness, and the British night bombers were probably still assembling over the North Sea before another raid on German towns.

Secondly, it had been quite some time since I had flown at night and there was nothing better than a few circuits in the growing dusk to get used to it again.

Granted, I had made all my operational flights and booked over 2000 flying hours on the Ju 88 both by day and night, but more than six months had now gone by since I had had a big aircraft under the seat of my pants. It was really high time I got used to that again, and indeed acquainted myself with the various innovations that had been introduced in the meantime.

In our detachment we had both versions of the Ju 188, the Ju 188A powered by Jumo 213A-1 (1750 hp) inlines and the Ju 188E with the BMW 801G (1800 hp) radials. These engines developed a good 400 hp more than the Jumo 211F and J (1340/1420 hp) fitted on the Ju 88 that I had flown previously. As the Ju 188 was only slightly heavier than the 88 this meant that it should be capable of considerably better performance. I had been told that, as far as the flying characteristics were concerned, the Ju 188 did not differ all that much from her older sister, so that the main thing for me and my crew was to get acquainted with the considerably different technology of this new aircraft. For that reason our familiarization flight was more like a 'dry run' followed by a joy ride.

On entering the aircraft, an old Ju 88 hand was immediately struck by the completely altered forward cabin. The fully glazed nose section was of streamlined shape, without the 'step' below the pilot's windscreen. This configuration gave an unobstructed view forward continued almost vertically downwards. As on the Ju 88, there was an electrically heated Plexiglas panel fitted in the floor between the rudder pedals so that the pilot could have a good view underneath as well.

The layout of the instruments and the various control levers differed completely from the Ju 88; the pilot's vision was no longer obstructed by instrument panels or other fittings. An instrument panel with the most essential navigational instruments was attached against the cabin roof to the right of centre; all other instruments and devices were fitted in special panels alongside the port and starboard walls of the cabin.

The control column was in the centre, to the right of the pilot. The control wheel horns were attached to a swing arm that could be moved across to the pilot or navigator as required. The seating arrangements for the pilot, observer, radio operator and gunner were the same as in the Ju 88, although in the Ju 188 there was place for an additional crew member, another gunner operating the dorsal gun. It was mounted in a turret above the cabin and the 20mm cannon was laid by electric servo-motors controlled by a small lever similar to a pilot's control column. This cannon certainly represented a considerable strengthening of the defensive armament if it was used the way it should. However, of what use it could possibly be on our stealthy nocturnal flights was another matter. The *Oberwerkmeister* who assisted us in our familiarization told me that these weapons had not fired a single shot in service at *Olga*.

On the spot I ordered that these installations should be removed from all the aircraft. This not only saved us almost 400kg (880lb) in weight on each machine but also made room for another man in the cabin.

Another important difference compared with the Ju 88 was the operation of the undercarriage landing flaps and dive brakes – in short, everything that was moved hydraulically. Where before the controls were moved by direct rods activated by levers on the pilot's

33

instrument panel, all these had now been replaced by electrical circuits, switches and press buttons. The hydraulic controls were activated by magnetic relays.

After each of us had carefully studied his own place we really felt at home in this brand new bird.

However, before anything else we had first thoroughly to work our way through the various service manuals. It was not enough for one to know where all the levers, press-buttons and instruments were in a large aircraft and how they functioned. That would be sufficient, after an appropriate retraining, to fly the aircraft under normal circumstances, but not if there was some technical fault or in case of unforeseen flying conditions. In such cases lack of technical knowledge could be fatal.

Generally speaking, in wartime when one has to fly in enemy airspace where unforeseen weather conditions can be expected and when frequently the aircraft has to be flown to the extreme limits of its range without any reserves, the demands on the aircrew's capabilities and knowledge are incomparably higher than in peaceful civil air service where every avoidable risk has been eliminated.

Here in the Ju 188 we had an aircraft that differed in so many technical details and its flying performance from all other comparable machines, that its safe and successful operational use depended completely on how familiar the pilot and his crew were with it.

We started the engines and carried out all the checks necessary before a take-off. Everything was in order, and the Ju 188 vibrated in anticipation.

The following flight in the dimming daylight carried us at low level over wide areas around Frankfurt. For me, it brought on a feeling of sheer enjoyment I had not felt for a long time, to be able to fly in a big and fast aircraft without specific orders or instructions over the late autumn landscape. The two Jumo 213A-1 engines with their total of 3500 hp take-off power almost made this unladen bird into a sports aircraft, giving all of us an exhilarating feeling. The Ju 188 responded eagerly to everything we tried: the electro-hydraulic operation of the landing flaps, undercarriage and dive automation, the fuel and oil transfer pump system, de-icing equipment, radio equipment, weapons, bombing automation, engine controls, as well as the emergency operation of hydraulics – in short, all the operations necessary for a safe flight – until we knew how to do it blindfold.

During the subsequent landing trials in the darkening evening I

34

found the advanced layout of the pilot's seat and controls a real boon compared to that of the Ju 88. Coming in for landing in the previous model I first had to loosen my harness straps to be able to reach all the necessary levers on the long instrument panel with my left hand. Not any more: on the Ju 188 the whole procedure was made easy by a set of switches and press-buttons at a handy distance around the seat. For instance, trimming of the elevators which regulated the landing speed and gliding angle, was done by just one switch button on the control column horn; it was no longer necessary to turn a hand-wheel somewhere on the cabin wall.

All indicators and visual displays for the positions of the undercarriage, landing flaps, trim and propeller pitch were concentrated in one single multi-display instrument which conveyed the information either by means of light signals or symbols. Thanks to this the pilot was informed at a glance of the momentary situation of the aircraft and had almost unlimited time to concentrate on landing and what went on around him.

When we climbed down the steel ladder after our last touch-down in the darkness and felt the ground under our feet again we were satisfied. At least as far as the aircraft was concerned, we should be able to cope with our tasks at *Olga*.

Twenty-four hours after we had witnessed the dramatic preparations the day before, we climbed into our cabin to take off on our first night operation as a KG 200 crew. I had detailed myself for the first operational flight right after taking over command of the detachment; it was the night of 23/24 November, 1944.

Our task was a round flight that would take us first to Holland, and then over Belgium to the area north-west of Paris and back again. In Holland a group of *V-Leute* were waiting in the area south of Rotterdam for some urgently needed supplies, while a man we had with us in the cabin had to be dropped over Belgium. For a spot near the Seine, barely 62 miles north-west of Paris, we had a PAG with three somewhat scared Frenchmen.

Two other Ju 188s had already taken off before us, we were the third and last that night; no other aircraft were serviceable.

The night was still pitch-black as we taxied over the field to the end of the take-off runway, directed by the flight controller who blinked his light at short intervals.

I rolled on the concrete runway and turned the aircraft into a take-off position. Then followed a careful check of the whole aircraft and

35

our pre-flight preparations. All this would seem to be a simple routine matter following our previous familiarisation flight and the countless night flights with the 'older sister' of the Ju 188; however I never let any operation become too routine in my whole career as a pilot. Quite the opposite in fact: as the years went by I became even more pedantic in these pre-flight checks and preparations and have never been content just to run up the engines. Only when I had found everything in order – the engine revolutions, propeller pitch automation, temperatures, engine boost pressure, electrical system, generators, navigation equipment, fuel and oil supplies, their transfer pumping system and the rest of the technical checks – did I give the flight control a signal. Next moment the green-white-red runway lights came on and I could take off.

That faint queasy feeling in the stomach that I always felt before an operational flight disappeared as soon as I pushed the throttle lever forward and we began to build up speed. It was always the same, whether on the first or the three hundreth sortie, and it was the same now. From then on, one only had eyes, ears and a 'feel' for the aircraft and what went on in the tight enclosure of its cabin.

I was airborne after a surprisingly short take-off run – the considerably bigger power reserves of the Ju 188 became noticeable. In addition to that I was of course used to take off on operational flights with aircraft that had been loaded to their limits while my present machine had relatively little to carry.

The time was exactly 2000 hrs.

In a flat climbing flight I was just past the airfield boundary when the runway lights were switched off. One after another, my crew members reported 'all clear' from their positions, the aircraft was functioning perfectly – we were on our way.

While preparing for this operation we had arranged with the air observer posts that we would fly over the Rhine south of Cologne. From then on I would remain at low altitude until our first target south of Rotterdam. Somewhere west of the Rhine I would then be crossing the front, it had not proved possible to determine its exact line. Likewise, I could not get any information about possible defences, either anti-aircraft guns or night fighters.

The fluorescent figures on the clock on the instrument panel showed 2010 hrs when I switched in the auto-pilot, set on a course of 325 degrees. That would take us over the Rhine at the plotted spot – and would also be the first point on our route where, despite the complete blackout, we could check our true position.

Nobody spoke a word. I observed the various instruments reflecting the current engine performance, temperature and fuel consumption, as well as the altimeter and the clock. Apart from some briefly flickering lights everything was pitch-black down below.

Although we were still over our own territory we had the same eerie feeling as on an operational flight deep in the enemy's hinterland. We felt especially alone and forsaken – as, in fact, we were. A properly functioning ground organisation that would know about and keep track of our aircraft movements had ceased to exist some time ago. We could imagine how the people down there in the villages and townships – both civilians and soldiers – might prick up their ears nervously as they heard our aircraft approaching. Here and there even an air raid siren might start to howl.

The whole situation was spooky and uncanny for us. And not only that, it was also somehow deeply depressing. Here we were on our way to an operational flight deep into enemy territory, still over our own homeland – and were nevertheless somehow regarded as foes and suspiciously observed. I could almost feel this enmity towards us. It was very weird indeed.

Hans Fecht, my observer, became a bit restless: according to the clock we should be at the Rhine in a few minutes. He let a fleeting flash of his pocket torch slide over the map once more to memorize the features we should expect at the river. In the next moment we had confirmation that we had arrived in the right place at the right time to cross the mighty Rhine. Indeed we could only spot a few bends of the river shimmering in the darkness but that was quite sufficient to determine our position, set course for the next sector and press the stopwatch once more. Now ahead of us we could already see lights shimmering on the horizon, at first only indistinct but rapidly becoming clearer. That would be the front-line!

I was not sure if I should go highter or better stay close to the ground.

We did not know what to expect 'over there' – and we did not know how we were looked upon this side either. Indeed, we did not even know exactly where the borderline between 'this side' and 'over there' ran!

I was at about 3280 ft altitude and I decided to keep it that way for the time being. It was just the right height for either climbing or losing height depending on the situation in the combat zone. I shot a quick glance at the airspeed indicator: it was just 230 mph.

Time and again the sudden flaring of pillars of light on the horizon gave us an overall view of the battle that was going on on the ground. There were all kinds of flares, coloured tracers and searchlights – a whole kaleidoscope of lights. Suddenly, streams of tracer from light anti-aircraft guns rose towards us from ahead and from behind us. This was really novel, with both sides firing at us at the same time! I pushed the nose down a bit and opened the throttles. The Ju 188 reacted at once, the airspeed indicator needle wandered to the 250 mph mark, and in the next moment we were out of range.

The scene that now met our eyes takes some describing. We were now pretty low over the immediate enemy rear area and we immediately took in a visual impression of the vast numbers of American troops and the immense amount of supplies that were being brought up. Apparently all blackout and air defence regulations had been scrapped: as far as the eye could see, there were long columns of vehicles moving up to the front – with their headlights full on!

All the main roads could be clearly distinguished, with smaller secondary roads spreading fanwise out of them towards the front. From our altitude we had visibility of some fifty to seventy kilometres (or 30 to 40 miles) into the hinterland, and there did not seem to be a single road, no matter how small, that was not filled with a continuous worm of light moving in both directions. We had never seen anything like it in all the years of war, even all villages, towns and railway stations were brightly illuminated. It was impossible for us to even guess at this massed array of strength either in men or tons of equipment.

In the meantime things had become more lively in our aircraft as we drew one another's attention to our own observations. What we could see below made it as clear as anything that we could no longer hold up this advancing mass with our own forces; the enemy superiority in material and troops was plainly overwhelming.

And another thing: nobody seemed to pay any attention to our presence in enemy airspace. Not a single searchlight, nor an anti-aircraft gun shot at us – nothing. It appeared that the Americans no longer seemed to bother about German aircraft; they obviously did not think it worthwhile to set up an air observation or air defence organisation at this stage.

With all this illumination it was not difficult for us to navigate and, although the ground below became dark again, we were soon in our target area. Ahead of us, on the horizon, was a clearly visible dome of light in the sky – that would be Rotterdam. The road network, marked by snaking lights, was also pointing that way. And then we were there.

We flew exactly over our initial point, a road fork north of Breda. I throttled the engines, shut the radiator flaps, reduced the airspeed to 155 mph, let out the landing flaps half way and began an accurately measured descent.

The seconds were ticking away on the stopwatch. My observer was now using his pocket torch quite freely; here it no longer seemed necessary to be as careful with lights as we had learned to be over England.

The ground came closer, and we could begin detailed orientation. The spot where they were expecting our cargo must be just ahead of us. The Dutch *V-Leute* had been notified by radio of our probable arrival shortly before the take-off. The message had been acknowledged, so that we could expect the agreed recognition signals at the right place: three flashing pocket torches set in a triangle, with its apex pointing north. Our cargo had to be dropped just there.

It was also specifically agreed that the aircraft would not fly any search patterns or 'loops' if the place was not spotted on the first go. This did not seem to apply now – thanks to the brightly lit-up villages and unmistakably recognisable road system, an accurate approach flight was no problem.

I was expecting to see the flashing pocket torches at any moment. We had already wound open the hatch under the ventral gunners' position and the despatcher stood ready to push out the two oblong wooden boxes at the right moment.

I gave a bit more throttle and let the propellers turn at higher revs to make more noise, and that did the trick: at the same time my observer and I spotted a faintly blinking light ahead of us. At first we saw only one, then another light further away, but there was no sign of the third. However, as we were absolutely certain this was the right spot, I turned into the drop direction, held the machine towards the northerly torch and then gave the signal to let go of our cargo.

The altimeter showed exactly 820 ft over the ground as the two wooden boxes, each $50 \times 20 \times 20$ cm ($19\frac{3}{4} \times 8 \times 8$ in), tumbled out of the ventral hatch. If everything functioned as it should, fifty metre long red and white linen ribbons were now unwinding from each box to facilitate their location.

Both engines again set at cruising revs, I banked the machine on the new course in a south-westerly direction according to the bearing notified by my observer. My first operational task for *Olga* had been fulfilled.

The mood aboard our aircraft was now more high spirited; we were back in business. The next leg of our flight to the spot where we had to drop our Belgian was estimated to take just 20 minutes, and everything went according to plan – simply because the brightly lit inhabited places and roads made our navigation as easy as in peacetime. We wished our agent all the very best before he slid through the hatch with his pack and parachuted exactly over the agreed spot. In the light of the risen moon we could even observe both parachutes opening as we left the scene. Now for the final part of our operational task!

While we busied ourselves setting the new course towards the next target, our radio operator 'Hein' Haller suddenly drew our attention to a mysterious apparition in the night sky. He had spotted what seemed like an aircraft with a fiery trail flying behind and across our flight path. Immediately we became alert. I pushed the Ju 188 down to gain more speed and we streaked along closer to the ground. Now we could observe the fiery trail better; it continued unflinchingly to fly in a northerly direction, towards the coast, and soon disappeared from our sight.

A short while later we observed two more such fiery streaks flying at medium altitude crossing our flight path behind us. There was no doubt: these were the V-1s, the flying robot bombs on their way to the English coast. At long last we had seen these marvels in action with our own eyes – met them in the air, even!

All the German hopes for a change in the catastrophic course of the war in those weeks and months were sustained by the promise of these 'wonder weapons', long since announced by the political leadership: the V-1 'flying bomb' (Fi 103), the V-2 long-range rocket missile (A4), the super-fast new aircraft powered by the revolutionary rocket or turbojet engines the Me 163, Me 262 and Ar 234, the bombs that could be remotely guided onto the target from the launch aircraft, the remotely-controlled anti-aircraft rocket missiles that could hit any-thing flying, the novel radio and radar devices, and the new big aircraft capable of reaching almost undreamed-of distances. Even if the numerical superiority of the enemies seemed to be overwhelming, these technically superior weapons would shortly lead to a turning point. At the very least, they would force the enemies of Germany to start negotiations.

And now we had seen them – a whole three of them!

In view of the gigantic concentration of force taking place below us from horizon to horizon, and apparently extending like a spider's web right into the western hinterland, it would have needed thousands and thousands of such superior weapons right now even to hold up the enemy. Where were they?

In the meantime we had gone into a gradual climbing flight so as to have a wider overall view for better orientation. The Belgian-French border was coming closer.

Suddenly the lights of an airfield were switched on right in front of us. An ice-cold fear gripped me and triggered a lightning reaction! With quick grasp at the switch I un-coupled the auto-pilot and banked steeply into the darker side of the skies. While doing this, I was fully aware that the clumsy PAG with its human cargo still hung suspended under my aircraft, and I had no idea how it would react to such acceleration. Of course, I could not risk losing the plywood cask and tried to bank as gently as I could, at the same time trying to get away from the airfield as quickly as possible.

As I was turning away my ventral gunner reported the next surprise: they were firing green flares from the ground! No anti-aircraft guns or night fighters or other devilries as we had experienced in constantly changing variations during our night operations over England. This time we were requested to land! What shall we do now?

– 'Amiens.' my observer Hans Fecht mentioned laconically on the intercom, calm as anything.

It was obvious they had taken us for one of their own aircraft that was either expected at this time or had apparently lost its way. Whatever it was, one thing was now clear: from now on they would keep an eye on us and note our further progress over the landscape.

This really was something new. In near enough six years of war we had not experienced anything like it: there we were, on an operational flight at night deep in the enemy's territory, they had us detected, but 'identified' us not as an enemy but a friend! How should we behave under these circumstances and yet be able to continue our mission? Apart from everything else, we were not a 'normal' aircraft but a special vehicle for spies! Whatever happened, we could on no account lose our 'disposable load' in some emergency or drop it somewhere else than planned. Should we now abandon our operation and hot-foot it back to our own territory? Or should we play along and

41

simulate 'distress', perhaps by switching on our navigation lights?

While I continued on our course we weighed the pros and cons against each other until my observer estimated that we should reach our last target in just 25 minutes. That decided the issue: we were going to carry on as if nothing had happened.

The airfield with its no doubt puzzled flight control gradually disappeared behind us and darkness again spread its protective wings around our Ju 188. And that was it. In fact, after all that, we were bothered only once more, by a group of three adjoining searchlights that flashed some signals we could not interpret, before we recognized the characteristic loops of the Seine ahead of us.

We contacted our Frenchmen in the PAG via the attached intercom and informed them that we could see the target area and would soon set them down in the agreed spot, a strip of meadow within a U-shaped Seine bend.

Naturally, we did not tell them anything about the previous episode, that we were regarded as one of 'their' aircraft. It would not make any difference to them, but could affect our future flights if one of them, for whatever reason, decided to talk.

Releasing the PAG was much less dramatic than dropping our Belgian with his parachute straight from the cabin.

With throttled back engines I let the 188 fly on at slow speed in a flat glide towards the clearly discernible target and passed over the river bend in a westerly direction at 820 ft altitude. The moonlight was quite sufficient to help me avoid overflying any houses and once I had reached the right spot it was only a matter of pressing on the bomb release button. Then the aircraft jumped in the air, now almost 800 kg (1760 lb) lighter, and then a second jolt as the strong steel ripcord jerked off the cap and pulled out the parachutes.

Without opening the throttles I continued flying in the same direction to avoid drawing the attention of any casual observer to the PAG dropping area. Only when the ground had come dangerously close did I carefully open the throttles and slowly began to gain height again to make a wide curve in a southerly direction before setting the course for home.

In the meantime, the crew of course had attentively watched the falling PAG, a novelty for all of us. The parachutes had opened perfectly not far from the ground, but they could not observe the actual landing; my 188 had already lost too much height for that. However we were sure that our device had proved its worth. Thanks to good visibility and the well-chosen dropping area we had done our part as planned. It only remained to be hoped that the trio had succeeded in reaching a safe haven without drawing any attention on themselves. It had been agreed beforehand that they would confirm their successful landing by radio to their group leader and controller in Germany the following day.

Our return flight path led us north at a respectable distance past Paris and then directly to Frankfurt. Right on time we were over the endlessly moving lights on the ground, filling all the main and secondary roads leading to the front, but we were now long since used to that display. On looking back we could clearly see a bright spot on the southerly horizon – Paris.

Suddenly, my observer poked me in the ribs and pointed ahead, drawing my attention to moving red and green lights. These were unmistakably navigation lights of an aircraft crossing our flight path at the same altitude. Almost simultaneously, a searchlight beam stabbed vertically into the night sky ahead to the right, and then we recognized the illuminations of an airfield on the horizon. I withdrew a bit to the north to remain unnoticed.

In the next moment we spotted several other navigation lights moving through the sky, and it became clear that we had inadvertently got in between the night flying operations of an enemy airfield. From the way the machines were lining up in the air, they were flying a left-hand circuit.

It all seemed so peaceful that I could not resist the temptation to join in the circuit. There was the airfield, fully lit up. And here was a German aircraft, unnoticed and unrecognized, taking part in the enemy's night flying operations! It seemed that all I had to do now was to switch on my own navigation lights and go around again without being challenged. What a night!

Below us on the ground were hamlets and villages, all lit up like in peacetime. All streets and roads were busy with traffic, with full headlights. And there was an airfield, lit up like a Christmas tree.

For a moment the thought crossed our minds to hang on behind one of the enemy aircraft and shoot it down with our turret guns (we still had them), or at least to roar at low level across the airfield and scare the lot, but just as quickly decided not to. What was the point, anyway? It would have been just as useless to fly some low-level attacks with our wretched guns against the endless motor vehicle columns. All we might achieve was to 'trample on our own salad', as we used to say, if we drew their attention to us.

Leaving the busy airfield behind, we continued on our previous course towards Frankfurt. The vehicle lights on the roads below began to swarm out fanwise, a sure sign that the front-line could not be very far off.

I let my Ju 188 gradually gain height because we could soon expect to be shot at by light anti-aircraft guns from front-line infantry positions. From this higher altitude we also had a better overall view, the same as we had when crossing the lines going west – irregular flashes of exploding heavy artillery shells, more distant flashes of the guns themselves, then coloured chains of tracer snaking across the ground. The combat zone!

I pushed the throttles forward and went into a slightly inclined flight to gain more speed. It was magnificent how the lightened Ju 188 could accelerate, a sheer joy to have your hands on! Then came the light anti-aircraft guns as expected, only this time way off.

And then suddenly it was peace again around us and under us. Despite the moonlight the night again seemed pitch-black – the German side had crawled into complete darkness.

The sudden change hit us like a physical blow: everything was dead. Only here and there came a weak reflection of the moonlight in some window or on the water surface, otherwise nothing. Never before had the complete superiority of the enemy become so evident to us: over there carelessness and lively activity as in peacetime, and an enormous concentration of men and material; on this side, total helplessness, fear and weakness.

We looked at each other and were unable to utter a single word.

We had long since had the navigation radio beacon near Frankfurt fixed in our direction finder, and it was now only a matter of making some minor corrections to be on the last homeward leg. From that, we estimated our landing for fifteen minutes' time.

A brief radio signal conveyed our estimated time of arrival and was acknowledged from the airfield.

We reached the base right on time and were greeted by the runway illuminations. Engines throttled back, landing flaps out, propeller pitch changed, auxiliary pumps switched on – I completed all these necessary tasks as of old while going into the landing turn. And then we were back on the ground again. The runway lights were switched off even before we had finished taxiing, but then a green light flashed from the direction of our parking slot near the edge of the woods.

I taxied carefully that way, making every effort to avoid the bomb craters. And then we were home. I switched off the engines and looked at the clock: our operational flight had lasted almost five hours.

In the sudden quiet we climbed down from the machine, and only then found the first words to express our impressions of this night.

Surely, the military and political leadership must know what it looked like on the other side of the front-line, but in spite of the overwhelming superiority they carried on as if our own situation was only a temporary setback. It seemed they were more convinced than ever that we could reverse our military fortunes with one final massive blow. Could it be that whispered hints of 'wonder weapons' had made final victory seem believable once more?

Nobody was really aware what these weapons were supposed to be. We already knew of some of them from our own observations and from hearsay – the new turbojet and rocket aircraft, the V-weapons, the guided bombs, the anti-aircraft rockets, but hard experience to date had also shown that these new weapons were nowhere near sufficient to turn the tide. In fact, this was already an open secret.

However the German leadership and propaganda machine kept promising new weapons of ever greater destructive power. This could only mean that the real 'wonder weapon' was still to come. Some still believed in it, others had given up hope long since. Or had they?

Before I got busy together with my observer preparing a detailed report about what we had noted behind the enemy lines, I informed the controllers of our now positioned *V-Leute* that everything had gone according to plan. It was always a touch and go business, everything considering.

But it was while writing down our observations and impressions that once more it became oppressively clear what kind of avalanche there was rolling towards the German lines. The whole thing was so overwhelming that we could hardly find the right words to give a more or less accurate description. For one thing, it was absolutely impossible even to give any figures or estimates. We tried to draw comparisons with Soviet supplies in winter 1941/42, the only other criteria we had. Despite the enormous amounts of troops and material we had then seen moving forward in an unbroken stream day and night, the impression remained that what was now happening here in the West was many times greater than the gathering of military power that had stopped the German Army on the Eastern Front in that winter.

4. A *Geschwader* Like no Other

A new task tackled by *Olga* was an exercise that did not involve deep penetration flights of enemy territory.

At the time when the front line had reached the Rhine we had an agent somewhere in the Paris area equipped with a VHF radio transceiver. We never found out his exact place of residence or his task – we only knew his covername, which was also frequently changed.

In contrast to his 'colleagues' who were all equipped with short-wave radio sets for sending transmissions, he could no longer contact his control post this side of the lines. This was because the wave characteristics of the VHF band allowed transmissions over great distance with relatively low power, but only when the transmitter and receiver are in a straight alignment. In other words, the operational range is limited by the curvature of the earth which between two ground stations would correspond to a distance of 30 to 50 km (18.6- 31 miles). However, if one of these stations is fitted in an aircraft that can reach high altitude, the effective operational range is increased to several hundred kilometres.

As it happened, the stay-behind agent had been given a FuG 16 set before he let himself be over-run by the advancing Allied forces. This was the same type of VHF set carried in our aircraft, enabling us to keep excellent contact with our informer. Of course, there was a strictly set timetable for these transmissions, limited to those nocturnal hours when an aircraft from *Olga* would be flying over French territory. The constantly changing speech code was based on a numerical key.

Of course, we were not at all pleased about this additional task, to take an extra man with us in the aircraft who would then carry on long-winded radio conversations with his agent. After all, the basic principle for us all was to keep absolute radio silence over enemy territory, and there we were, chatting away. Apart from that, the place occupied in the aircraft by this *V-Mann* controller was always lost for the possible transport of an agent. In addition to that, it was soon obvious that these radio conversations were unnecessarily prolonged because the *V-Man* controller lacked sufficient practice, and was also

46

somewhat inhibited and frightened.

Finally, pursuing the interests of our own safety, we were able to leave the controller on the ground and were authorised to carry out the necessary radio conversations ourselves. This speeded everything up, was safer for all of us, and we managed to remain free of critical transmission errors.

I can recall another flight we carried out at that time. It was a bright moonlit night over France, and it was past midnight getting on for one o'clock. We were flying past Paris in the westerly direction carrying a PAG with three men and their equipment underwing destined for the Brest area. Two other Frenchmen with their little suitcases crouched in the cabin, nervously following the progress of the flight and every move of the crew with staring eyes.

The observer pulled out a paper from his map case and prepared to write. He had to switch on a small lamp that was dimmed sideways, but was nevertheless bright enough. From the plan he noted the frequency allocated for that day, as well as the current call name of the lonely man on the ground. Meanwhile we were flying over brightly lit villages and towns, with their streets and squares already decorated for the coming Christmas.

Exactly on the agreed minute the observer pressed the voice button on his transmitter and spoke: -'Station from Locomotive – please report!'. The reply came right away : 'Locomotive from Station – I read you loud and clear!' – 'Please start!' – '91864 – 37368 – 12509 . . .' My observer began to take down the long series of numbers that took quite some time to transmit while I watched the minutes creep by on the cockpit clock. At long last came the 'Fini' from the darkness below – 'Understood!' was the only word spoken in reply by my observer, a word that had to express simultaneously a confirmation, farewell greeting and best wishes.

With the same breath the observer began to call out number combinations for his part, reading from a small piece of paper. Nobody knew what these numbers meant, perhaps this time they contained Christmas wishes in addition to other instructions.

I followed this radio conversation impatiently, wishing it to end. I was certain that we were being monitored by the enemy, and those few minutes were quite enough to identify my aircraft as one of the partners in this conversation. This being so, I had to assume that our flight might now be tracked from the ground which could endanger the success of my main task, the release of the PAG with it human cargo. I had to be prepared to face anti-aircraft fire and even night fighters from then on.

Of course, we could have had this prolonged radio conversation on the way back, after completion of our main operation, but the agreed timetable for air-to-ground contact precluded that sensible solution. Indeed, things could have been better organised but unfortunately there was no proper coordinating centre that could sort out such problems. It was the same old story: in case of active enemy defence I had to immediately abandon my flight and return home. There was no point in trying to carry on with such highly secret tasks as setting down agents in the enemy hinterland once the enemy had joined in the game. Apart from the immediate risk, it might also endanger the safety of all future agent flights. All this was quite understandable, and for these reasons all *Olga* aircrews had strict orders to immediately give up their operational flight if they suspected being identified by the enemy.

Naturally, the final decision was always left to the pilot, and it was never an easy one. After all, we would rather land back at home with the feeling of having accomplished our task than to report a failure. Apart from that, in those winter days with frequent bad weather we were already overloaded with operational requests and every single return meant another delay. It was a problem we had to solve somehow, but even every effort of the technical personnel working on our aircraft outside in all weathers in their widely dispersed bays was to no avail.

To have aircrews standing by to fly operations in unfavourable weather conditions also did not make much sense if there was no guarantee that the secret target could be found, and that there would be sufficient visibility for an accurate and unnoticed drop of people and material.

Unfortunately we received very few acknowledgements from our task masters regarding the success or otherwise of such operations. This was mainly due to the standing and strictly observed secrecy, but it would seem perhaps that gradually more chaotic communications also played a certain part.

Be that as it may, we developed a kind of half open collaboration with a few agent controllers and their organisations. These were our 'permanent clients' so to speak, people we got to know better in the course of months, at least as individuals, even if hidden behind the ever present screen of cover names. We occasionally heard from them what had happened to this or that of their protégés after we had seen them

48

disappear under our aircraft in the darkness.

In any case, it was critically important to carry out these flights as inconspicuously as possible. This was finally realised by the controllers of that radio operator near Paris. As a result, every effort was made to shorten the conversations both ways as much as possible. From then on we no longer felt that the radio agent might be discovered at any moment, or that our flights could be connected by the listening enemy with these ethereal messages. In fact we remained in contact with that particular agent until the very last flights of *Olga* crews made over French territory shortly before the end of hostilities.

This kind of activity had become daily routine both for the aircrews of *Olga* and the specialists on the ground. However, the many legends woven around KG 200 have eventually led to the question: what actually did go on in this mysterious formation, what did it do? How much truth is there in those stories of 'suicide actions', *coup d'état* attempts, cyanide capsules for the aircrews, various assassination plots in the best tradition of Hollywood films, composite aircraft, and other exotic weapons?

The fact is that KG 200 was the most secret unit of the Luftwaffe in its own lifetime, but whatever was revealed to the public in detail after the war soon built into a legend that contains more misleading inventions than truth. Yet the truth is adventurous enough.

To begin with, all operational activities carried out by KG 200 were 'especially secret' – but if it comes to that so were the existence and activities of any other military unit in wartime. Looked at this way, KG 200 was nothing exceptional.

Its personnel were made up of ordinary Luftwaffe soldiers, just like any other *Geschwader*, the only difference being that they were selected according to their proven abilities and experience to carry out special tasks. There was no special 'KG 200 oath' or some special swearing of loyalty, just as there is no truth in stories about poison capsules the aircrew were supposed to have carried on operational flights to evade capture by commiting suicide. All that belongs in the land of fairy tales.

The official order authorising the formation of KG 200 was sent out on 20 February, 1944. It happened at a time when the activities of the Luftwaffe were limited mainly to the defence of the Reich against the constant raids of the Anglo-American bomber fleets. Due to the shortage of fuel, German bomber squadrons were largely grounded, and whatever fuel was available went almost without exception to the day and night fighter defences. The transport and reconnaissance *Geschwader* and smaller formations were in the same predicament. Production and supply of aircraft and fuel, as well as training, were fully geared to the so-called 'Fighter programme' aimed at 'sweeping the skies over Germany clear again', as Hermann Göring and the propaganda machine had promised.

The remnants of the bomber, transport and reconnaissance formations were units entrusted with special tasks or equipped with special weapons. These included KG 100, operational with the Hs 293 and Fritz X glide bombs against special targets, and parts of KG 66 and KG 30 equipped with *Mistel* composite aircraft (also known under the cover designation of *Beethoven* or as *Vater und Sohn* = Father and son). A small number of transport and reconnaissance *Gruppen* were also still functioning, such as FAGr. 5, partly equipped with the Ju 90 and Ju 290 long-range aircraft flying long-range reconnaissance missions for U-boats over the Atlantic, but also available for special long-range transport tasks. The same applied to the *Versuchsverband Ob.d,L.* under the direct control of Luftwaffe High Command, used for special activities beyond the capabilities of normal *Geschwader* such as very high altitude reconnaissance, operating at heights of over 12,000 m (39,000 ft), as well as testing, conversion and operational use of captured enemy aircraft and other material.

Even if under the pressure of conditions in early 1944 all these operational activities and tasks had been limited only to the barest minimum, a certain very special mission remained constantly urgent – in fact, became even more important: the placing of our own intelligence and sabotage agents in enemy territory, their regular supply and – in certain cases, their return. Regular soldiers too were set down from aircraft behind the front lines when the tactical situation required, or when it was a matter of carrying out certain reconnaissance tasks; they did not necessarily have to be trained paratroopers.

Before the formation of KG 200 such tasks were always entrusted to selected aircrews drawn from normal transport, reconnaissance or bomber units. The determining factors were solely the qualifications of the aircrews and the required aircraft type, again depending on the operational task. Was it a matter of deep penetration flights? Did it involve the transport of especially large loads? Would it be advisable to use the fastest possible aircraft (generally applicable to operations near the combat zone), and so on.

One of the chief reasons for the setting up of KG 200 was that it was becoming increasingly difficult for the controller of such clandestine agent flights (mainly the RSHA of the SS and the military *Abwehr*) to get hold of the necessary aircraft, aircrews and servicing personnel from the already shrinking transport and bomber *Geschwader*. Apart from that it was only sensible to form an independent formation for all flying tasks that carried the 'special' label. In this way, the 'task master' need only have a single authorized partner to address when it was a matter of getting hold of custom-made components suitable for the task in hand. Another important advantage was that training, choice of aircraft and crews, their technical maintenance and supply could be better coordinated and more effectively managed. The advantages were obvious also on higher level, relations with the various secret offices of the political and military leadership were more clearly defined and no longer dissipated among all possible command posts and combat formations of the Luftwaffe.

Once the formation of KG 200 was authorized, things began to move quickly. On 29 February 1944, only nine days after activation, the *Geschwaderstab* (HQ) and *Stab* of I *Gruppe* were in being, and *Luftflotte Reich*, to which KG 200 was subordinated, was notified accordingly. The *Versuchsverband Ob.d.L.* – formerly *Aufklärungsgruppe Ob.d.L.* (with a tradition stretching back to prewar times) and *Transportkolonne XI Ost* formed the nucleus of the planned three *Staffeln* of I/KG 200. At the same time, the long-range Ju 290s of FAGr. 5 were recalled to Germany from their bases on the Atlantic coast and put at the disposal of I/KG 200.

II/KG 200, formed soon afterwards, was initially intended to take over the technical care and maintenance of the various aircraft types and also function as a training *Gruppe*. From then on KG 200 developed and took shape very quickly. In the course of this rapid build-up a confusing chain of changes resulted in the internal structure of the *Geschwader*, just as the scope of operational tasks kept expanding. Basically, only the build-up of I/KG 200 took place logically and as planned. Under its commanders *Major* Gartenfeld (February 1944-March1944) and *Major* Koch (April 1944-end of the war), I/KG 200 activated three operational *Staffeln* one after another, and a well-equipped technical company with its own large workshop. This uninterrupted build-up was necessitated by the urgent tasks entrusted to the *Gruppe*. It was to be the flying formation that had to carry out all air transport operations connected with intelligence and sabotage agents over enemy territory. It had also to carry out all transport flights that involved any kind of behind-the-lines special operations.

The main clients of the *Geschwader*, RSHA of the SS and the *Abwehr*, were to prove very useful in the critical times when aviation fuel, equipment and personnel became very scarce; their supply to KG 200 had priority.

Within I/KG 200 the tasks were shared out as follows:

1. *Staffel* : long-range operations
2. *Staffel* : operations near the combat zone
3. *Staffel* : replenishment and training.

The *Staffeln* served as a basis for so-called *Kommandos* or detachments which received their operational orders directly from the *Geschwader* HQ but otherwise were largely independent. The commanders of these detachments had the disciplinary powers of a *Staffelkapitän* leading an independent *Staffel* because these detachments were some distance away from the *Gruppe* HQ and operated as completely self-sufficient units. Their bases changed according to the task in hand, and the front situation. From time to time such detachments operated on the northern sector of the Eastern Front (for instance, in Finland); in the Balkans for operations behind the southern sector of the Eastern Front and the Near East; in northern Italy, covering southern Italy and Africa; and in western Germany, covering the entire Western Front (France, Belgium, Holland), and later also including Italy, North Africa, Spain and the British Isles.

Of course, to conceal their real relationship all these detachments were known only by their cover names, such as *Olga, Carmen, Tosca, Clara* and so on. Their strength changed constantly, fluctuating from that of a reinforced front-line *Staffel* to only a few aircrews just about able to carry out a limited operational task.

The commander of such a detachment, especially a larger one, had his hands full: he had to be a pilot, operational commander and paymaster at the same time. In addition to that he was responsible for the security of all special operations both within and without the detachment, and he also had to see that the various controllers and their agents who came his way, did not get to know each other. This went as far as ensuring that there was nothing that could indicate to an agent the name or location of the airfield from which he would be taken off into the unknown.

The detachment commander and his specialists also had the final word regarding what an agent could take with him and its packing into

Oberst Werner Baumbach, *Kommodore* of KG 200 from October 1944 to the end of hostilities. Best known for his daring and successful dive bombing attacks on shipping with the Ju 88, Baumbach was also a strong personality who never lacked the courage of his convictions. After release from British and then American captivity Baumbach collaborated with Prof Dr Bruce C. Hopper of Harvard University in producing a valuable study of the Luftwaffe in World War II. He was killed flying an Avro Lancaster bomber in Argentina on 20 October 1953.

The author, Peter W. Stahl with his crew in autumn 1940. From left to right: Theo Goertz (gunner), Hein Hallert (radio operator), the author, and Hans Fecht (observer/bomb aimer).

A Ju 88A bomber displaying washable temporary night camouflage often applied in 1940/41.

Ju 188A-3 crew preparing for an operational sortie. The flexible 20 mm MG 151/20 cannon in the nose and 13 mm MG 131 in the electrically-operated dorsal turret are shown to advantage.

Ju 188A-3 torpedo bomber 3E+KK of 2./KG 6 being loaded with two LT 1B torpedoes.

Ju 188F-2 reconnaissance bomber shortly before take-off. This version dispensed with the forward-firing MG 151/20 cannon and usually carried 2 × 200 1 (44 Imp gal) drop tanks for extended range.

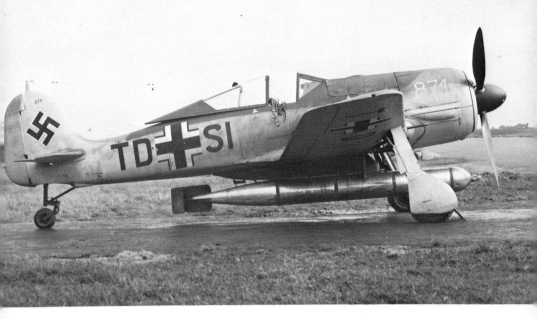

FW 190A-5/U14 torpedo fighter with LT F5b torpedo on ETC 502 fuselage rack. Note the lengthened tailwheel leg and enlarged fin. The FW 190(BT) version briefly used by III/KG 200 was a later modification of the FW 190F-8 carrying either one 2094 lb BT 950 or even 3087 lb BT 1400 bomb-torpedo, but were never more than conditionally operational.

The SD 1400 X was an experimental HE variant of the armour-piercing PC 1400 X free-fall guided bomb generally known as Fritz X. Its most notable success was the sinking of the fleeing new Italian battleship *Roma*, of 46,215 tons maximum displacement, with one direct hit on 9 September 1943.

The variety of aircraft used by KG 200 included such widely different types as the FW 189 tactical reconnaissance, Ju 352 *Herkules* transport and Go 242 cargo glider.

Captured French aircraft converted for KG 200 use included the obsolete Amiot 143 bomber-transport, the more modern Lioré et Olivier LeO 451 bomber, and at least one Bloch 161 civil airliner.

Arado Ar 232A twin-engined combat transport during trials. Its large main wheel undercarriage with hydraulically extending legs combined with 11 pairs of smaller idler wheels enabled the Ar 232A to land on unprepared fields and earned it the nickname 'Tatzelwurm' (a mythical Alpine dragon).

The Italian Piaggio P.108C four-engined transport was another foreign aircraft type impressed into KG 200 service. These illustrations show the J4+HH and J4+JH operated by LTS 5 (*Lufttransportstaffel 5*).

Other commandeered Italian aircraft types used by KG 200 were suitably converted Savoia-Marchetti SM.79-II Sparviero torpedo-bombers and SM.82 Canguro heavy transports.

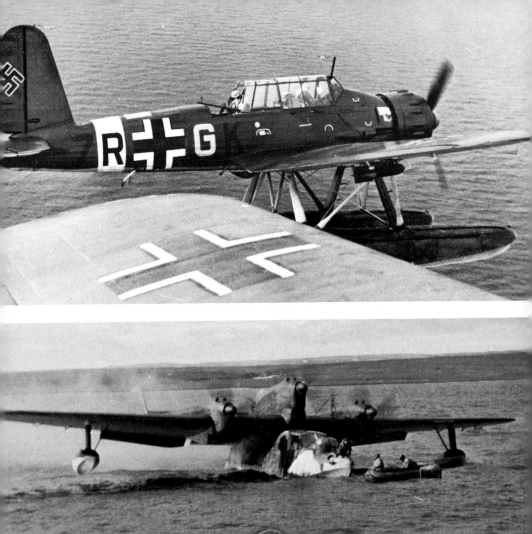

A variety of seaplanes were also under KG 200 command and included such diverse types as the Ar 196A, BV 138C (shown here equipped with ASV radar), and even some old He 59D float biplanes. A few Ar 196A-3 floatplanes were used by KG 200 to supply agents in Soviet Karelia, landing on one of the many lakes. According to Finnish archives two of these aircraft were coded A3 + AC and A3 + BC.

The few surviving BV 222 Wiking flying boats were also attached to KG 200 and held in immediate readiness, but plans to use them to transport a group of State and Party VIPs to Greenland shortly before the capitulation never materialised.

A more unusual type in KG 200 service were two Lioré at Olivier LeO H.246.1 flying boats. Three of these French civil seaplanes were commandeered by the Luftwaffe in 1942, modified to carry 21 fully equipped troops (or 14 casualties) and fitted with a defensive armament of five flexible MG 15s.

The two H.246.ls flown by KG 200 crews were coded A3 + HC and A3 + KC and used to transport Finnish long-range reconnaissance patrols deep into the Soviet hinterland; there was no shortage of suitable lakes in the tundra. The top illustration shows the H.246.1 coded 24 + 62 at Santahamina seaplane base south of Helsinki.

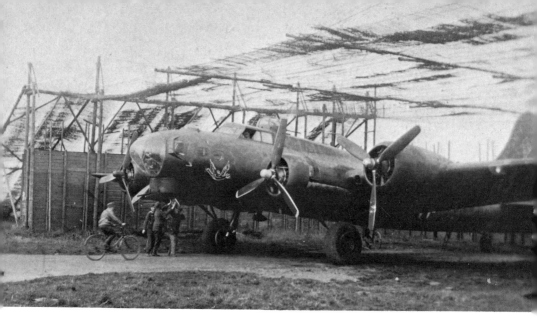

A captured Boeing B-17G Flying Fortress converted for special transport duties in KG 200 service at Hildesheim in April 1945.

The insignia based on a Nils Holgerson fairy tale is of Luftwaffe origin.

A KG 200 B-17G shortly before take-off. Its former identity has been completely oversprayed and replaced by clearly visible Luftwaffe markings.

Another carefully camouflaged KG 200 B-17G in its revetment at Hildesheim in April 1945. Note the special wooden 'splinter walls'.

A captured and converted Consolidated B-24J Liberator in KG 200 service at Hildesheim on 6 April 1945.

Arado Ar 232B 'Tatzelwurm', the four-engined version of this combat zone transport, could carry 50 per cent more useful load than its twin-engined counterpart but otherwise had lower performance characteristics.

The Ar 232B used in 'Operation Zeppelin', the unsuccessful attempt to assassinate Stalin in September 1944, after its alleged forced landing at Karmanovo, about 90 miles west of Moscow.

practical size loads that could be dropped together with an agent and would not go astray. He also had to see to it that all agents were instructed how to behave during the parachute jump and on landing, because as a rule none of them had had any training. Some of them had never even seen a parachute before, and it was up to the detachment commander to boost their confidence and help overcome fear.

And of course a detachment commander was completely on his own when dealing with the local administration, Nazi Party and military authorities.

The diversity of tasks required of I/KG 200 is best indicated by the wide variety of aircraft types this *Gruppe* had at its disposal: Arado Ar 96 trainers, Ar 196A reconnaissance floatplanes, Ar 232A '*Tatzelwurm*' 2-engined transports, Ar 232B 4-engined transports, Bücker Bü 131 Jungmann trainers, Bü 181 Bestmann trainer/liaison, DFS 230A cargo gliders, Dornier Do 217 bombers, Fieseler Fi 156 Storch STOL liaison, Focke-Wulf FW 44 Stieglitz trainer/liaison, FW 189 tactical reconnaissance, Gotha Go 242 cargo gliders, Heinkel He 111 bombers, He 177A Greif long-range bombers, Henschel Hs 126 short range reconnaissance, Junkers W 34 utility transports, Ju 87 dive bomber/close support, Ju 88 dive/level bombers, Ju 188A and E bombers, Ju 252 transports, Ju 352 Herkules transports, Ju 290A large-capacity transport/long range reconnaissance, Klemm Kl 35 trainer/communications, Messerschmitt Bf 108 Taifun liaison, and Siebel Si 204 communications aircraft. This long list was augmented by various sailplanes, and the following seaplanes: Heinkel He 59, He 115, Blohm & Voss BV 138, BV 222 Wiking and Dornier Do 18.

In addition, I/KG 200 also disposed of the following foreign and captured enemy aircraft types: Amiot 143, an obsolete French bombers converted for transport role; Bloch 161 French short-range 18-seat passenger transport; LeO H-246, 4-engined French flying boats; LeO H-451 2-engined French bombers; Savoia-Marchetti SM 79, 3-engined Italian reconnaissance bombers; SM. 82, 3-engined Italian bomber transports; Douglas DC-3 passenger airliners; Boeing B-17 Flying Fortresses and Consolidated B-24 Liberators.

For various reasons II/KG 200 never got around to looking after its intended duties as a replacement and training unit. It first appeared in September 1944 equipped with a number of FW 190(BT), a standard fighter modified to carry a bomb or aerial torpedo up to 1400 kg (3090 lb) in weight. It was planned to form three *Staffeln* with these machines but it never got that far. The main reason was that the FW 190 was really stretched carrying such heavy loads under operational conditions. There had been a number of bad accidents during trials and retraining, mainly because the undercarriage and the tyres in particular just could not stand up to this load stress.

Nevertheless, a few FW 190 (BT) fighter-bombers from II/KG 200 based at Stavanger/Norway did eventually fly some individual attacks against British warships in the North Sea.

In mid-November 1944 III/KG 66 was incorporated into KG 200 and formed the nucleus of the new II *Gruppe*, while the existing II/KG 200 was redesignated III/KG 200(BT). In addition to the *Mistel* composite aircraft the new II/KG 200 also had on hand some He 111 and Ju 188 escort bombers and flare-carrying 'illuminators' (*Beleuchter*).

November 1944 also saw the formation of IV/KG 200. This *Gruppe* was to be responsible for the whole training and instructional programme for KG 200. Its personnel came mainly from the previous III/KG 200, which had become II/KG 200. From sheer embarrassment IV/KG 200 also had to take under its wing the 80-100 so-called *Totaleinsatz* ('total effort') men, volunteers for suicide operations, whose care and control had remained stuck with KG 200.

The central technical base of the *Geschwader* was established at Finow airfield near Berlin. It was here that the aircraft were prepared for operations, and any necessary conversions carried out. These particularly concerned the captured American B-17 and B-24 bombers. (Later it has been repeatedly asserted that KG 200 had hundreds of these captured bombers. Such statements only show how much the former enemies have overestimated the possibilities of the *Geschwader*, and their own losses). Finow was also the depot for spare parts, and accommodated KG 200 specialists for parachute and cargo dropping.

The first commander of KG 200 was *Oberst* Heigl, who was replaced by *Oberstleutnant* Werner Baumbach in autumn 1944.

Shortly before the end of hostilities an order from the highest authority completely disbanded the *Geschwader*. By that time however the *Gruppen* and all the various detachments were scattered to the winds and this order did not reach all flying units. As a result, some detachments and individual crews carried on with their secret duties right until the capitulation and even beyond.

After the end of the war the Allied military authorities instituted a specially vigorous search for all former members of this 'Hitler's Spy *Geschwader*'. Contrary to anything they might have expected they found only ordinary soldiers and officers of the Luftwaffe who had done nothing else than their airman's trade, who could not tell them any details of the secret operations carried out during the war, and who did not even know the names of people and authorities who had been their 'controllers'. They did not know simply because the names and designations known to them at the time were just cover designations.

As far as their activities were concerned, the transport of agents and their supply had been just one of the many tasks demanded of, or carried out by the *Geschwader*. There were many others, including the planning of strategic bombing raids with 'special weapons' against the Soviet energy supply system; preparation of long-range aircraft for the transport of strategically vital materials from the Far East (for example, from Japan); attacks on specially important targets in key positions with bombs and remotely-controlled missiles; testing of new weapons; and finally, preparing land and seaplanes to enable high Party officials to escape.

Some of this remained in the planning stage, some did not get past the half-way mark, and in one case they even fell into a trap set by the enemy. Be that as it may, the members of this *Geschwader* never performed, or were asked to do anything that contravened the international rules of warfare. Was that all?

If one was strictly accurate, yes. On the other hand, operating in this unique military formation, amazing ideas could grow into firm plans and there was no shortage of adventurous and imaginative people eager to carry them out as actual missions!

5. Operation Zeppelin

One of the more fantastic episodes involving KG 200 embodied all the elements of a modern thriller – this was the operation codenamed *Zeppelin*.

Typically of the period, a hare-brained scheme had matured into an operational plan and then actually been carried out. But let's start at the beginning:

As happened very frequently, the operational command of KG 200 was requested to prepare aircraft suitable for landings behind enemy lines. Such requests had to be refused as far as the Western Front was concerned simply because the geography of that densely populated area would have permitted such operations only in extremely exceptional cases. Of course, it was not always easy to explain this to the armchair fliers from the RSHA and the *Abwehr*.

However, the situation was quite different in the enormous expanses of the Soviet Union. There were enough large flat areas quite suitable without any special preparations for unnoticed landings of aircraft. There were areas there so thinly populated that provided the landing places were carefully chosen, absolute secrecy for landing and even taking off could be guaranteed before the enemy was in a position to do anything about it.

In July 1944 the KG 200 Operations Officer was called for a secret discussion to the RSHA in Berlin. It was not the first time, and also did not necessarily mean anything special. Usually, he was given the operational requests for the next few weeks, accompanied by some veiled or quite open reproaches for agent flights not completed in the current period. Then again, seldom as it was, perhaps he might receive some appreciation for this or that successful operation. Whatever was in store, it was certain that they would be requesting more than the *Geschwader* was in a position to cope with – provision of even more aircraft for the RSHA tasks, flights over countries and continents far outside the range of available aircraft, or transport of cargoes amounting to whole shiploads. Apparently in Nazi Party and SS circles the word still had not got around that it was 1944, that the German armed forces and the war economy were fighting with their backs to the wall and were absorbing massive blows from the enemy every day.

'To the German soldiers nothing is impossible!' – was still the slogan there. In the RSHA building the Luftwaffe *Oberstleutnant* was led directly into the Chief's office and asked to take a seat. The doors were shut behind his back, only the two of them were in the room.

Ernst Kaltenbrunner, head of the *Reichssicherheitshauptamt*, the Reichs Main Security Office, cleared his throat. He would like to discuss a certain matter that came under the highest secrecy classification. He was the only one in this building who knew about it, but as yet he still could not reveal any details.

That was not all that unusual. It was very seldom that the operational command and KG 200 aircrews got to know anything about the tasks of their secret 'parachute passengers' whom they had to drop somewhere over the enemy territory. If it came to that, they were no longer curious either: habit makes one indifferent.

However, when the all-powerful Chief of the RSHA made a personal appearance, then it could not have been just the 'ordinary' secret task any more; it must be something much more important and urgent.

'I can tell you this much. Your KG 200 has to provide an aircraft that is capable of flying almost to Moscow, land, and unload a sizeable amount of cargo and one or two people safely and unnoticed. The whole operation is very important, perhaps even decisive to the outcome of the war. It must be carried out as soon as possible, at least before the autumn, not to mention the winter weather sets in. The landing place must not be further than 100 km from Moscow, and it is essential that there is a road nearby that leads directly to the capital.' – Kaltenbrunner lowered his voice:

'Your task will be to land a man who would operate on his own in Moscow. This man has to cover the distance from the landing place to Moscow in a motor vehicle which will be carried in the aircraft. You have to know at least these details because you have to select the most suitable aircraft.' And after a short pause: 'Do you think this can be done? The time limit for your preparations is just four weeks because this operation has been ascribed the greatest urgency by the highest command circles.'

In the course of further talks it was unavoidable that the KG 200 Operations Officer got to know more than his 'taskmaster' really wanted to reveal. According to everything insinuated in these discussions it could only have been an attempt to assassinate Stalin himself!

Apparently this operation had been prepared with great care. The central figure was a Soviet officer who had deserted to the Germans and had volunteered to kill the 'Red tsar'. On the German side they expected great things from this deed. It seemed they were taken in by the notion that following Stalin's death the Western Allies would critically re-examine their military alliance with the Soviets and possibly revise or even renounce it. And in such a changed political situation cautious diplomatic initiatives regarding an armistice could begin. They were also probably hoping to be able to concentrate German forces on the Eastern Front to hold up and even finally defeat the Soviet masses.

'As far as the flying side itself is concerned,' the KG 200 Operations Officer said finally 'this should be no problem. We have at our disposal some Arado 232A and 232B assault transports and these two- and four-engined aircraft can carry a useful load of up to four tons. The rear end of their fuselages can be lowered to the ground and thus serve as a loading ramp. Even large vehicles can drive straight into the fuselage, and unloading is no problem either. The Ar 232 undercarriage is designed for landings on unprepared grounds, so that we can even consider bumpy meadows for our purpose. This undercarriage consists of three larger and twenty two smaller wheels, hence the nickname 'Tatzelwurm' ('Winged Dragon', a legendary Alpine animal) bestowed to this machine. Thus equipped, the Ar 232 can land in places where an ordinary aircraft would crash.

The distance to the Moscow area too should be within the capabilities of this aircraft.'

Kaltenbrunner looked up: 'Would you then consider that this task could be carried out with equipment already on hand?'

'From the flying point of view, yes,' replied the Operations Officer. 'Of course, such details as the exact times of the approach flight, landing and return flight will depend on the chosen landing place, which still has to be reconnoitred. The weather situation too can turn the scales one way or another. For example, it would be preferable to use low cloud cover both for the approach and return flights. Under those conditions the aircraft would only reveal itself when going down to land and climbing away again, provided the landing place can be found without undue difficulties. It would also be possible to land at night, in bright moonlight, but in that case the landing place would have to be almost like a normal airfield. The early morning twilight too has its points for a reasonably unnoticed landing, only in such a case the return flight in full daylight could be difficult. If there is no closed cloud cover in which the aircraft can hide, it will most certainly be shot down by Soviet air defences somewhere along the 370 mile long way back. That could frustrate the successful outcome of the whole operation, or at least make it questionable. In short, before we can give a positive answer regarding the feasibility and date the *Geschwader* has to clear up a whole series of questions and make preparations accordingly.'

Like it or not, the all-powerful Chief of the RSHA, impatient as he was, had to agree that a proposal outlining the feasibility of this difficult flying task would have to be prepared and submitted 'as quickly as possible'. Only then it would be possible to look further ahead.

For several weeks afterwards, there was a real to and fro between the RSHA and KG 200, during which the airmen had to argue against the unrealistic notions of the SS time and again. Finally, an agreement was reached regarding the landing place near the highway between Smolensk and Moscow, as well as an alternative field in the Rzhev area, and their detailed reconnaissance by an advance detachment. This detachment was to be dropped by parachute 'right away' to carry out detailed orientation on the ground, to find out how much things had changed since the German withdrawal – not only in respect of ground conditions but also as regards the population and local Soviet administration measures, and so on. Most important of all, they had to determine if the planned operation could be carried out there without being spotted. This could by no means be expected in this relatively densely populated area so near the capital and not very far away from the main highway and an important railway line.

A group of suitable volunteers, mostly former Soviet POWs whose reliability and loyalty had long since been proven, was then organised in great haste, quickly instructed, and equipped for the task even faster. Their transport to the operational area was then an almost routine job for the KG 200 crews.

A detailed report from the commander of this advance detachment came in after a surprisingly short time. He had found a suitable place that fulfilled all the requirements east of Smolensk where an unnoticed landing could be carried out. According to his description, it would also be quite easy from there to reach the main road to Moscow in a motor vehicle.

59

Similarly favourable conditions were also offered by the selected alternative landing place about 31 miles further north-east. However, this was already dangerously close to Moscow and for that reason was only intended for use in an emergency.

Thanks to the well-functioning radio contact, excellent local knowledge of the men, and the favourable weather conditions, the task of this advance detachment was completed sooner than feared.

From then on brief radio messages were exchanged only at longer intervals. The interest from this side was mainly about weather, but also about all other conditions that could affect the safety of the aircraft and the agents in their daring undertaking.

Of course, these radio calls also had a control function. It had happened often enough that espionage or sabotage agents would sooner or later begin to play a false game, being forced to do so once they had been discovered by the enemy. The radio traffic would go on as if nothing had happened, the aim being to spread disinformation, attempt to directly mislead the enemy, or try to obtain important information from the previous employer.

In the meantime KG 200 staff had completed all the necessary preparations for Operation *Zeppelin*, as it had been named. The aircraft, an Arado Ar 232B, stood ready. The four-engined version of this assault transport had been chosen for added safety reasons. Its aircrew, commanded by an *Oberleutnant*, was also on hand. All they had been told about the forthcoming operation was what was necessary for the execution of this difficult flying task: they knew the details of the intended landing place and the alternative field from maps and every other possible source. They knew that a man – possibly accompanied by a woman – and a motorcycle with a sidecar would have to be set down unnoticed. And they had orders to take off again immediately after unloading the agents and their motor transport without bothering about their fate. The shorter their stay on the ground, the better.

The aircrew had not volunteered in any way – to them, it was just another flying task requested by the KG 200 command. None of the I/KG 200 airmen were 'death or glory' boys who had volunteered for do-or-die missions, but ordinary soldiers fated to serve in this Luftwaffe unit that had to carry out unusual flying tasks. It could be that some of them might have pulled a few strings to get there, hoping for more exciting and interesting experiences, or because they believed that this kind of flying involving secret tasks would be especially rewarded. But as a rule it was special flying qualifications that decided such transfers to KG 200. One also had to remember that, generally speaking, flying for KG 200 was actually less dangerous to life and limb than serving with a 'normal' Luftwaffe combat formation because all contacts with the enemy had to be strictly avoided.

On the other hand, once captured by the enemy, KG 200 crews had to reckon with the possibility of being treated the same way as the spies and saboteurs they had transported. It was a matter of convincing their captors that they had really nothing to do with the agents and their mission; they only served as transports. This applied particularly for operations behind the Eastern Front where it was well known that the Soviets were not exactly tender already in their behaviour towards ordinary POWs.

The voluntary principle came in only as far as an aircrew always had the chance to ask to be relieved from flying an operation, but then the reasons had to be valid: the required task really had to be beyond their capabilities.

In short, *Zeppelin* aircrew consisted of ordinary airmen doing their operational duty; the only difference might have been their experience and capabilities.

The chosen take-off airfield was in Latvia, near Riga, the capital, then still in German hands. From there, it was about 370 miles to the target area, the shortest route still available at that time. This was an important point because a longer approach flight would have resulted in a certain reduction of the useful load displaced by more fuel for the return flight.

The Ar 232B was then flown by its crew, with the necessary technical personnel, to the chosen jump-off base and kept in readiness. All the preparations had been carried out as routine and under observation of the strictest secrecy.

In Berlin the KG 200 operations command and the SS planning experts were already determining the point of time, considering such factors as clear full moon nights, early morning twilight, evening dusk, weather conditions and security in the landing zone. A small RSHA operations staff had also been transferred to the airfield near Riga and established contact with the small KG 200 operational detachment stationed there.

With all these moves the Ar 232B crew had also got to know a lot more about the hitherto closely guarded secret details of Operation *Zeppelin*. At their new base they met a Soviet major who was to be their 'flying guest', as well as a young Russian woman, reputedly a former lieutenant of the Red Army who was also to be set down together with the major near Smolensk. This otherwise unobtrusive young woman was a late addition, her task being to look after the radio traffic to the 'centre' in Germany. During the preparations and training for their dangerous task both Russians had developed such a close relationship that they had spontaneously decided to get married.

Together with the newly married couple, the KG 200 crew now excercised in loading and unloading the aircraft, gradually speeding up the process to reduce the risk of discovery to the minimum and ensure leaving the place without delay. The vehicle in question was a captured Soviet Type M-72 motorcycle, in the sidecar of which was stowed all the equipment necessary to carry out this operation, including weapons, explosives, radio and provisions.

The nerve-racking wait for favourable weather conditions did not take long. An extensive front of bad weather was coming in from the west and seemed to create the right conditions for 'invisible' outgoing and return flights in the clouds.

The conditions were just right for the night of 5/6 September: the target zone reported closed cloud cover with a ceiling of only a few hundred metres from the ground – ideal for an unnoticed landing in the early morning twilight.

The pilot and navigator had their final consultations with the weather experts; it was essential to know as much as possible about the direction and strength of the wind in the landing area. Another important point was to know at what altitude they could expect icing to develop on the wings; all this could affect their flight.

Navigation had to be very accurate of course. Unfortunately in this case there was no friendly radio beacon available, although the Soviet radio station at Petrozavodsk near Lake Ladoga might be used to take radio bearings. 'Better than nothing,' retorted the crew, even if because of the great distance and unfavourable angle it would be almost impossible to obtain an accurate bearing.

Right on the minute, the heavily laden Ar 232B took off and climbed slowly into the night sky. The sound of its engines gradually faded in the east – Operation *Zeppelin* was on!

The few people in the know who had watched the take-off returned shivering to the provisional command post. The night was cold. They looked at the clock and knew that they would have to wait at least five hours before they would know if the first stage of this risky undertaking had succeeded or not.

The pilot had been given instructions – not that they were necessary for a KG 200 airman – not to take any risks and return if he suspected something in the target area that might endanger the execution of his task. He was also forbidden to use the radio under any circumstances – both sides were only to listen to each other.

At long last the morning twilight appeared on the eastern horizon and the surroundings near the airfield began to take shape. Grey, low-hanging clouds covered the sky.

Then came the time of the earliest possible return, but there was nothing, no engine noise, no radio message announcing an expected landing. The tension rose, while the clock relentlessly advanced the time. In Berlin too, nerves were being strained to breaking point, all they had had was the terse message announcing the start of Operation *Zeppelin*, received hours ago.

To the small group of men of the KG 200 operations detachment near Riga it was now clear that the Ar 232B had long since used up its fuel and could no longer be expected back – unless, of course, it had been held up for longer on the ground than planned and had had a late take-off. All one could do was to wait – and hope.

It was then decided to break the strict radio silence with a direct inquiry to the Ar 232B crew, but there was no reply to this or subsequent radio messages.

There was another possibility, the last chance, that the aircraft had landed on another German-held airfield in the combat zone within its range, but all inquiries proved negative.

Then, after many hours of waiting, came news from Berlin: the RSHA had received a radio message from the ex-Soviet major! It read: 'Aircraft crashed on landing, but all crew members uninjured. Crew has split up into two groups and will attempt to break through to the West. We are on the way to Moscow with our motorcycle, so far without hindrances.'

So that was what had happened! With heavy hearts the KG 200 operational control had to write off the *Oberleutnant* and his five men crew: only an optimist who had no idea of the true conditions could think that the missing crew could cover 370 miles – as the crow flies – on foot, without being apprehended. They had to cross too many rivers and other obstacles where it would be impossible to move without being spotted by the enemy.

True enough, the Ar 232B aircrew were trained and equipped for just such a case. They were supplied with a sufficient amount of Soviet money, and even Soviet cigarettes and provisions to help them cover up in an emergency. They also carried maps on their bodies that would make it easier to orientate on the way back. And people who knew Russian conditions – and there were many in the German armed forces – had trained them and provided tips on survival from their own experiences, had given them advice how to behave in Soviet hinterland, and had warned them of all possible dangers. All this had been an obvious part of their preparations for this operation.

However, they were not provided with any false documents – Russian, for instance. These would not have been of any use anyway because the men would have to know Russian or at least one of the Baltic languages. Apart from that no regular soldier (and that is what these airmen were) could afford to put himself outside the Hague Warfare rules or the Geneva Convention that protected him as a POW.

The only hope was now the portable radio set they were equipped with, and from then on all principal radio stations were asked to listen in for a sign of life from the Arado crew on all possible frequencies day and night. And in fact a contact was established 24 hours later when a brief radio message confirmed the ex-Soviet major's report: 'Aircraft damaged on landing at alternate place. Returning on foot in two groups'.

But that was all; no other radio message was ever received from the crew. After several days of monitoring and listening it had to be accepted that they had been captured. Another six letters joined similar ones being sent to the closest relatives: '. . . I am sorry to have to inform you that your . . .'

In the meantime, the 'Stalin killer' was reporting an almost uninterrupted progress of his mission: he had managed to get to Moscow unchallenged; he had moved into the prepared hiding place; he had contacted a middleman, a German agent in the Kremlin; and that he was now carefully preparing to carry out his mission.

The whole thing sounded too good to be true somehow, and a few people at the RSHA became a bit suspicious. The only way to find out was to send some control and 'catch' questions, using all the tricks of the trade to unmask radio messages in fact controlled by the enemy.

It did not take very long before they had to consider Operation *Zeppelin* as a failure. The reports sent by the ex-Soviet major and his wife were false – possibly transmitted under duress. It would seem that the agents were captured shortly after landing. Something had gone wrong, but what? The radio game was abruptly broken off.

Months later some light on this mystery was shed by a returned *V-Mann* who had been a member of the advance detachment parachuted near Smolensk. A former Soviet POW, he had volunteered to work for the German *Abwehr*, and after many adventures had succeeded in breaking through on foot to reach the German lines again.

He reported that the advance detachment was spotted by the enemy while they were still reconnoitring likely landing places and, after capture, forced to carry on with their preparations. Under duress, they had to establish the agreed radio contact with Berlin as if nothing had happened, avoiding causing any suspicion.

When the reports about the position and state of the chosen place arrived in Berlin, nobody there could imagine that preparations were also going on to storm the aircraft after landing and capture its 'cargo', the contents of which were still unknown to the Soviets. Of course, the assertions by the captured members of the advance detachment that they had no idea about the purpose or timing of the planned action were at first disbelieved, but eventually the Soviets had to accept it. The captured group was held near the selected landing place which was surrounded by a strong Soviet detachment, large enough to prevent the escape of the aircraft. When, early in the morning of 6 September, the Arado broke through the cloud cover and prepared to land, something must have gone wrong: all at once, Soviet anti-aircraft guns opened fire.

According to the returned agent, he had used the ensuing general confusion to escape and after months of wandering under most difficult conditions had managed to get through to the German side again.

We could only rack our brains as to why the Arado pilot had not immediately turned around and flown straight back home with his 'highly explosive' cargo – assuming of course that he had not been shot down by anti-aircraft fire. It will remain his secret why he did not realise that the enemy would be waiting with open arms at the alternate landing place also.

Of course, once the crew was posted missing, KG 200 command immediately considered what could be done to rescue them. A high-speed Ju 188 was sent to the target area, where, despite intense anti-aircraft fire, the crew managed to spot the wrecked Ar 232B, but there was no sign of the escaped crew.

After the end of the war several accounts of this episode have appeared in the Soviet press. The rest of the story, from the Soviet side is given here. There are some reservations, but it does not lack a certain racy note.

The Arado 232 had in fact flown to the alternative place which turned out to be unguarded. Apparently the Soviets must have been so sure that they already had 'the fish in the net' where they were so perfectly prepared for it that they had not bothered about the secondary landing ground.

The anti-aircraft fire seems to have been caused by a misunderstanding. Apparently the channels of command and level of competence were just as ambiguous as on the German side. In any case, the Arado had turned away and flown in the direction of the alternate landing place. East of Vyazma the aircraft was detected again – it had chanced upon the Moscow air defence positions. The pilot had then flown in a northerly direction before turning west again.

By that time the Soviet air defence posts had the Arado under observation all the way. The constantly changing course indicated that the pilot was 'an old fox' who knew his job. They already wanted to scramble fighters to intercept it when the Soviet security authorities interpolated and managed to get their way, the Arado just had to be observed and accurately tracked from the ground, and reported immediately it had landed somewhere.

At about 0300 hrs local time it was established that the aircraft had gone down near Karmanovo, and this was reported to the nearest State security offices. Immediately a strong detachment was despatched to the area, where their task was made easier by a fire burning on the ground. Apparently the landing path had been too short and while rolling to a stop the aircraft had run into a tree with its starboard wing. The starboard outer engine had been ripped out and thrown forward, where it caught fire, and thus acted as a guide to the Soviet detachment.

The place itself was empty; there was no trace of the crew. An immediate search of the surrounding area was also unsuccessful.

In the meantime, a motorcycle with a sidecar carrying two muffled figures was speeding towards Rzhev. The visibility was poor. Suddenly, a road block came into sight and the motorcycle had to brake sharply; the heavy machine skidded on the wet highway. A shivering sentry demanded documents, and the driver handed him paybooks in the names of Major Tavrin and Sub-Lieutenant Shilova, as well as front leave papers and authorisation for the motorcycle. Everything seemed to be in order. As the major was pulling out the documents the sentry had caught sight of the Gold Star of the Hero of the Soviet Union flash on his uniform blouse. He was just about to return the documents and let the couple proceed when the major made a fateful remark: 'Hurry up, will you please. We have been on our way all night!'

The sentry hesitated. Until just a short while ago it had rained in streams – yet the clothing of the motorcyclists and their machine were remarkably clean and dry. He raised the alarm, and that was the end of Operation *Zeppelin*.

Today, it is just idle speculation to consider what would have happened, if . . . .

The agents had undergone a long and thorough preparation. In Moscow, an accommodation was waiting for them. They were armed with conventional weapons and poisoned ammunition, magnetic mines and radio fuses; carried over 428,000 Roubles in genuine Soviet banknotes, possessed 116 real and forged rubber stamps, various forms and blank personal documents. They had everything that could be needed for such an undertaking – except luck.

Or could it be that, as usual with the Prussians, an MT sergeant would not have thought of delivering vehicles and equipment, even a captured Russian motorcycle before it was neatly and properly cleaned? After all, he would not have known what these things were required for; his duty was to look after them.

Perhaps the whole planning of this operation should not have been left exclusively to the military. With such a fantastic affair it would not have been amiss to have a film director on call. He of all people would have thought of covering the machine and the uniforms with a suitable patina before loading them. And then?

6. Much Daring in Vain

During June 1944 long range Ju 290s of KG 200 flew agents from Zillistea in Romania to points behind the Soviet lines on the Eastern Front. In the course of these operations the large four-engined aircraft also had to make landings on unprepared ground in the Kalmuck steppe to pick up agents who had completed their missions.

On one occasion some people had to be brought back who had been dropped by parachute only a short while previously. According to instructions, they were supposed to reconnoitre a suitable landing ground for the Ju 290 and report its position by radio.

The aircraft landed in the morning twilight, but instead of being met by the agents it was surrounded by heavily armed Russians and the crew were captured.

In this case the enemy tried a radio game, ostensibly making the crew report that they were unable to make the return flight because of a technical defect in the aircraft; otherwise everything was in order. If it would be possible to send another aircraft with spare parts and experts the necessary repairs could be carried out on the spot. All this sounded plausible enough, but had one flaw; the radio operator's touch was quite different from the tell-tale signature of his usual transmissions. Nevertheless, a relief mission was mounted despite strong objections, only to be finally cancelled after two days delay when it became obvious that the Ju 290 crew must have fallen into Soviet hands. The only question was: with a serviceable or an unserviceable aircraft?

In this case the whole operation had to be abandoned without being able to do anything to save the crew or the aircraft. (The complete crew only returned from Soviet POW camps to West Germany in 1951).

On another occasion, a top agent had been dropped by parachute near Moscow. For quite some time afterwards he was supplied from the air, including photographic equipment. His task was to penetrate higher Soviet command staffs and obtain information and other secret material. It was agreed that after completing his mission he would be picked up by an He 111 from a landing place which he himself had selected near Tula, south of Moscow.

To carry out an operation of this kind in that relatively densely populated area only a landing at night could be considered. This settled, the agent was given instructions to mark the chosen landing ground with three fires.

The He 111 arrived on time, and made a safe landing.

As the agent was just about to start loading his bulky baggage into the aircraft – he had allegedly acquired complete plans of Soviet strategic concentrations – a heavily armed Soviet detachment also appeared on the scene. The pilot reacted at once, and just managed to take off again in blazing gunfire. He arrived back home without the *V-Mann* or his secret material in a bullet-scarred He 111. It was a close shave, but fortunately none of the shots had hit a vital part of the aircraft.

Whether this incident was due to the agent being 'turned' or because he had attracted Soviet attention by his careless behaviour, was never found out.

Perhaps a few words about the reliability or otherwise of parachute agents, particularly those used on the Eastern Front, would not be out of place here.

From among my circle of friends I quite by chance learned that one of the principal training and rest centres was situated on the Schwarzenberg in the Riesengebirge mountain range (now part of SW Poland). Not very far from the old Schwarzenberg House was an ultra-modern mountain hotel, originally built as a Luftwaffe rest centre, but then taken over by the so-called *SS-Jagdkommando G.* (Raiding Detachment G). This detachment was commanded by an Army (not SS) *Hauptmann* of Baltic origin – but that was only one of the odd things about this place. The whole area around Schwarzenberg had been declared a prohibited zone and the only access to it was by an adventurous ride in a cable car. The few houseguests who received permission to visit the hotel first had to pass through triple controls before they could enter the building. And they were not just ordinary patrols either: the sentries had orders to use their firearms at the slightest sign of suspicious behaviour.

Those who were allowed in were then met by a sight of plenty, in every sense of the word. It was as if one had suddenly been transposed back into peacetime, everything was in such abundance – cigarette packets were scattered about carelessly, even such rare brands as *Atikah*, in the sixth year of war! – and a just opened bottle of Remy

Martin stood deserted on a table. In a way it was rather comical that such things should first attract the attention of a normal mortal who has had to go short for so long!

Indeed, nothing was lacking or in short supply there. The house was full of choice food and other luxuries, and had a fantastic kitchen, there was a cinema where one could enjoy the latest films – and not only German ones; there was a complete Russian ballet troupe, and there were many pretty girls to keep one company – in short, everything that would make a return to this paradise seem as tempting as possible.

This however was not really the motive behind it all, because quite different criteria were used to select the agents. After completion of their training and before the first operation the candidates had to undergo a special test. This consisted of a trial task that would be similar to his 'real' operational activity. For example, the candidate would be given an order to attach dummy explosive charges at a specific place to a certain bridge over the Rhine. All bridges in Germany, as in other countries, were of course closely guarded in wartime and the aspiring agent's problem was to carry out his task technically correctly without being spotted by the security forces. In case they were apprehended, all agent candidates carried a sealed envelope to identify themselves, but this naturally involved checking with the RSHA and meant that he had failed his test. There were candidates who would rather risk their lives than make use of these envelopes, and that surely speaks volumes for the attitude of these people, even in February 1945.

Gathered together at Schwarzenberg were in the main former Soviet POWs who had volunteered for German service, but there were also a number of Germans, such as a Waffen-SS soldier wearing the Knights Cross who came from an old Baltic-German family. He had already been dropped by parachute behind the Soviet lines on the Leningrad Front more than ten times and after accomplishing his tasks had broken through on foot back to the German lines. Then there was a former nurse from Breslau who had lost her family in a horrible way, and others. Of course, each of these people had his or her own reasons for volunteering for such special duties, and all were fully aware of the great risks involved, but the determination to succeed was the same for all.

The success of some sabotage agents flown in by KG 200 had to wait six years to be confirmed.

Thus, according to reports by German POWs who returned from Soviet captivity in 1951-52, some had been employed in rebuilding a large power station on the Volga river which had been destroyed by saboteurs during the final phase of the war.

The total number flown behind the enemy lines by KG 200 crews in the West and East, in Africa, in the far North and the Near East amounted to about 1000 agents.

For the aircrews, these flights were always a most interesting task. Even if the feeling of being something special, wrapped in a cloak of secrecy so to speak, gradually lost its attraction, the often unique flying problems still remained a constant challenge.

Of course, there were grievous losses too, especially during the flights in the West, but compared to those of the bomber, fighter and transport units of the Luftwaffe they were relatively light.

There were also some really ambitious projects that failed despite prolonged and most careful preparations. An example that comes to mind was one of the earlier tasks required of KG 200.

In spring 1944 the Operations staff of KG 200 began preparations to establish a series of secret landing grounds in Africa. By that time of course the drama of the German *Afrika Korps* had long since come to an end, but nevertheless Africa remained a militarily and politically important – if sensitive – area. This applied in particular to some vital ports and staging points along the west coast and in South Africa, and naturally along the Mediterranean itself. Egypt was the key to the Near East where it was felt the local Arab tribes needed an unbroken demonstration of political and military dominance to keep them in line. This applied especially to upheavals after the German collapse and the post-war 'redistribution' of the world.

It was known to the Germans that the Allies had built up a well-functioning air transport service operating from various African ports. The focus of this service was the airfield at Fort Lamy in French Chad. Large amounts of military supplies were unloaded at the ports of Freetown and Monrovia on the west coast of Africa and Durban in South Africa, and flown via Fort Lamy to Cairo in Egypt.

Naturally, the German command was most interested to find out more details about these transport flights and, if possible, to effectively interrupt them. A large scale operation was already prepared when KG 200 was ordered to work out detailed plans for its execution and prepare all necessary flying arrangements. Basically, it concerned flying in a number of radio agents and saboteurs, keeping them regularly supplied and, when necessary, to exchange them.

However, it was far easier said than done at this stage of the war and considering the limited number of available long-range aircraft it was doubly difficult. In fact, it seemed an impossible task to begin with. The most southerly base still in German hands was the Kalamaki airfield in Athens, and the distance from there to Fort Lamy was 1864 miles. To the vital supply ports at the West African coast it was at least 3107 miles. No aircraft could fly that distance non-stop there and back, not to mention carrying any useful load.

It was thus obvious from the start that this operation would have to be flown in stages and required several bases between Athens and the targets in Africa where an aircraft could land, refuel and be technically maintained. But such bases did not exist – at least not for the Luftwaffe, and so it was decided to set them up secretly on our own. It was hoped to find suitable places in the Central and Western Sahara, and there was also a long-since abandoned Italian desert airfield that could be used. At least from there it would be possible to reach the supply ports and airfields along the West African coast.

Experts were found who knew the geographical and weather factors well enough to advise and recommend which areas would provide the best conditions for setting up such secret air support bases, and detail planning began at once. Time was indeed of essence, and the political leadership urged to carry out the operation as soon as possible. The provision and preparation of technical means were given the highest priority, and everything came under the 'most secret' grading.

The KG 200 aircrews planned, reconsidered and calculated again. Decisions were taken and possible flight routes mapped, only to be scrapped again; even the most experienced airmen were somewhat dubious about the feasibility of this operation. On the other hand, they were also fascinated by the challenge. It was still the period of pioneering discovery flights, the conquest of the air by aircraft. True enough, the war had blotted this out, but the thought of reaching out to new frontiers had something overpowering in it. It just had to be tried!

Technical experts were called in for consultation so that the KG 200 command could have an overall view of the actual requirements of material, aircraft and personnel. And there was the ever-present pressure to speed up things from the ministries and higher military authorities in Berlin.

Gradually, the plans began to take shape. The available possibilities and the required necessities were clearly defined, and the proposals based on these premises were accepted.

The first step was to reconnoitre the possible areas for suitable landing grounds. As aerial reconnaissance alone did not promise positive results an expert was to be landed as an 'advance party' at these places to examine the ground thoroughly and decide on the spot. However, this task could only be done by a small aircraft that could land on and take off from limited spaces. The obvious choice was the Fieseler Fi 156 Storch, but this well-known STOL aircraft had neither the range nor the speed for the job. After a thorough consideration of all other available machines it was decided to try the reconnaissance with a Messerschmitt Bf 108 Taifun. It was faster and had better flight endurance, but still not enough: the aircraft had to have a range of at least 2500 km (1554 miles) carrying two men and tropical survival equipment and provisions for at least 10 days. This meant that the range of this Bf 108 had to be 'stretched' somehow without loading it with extra fuel. There was only one possibility to do this: the Bf 108 had to be towed behind a larger aircraft part of the way, as had already been done operationally many times with cargo gliders. The most suitable towing aircraft, an He 111, was equipped with the necessary attachments and was ready after only a few days, and trials showed that this combination functioned well. The only critical point was starting the engines after dropping the towing cable. The Argus As 10C of 250 hp fitted to the Bf 108 was well known for its reluctance to start, and it had happened that engine fitters had tried to get the Argus to go for hours until the thing finally began to chuck.

The 'advance reconnaissance party' carried by the Bf 108 consisted of an *Oberleutnant* pilot and a particularly experienced *Feldwebel* radio operator and navigator. These two men were also the first who got to know something about this top secret undertaking. Naturally, both men were also asked if they were prepared to take this great risk. And risk it was, not so much because of the enemy air defences but because they could die of thirst somewhere in the desert. And this was a distinct possibility if several circumstances happened to take place at the same time – if the aircraft crashed while landing and lost radio contact with the Operations staff at home – or if for some reason this contact could not be established in the first place. Then there was only a very slim chance that our search aircraft would find them again.

It did not need much for something to go wrong half way – if the engine did not start after uncoupling from the towing aircraft a crash landing was a distinct possibility. In that case the crew just had to make their own way on foot – always assuming they were not injured in the landing.

For this eventuality both men carried a special 'pass' in Arabic, English and German that informed the finder about their indentity. The text stated that the bearer of this document was a soldier of the great German nation, and that the Germans and their great leader Adolf Hitler had always been friends and protectors of the great Arab peoples. In the knowledge that this bearer of greetings from Germany, at the moment in great distress, will be accorded help and the traditional Arab hospitality, the entire German people would be under an obligation, bound with an assurance of eternal friendship between the German and Arabic peoples.

This 'pass', carried by all Luftwaffe airmen operating in North Africa, in fact helped a number of shot down or crash-landed German aircrews. It could have been religious, but also political grounds that induced many Arabs to help German soldiers, to take them in, or even to hide them from certain capture and take them back to the German lines.

For these reasons a crash landing after release from the towing aircraft – assuming the men were not injured – would not necessarily be catastrophic. After all, the crew of the towing aircraft could remain in the vicinity until the engine of the smaller machine was persuaded to start, or until they could clearly observe and plot the crash landing site.

The chosen Bf 108 received the well-known Sahara-colour camouflage, and the final preparations began. The equipment was selected with great care: a double-panel tent, durable provisions, a petrol-fuelled cooker, weapons and ammunition, flare pistol, smoke cartridges, a hunting rifle, additional clothing, money in several currencies, all possible kinds of presents to the locals, and a considerable amount of water in sealed five-litre containers. Apart from that, the aircraft was equipped with a selected set of tools and precise maintenance and repair instructions.

On a dark but clear spring night in 1944 a He 111 began gaining speed on the concrete runway at Athens, pulling along a fully loaded and tanked Bf 108 Taifun attached to a 50 metre long steel cable. The long-range African operation was on!

Both aircraft left the ground almost simultaneously. It needed all the piloting skills to control the small aircraft in the bumpy air churned up by the He 111 propellers, but once the Bf 108 had managed to gain some height things became calmer and more pleasant. It was a kind of flying that needed experience. The airspeed of the towing aircraft had to be adjusted to correspond to that of the lighter 'bird on the line', meaning that the He 111 had to fly with throttled-back engines and landing flaps half-way down.

To avoid being detected by the enemy radar, the combination flew at low level across the Mediterranean aiming for a point on the coastline of the Great Sirte that should be unguarded. Ahead of them lay a tiring flight of almost 620 miles, nearly four hours of intense concentration. Looking ahead from his cockpit, the pilot of the Bf 108 could just about make out a dark shadow where the He 111 was, its exhausts having been carefully dampened.

As a matter of course, all the aircrew involved wore life preserving vests in case they had to ditch, but that was all. A rubber dinghy that was part of the standard air-sea rescue equipment had to be left behind because of weight considerations.

The take-off had been calculated to allow them to cross the African coast in darkness. Shortly after that the brief twilight would set in, changing quickly into a bright day. From then on, the towing flight would continue in 3280 ft altitude, climbing as quickly as possible to avoid being observed. Then came the first critical phase of the entire flight: releasing the towing cable and starting the As 10C engine. Immediately after release both aircraft had to go down to low level again, the He 111 in uncertain safety on its not exactly safe return flight in broad daylight, and the Bf 108 into the desert in a south-westerly direction. The area chosen for the preparation of the first secret base was about 124 miles inland from the coast.

All went well: after release from tow the Argus engine started at once, and the two men in the small cabin aircraft continued on their way according to compass and estimated time. There were hardly any other means of navigation; one could just about tell one's where-abouts by comparing the terrain formations with the map, but that was only approximate. However, they found the area marked as 'probably suitable' surprisingly quickly. It consisted of enormous sandy flats scattered with some kind of vegetation, and there were signs that this place had served as an auxiliary landing field some time in the past.

They circled the area for quite some time, then slowly flying over strip after strip of flat sand before deciding to land. The wheels touched the ground softly, while the pilot kept his hand on the throttle lever, ready to 'gun the engine' immediately they spotted an obstacle or the ground became too soft. But it was not necessary: the desert 'runway' was quite passable.

Both men climbed out of their tiny cabin aircraft 'in the middle of Sahara' and lit a cigarette. It was quite something: there they were, two Luftwaffe airmen with their machine, deep in the enemy territory almost a year since the last German aircraft had been based in Africa! But there was no time for long meditations, they had a job to do. First of all, with the help of their octant and the sun they determined the exact position of their landing place. Then they prepared the radio set and erected the aerial. By that time the sun had climbed higher over the horizon and it was becoming unpleasantly hot. The first radio contact with home base was established exactly on time, and turned out to be better than expected. A coded message sent them all good wishes and the news that their towing aircraft had arrived safely back in Athens. So far so good.

The next step was to erect the tent to have some shade: the murderous heat forced them to interrupt their work more and more frequently. Two days later the job was done and a report was on its way stating that they had prepared the place for landing larger aircraft.

Early one morning a B-17 of KG 200 appeared out of the desert twilight and landed the first load of more than four tons of material for setting up the air base, including drums of aviation fuel. The KG 200 Fortress had also brought a few more men to act as base personnel who immediately got to work.

Their first task accomplished, the Bf 108 crew began to prepare for the next flight in search of another suitable air base. That too was found and prepared successfully in the same way, as well as a third base near the target area, not far from the West African coast.

Thus in the summer of 1944, there existed a functioning German air supply system right across the Sahara desert which made it possible to transport people and material near important Allied key points in Africa, and bring them back again.

Unfortunately however already that very first action was to end in disaster: the agents that had been flown in with such care gave themselves away in the target area, the port of Monrovia, by having German cigarettes! As a result of this carelessness they were first observed, shadowed and then arrested and forced to disclose everything they knew. From them on it was only a question of days before the Allies found out the exact positions of the three landing grounds; they were all captured at the same time.

The KG 200 crew of another B-17 that had been sent to fly in an additional load of supplies only just managed to escape the trap and return. They reported that on landing at one of the desert bases they had just noticed that the field storehouse had been burned out when suddenly their Fortress was hit by heavy machine gun fire. Despite considerable damage the pilot managed to take off and get away, with difficulty reaching the southern shores of Greece where they made a successful emergency landing.

With that, an outstanding flying performance by KG 200 crews, and probably the most interesting mission they had ever undertaken, had come to an abrupt and inglorious end.

It is impossible to say how much all that effort put into the preparation and execution of the Africa mission was really justified. One thing stands out however – not enough was done to detect the weakest point that could topple everything, otherwise that misfortune with the German cigarettes would never have been allowed to happen.

7. Mosul and Back

The time was 1629 hrs on 27 November, 1944. The four 2000 hp engines of the Ju 290 A3 + HB howled into life and the big aircraft began to roll along the roughly patched-up runway of Vienna-Neustadt airfield, then accelerated, and finally became airborne. Only a few who watched the aircraft leave the enormous airfield knew anything about the real mission given to the Ju 290 aircrew that had just taken off into the gathering evening twilight. The roar of the powerful radial engines became fainter and then faded in the east.

The aircraft A3 + HB belonged to a KG 200 detachment under *Hauptmann* Braun that had been stationed at Vienna-Neustadt for some time, and the commander himself with his crew was aboard the Ju 290. His co-pilot was *Leutnant* Dipl.Ing. Pohl. The rest of the crew consisted of an observer/navigator, the first and second radio operators, the first and second flight engineers, and a flight mechanic. The latter was an 'extra' to the ordinary crew because the flight involved intermediate landings with refuelling and an experienced mechanic might be needed to put right some minor technical faults.

Until shortly before the take-off only the two pilots and the navigator knew the flight route and the destination: they were on the way into the Orient. Their task was to drop five men and a good ton of other cargo by parachute at a place south of Mosul in Iraq. One of the five 'passengers' who now had made themselves more or less comfortable in the large dark cargo compartment of the aircraft was an Iraqi General Staff officer, and on orders from the Grand Mufti of Jerusalem, Mohammed Amin Al Husseini, they were all to become active in their homeland. The Grand Mufti himself, the overall chief of the Palestinian Arabs, an enemy of the British and a passionate hater of Jews, had lived under Hitler's protection in Germany since October 1941. From there, he carried on his political intrigues which matched German interests in the Islamic region of the Near East.

As usual, the aircrew knew no details of the tasks and intentions of their 'passengers'; their responsibility was to transport them safely to their destination, drop them and the cargo, and make their way back again. But one could always make some 'educated guesses' from things that could not be hidden, the type of people they carried – intellectuals, soldiers or tough customers, their 'luggage' – weapons, ammunition, explosives, or their personal possessions such as clothing, money, jewelry, or presents of various kinds. In some cases their 'passengers' took with them – or had delivered later on – complete photographic laboratories, and of course radio sets were part of their standard equipment. Likewise, certain conclusions could also be drawn from their destinations, such as in the case of these five Iraqis.

On the other hand, knowing more than absolutely necessary did not really matter to *Hptm* Braun and his aircrew. For one thing, they had already flown too many similar operations to still find them sensational in any way. They had their own job to do, and did not bother much about the five 'passengers' in the cargo compartment of their Ju 290, unless one of the aircrew members had to do something in there and could spare time for an encouraging nod or a reassuring gesture. The only other conversation would be keeping the 'passengers' informed about the weather conditions in flight and expected in the target area. In the interests of their own safety, any details about the flight path, the present position, their own names, and the type of aircraft they were flying, were not divulged on principle. Another strict rule was that none of the 'passengers' were ever permitted to carry any arms, and all their weapons had to be stowed in such a way that they were inaccessible in flight.

The engines roaring in unison carried the big Junkers further into the night and although the sky was star-bright, it was pitch dark. The aircraft was still in a flat climb somewhere over Hungary, and the pilots checked their instruments. The airspeed was kept at 124 mph until they reached the cruising height of 9840-13,120 ft when they would continue at about 186 mph. The exact altitude was dependant on the weather, which could easily complicate matters. After all, the target area was some 1864 miles to the east, and in those latitudes weather conditions could change several times in the east-west direction over such a distance. This could often create unforeseen problems, especially under wartime conditions. For instance, the aircraft could suddenly develop icing that would force the pilot to go lower. This would affect navigation and that, in turn, the whole flight path. The problem here was that the flight path just could not be changed at will, almost every part of it led over enemy territory as it was, and all neutral countries had to be strictly avoided.

By late November 1944 the territory still held by German armed forces was hardly bigger than the area of Germany itself, and sizeable sections of eastern Germany had already been overrun by the Soviets.

The navigator was busy with his direction finder. At this stage it was still possible to receive emissions from German radio beacons and broadcasting stations. By the light of a carefully dimmed lamp he drew in the base lines on his navigation map which determined the position of the aircraft at any given time. By using a slide rule, he could then calculate the actual direction and strength of the wind and give his pilot the necessary corrections. Although each KG 200 aircrew was a closely-knit interdependent team, on such long-distance nocturnal flights the navigator carried the lion's share of responsibility.

The land below them was wrapped in inky darkness and it was impossible to make out any prominent features. There were no large towns, no rivers, and no coastline to help them orientate. A direct course would have taken the Ju 290 over the south-western part of the Black Sea and then over neutral Turkey, and that was something *Hptm* Braun was determined to avoid for obvious reasons. Instead, he had chosen a longer route that led them over Hungary, Yugoslavia and Greece. It was hoped that they would then be able to fix their position over the Greek islands and check if their estimated wind data were still valid. In fact, they had to. It was their last chance before setting off across the sea and into enemy territory. However, until then they still had a good three hours to fly.

The Captain lit a cigarette and offered one to his co-pilot. The intercom remained silent – there was no need for words.

On reaching a cruising altitude of 9840 ft for a short while there was some movement in the cabin. The pilot trimmed the elevators for level flight and the airspeed gradually began to increase. The engines were throttled back a bit, and the propeller pitch regulated for the most economical cruising flight. At the same time the engine cooling gill flaps had to be set in such a way that the engine temperature would not sink below their normal running rating: the higher the airspeed, the more cooling air would flow over the radial engine's cylinders exposed to the cold airstream. An experienced pilot was a living part of his aircraft and would 'feel' for it without being reminded by any instrument.

The door to the pilot's compartment opened and the figure of the first flight engineer was just visible in the darkness: – 'What's happening? Where are we now? How long before we get to the target?'

80

The change in the engine revs and the unusual sounds the airframe was making had also drawn the other crew members' attention. *Leutnant* Pohl silently lifted his left arm with the thumb upwards to show that everything was in order. *Hptm* Braun answered the second part of the question without taking his eyes off the instruments: – 'Still a good seven hours yet!'

For a long time afterwards everything remained peaceful. Only the navigator seemed to be working without respite, climbing into his Plexiglas astrodome at short intervals to take a star-shot with his octant. Down at his table he would then compare the measured values with tables in a thick book to determine the astronomical base lines which he would then draw on the map. The intersection point of two or more of such lines gave a 'fix' of his position.

Put this way, it sounds easy, but it was not. After all, the aircraft was flying at about 186 mph and it needed quite a bit of reckoning to determine the distance covered between 'shooting' the stars, the calculation of base lines, and the actual markings on the map. Page after page in the navigator's note book were filled with figures, and time and again he would press his stop watch to check elapsed time and look at the airspeed indicator. Then it was the turn of the slide rule to re-check the established data, and only then could he mark the lines on his map with the compass and ruler. Under favourable conditions a good navigator could be relied on to guide an aircraft by stars so accurately that deviations from the true course would not exceed a few kilometres. But such ideal conditions were few and far between in winter.

There were still some 1550 miles ahead of them, an enormous distance over an area where there was no longer any help from the ground – except perhaps that the rising moon might make it easier to orientate according to ground features. It was because of this uncertainty that the navigator had switched to astro-navigation. Thanks to his consistent and accurate work there was general agreement with the available radio navigation data. The aircraft captain nodded his head in satisfaction when this was reported to him. It was not the worry about possible enemy defences that kept tension up inside the big aircraft but rather the problem of navigation: the whole operation became questionable if the position of the aircraft could not be determined at any given time, darkness and weather conditions notwithstanding. After all, it was not only a matter of finding some Godforsaken point in the desert, but also getting back home again! And this final thought was as much on the aircrew's minds as fulfilling the wishes of their five anonymous 'passengers', or carrying out the orders of their equally anonymous controllers.

It was of course known to them that the endurance of the Ju 290 with the present load was not enough to fly non-stop from Vienna to Mosul in Iraq and back again, on the return leg they had to land somewhere to refuel. As the whole area covered by their flight from the Balkans over the Mediterranean to the Lebanese coast was in enemy hands, the whole operation would have been impossible if it was not for the island of Rhodes. Indeed, this German-occupied Greek island was quite unique, it was the most unusual 'prisoner of war camp' imaginable.

By autumn 1944 all the territory and bases in the Mediterranean area once held by the Germans had been retaken by the Allies, except Rhodes. This island with its German garrison of a few thousand men had been spared by the British, apparently because they considered the possible cost in blood and material in taking it an unnecessary effort. All they needed to do was to keep an eye on this forlorn bunch of Germans from a distance and let them stew in their own juice, so to speak. After all, the island with its German garrison and local population was completely cut off from outside supplies, and the German troops there no longer had any influence on the warfare in the Mediterranean area. Consequently it could be left to its own devices, at the same time saving all the effort and cost it would involve to keep such a large POW camp – for that is what Rhodes now was, in every sense but one.

Indeed, it was only with the greatest effort and by suffering many hardships that the German garrison managed to keep alive on this largely barren island. But Rhodes also had an intact airfield which the British had not deemed necessary to bomb as yet, and this airfield now served as the only lifeline with Germany and the military command. Considering the catastrophic military situation late in 1944 it was of course out of the question even to think of some kind of supply effort; it could only be a matter of the barest necessities. Ironically, it was a captured B-24 Liberator bomber flown by a KG 200 crew that visited this island with some regularity, sneaking in and out at night and in fog. But the only things it could bring to the cut-off troops were some urgently needed medicines and mail. On the return flights the B-24 would take out some critically ill soldiers.

This airfield at Rhodes was to be the refuelling place for *Hptm*

Braun's Ju 290 on the way back from Iraq. The necessary fuel was to be flown in by another Ju 290 the same night.

The planning of this operation and everything connected with it were like something out of adventure fiction. The dangerous imponderables, such as the weather, navigation problems and enemy reaction were all there, not to mention the questionable nature of the anonymous figures in the cargo compartment who often looked like they might go berserk at any moment. That apart, the task that *Hptm* Braun had taken on remained a flying challenge of the first order, but he did not talk about it. How could he explain all the problems involved to a non-airman, anyway? There you were, hanging in the clouds at night, completely blind. Whatever your eyes might perceive of the world around you, there was no tangible up or down, or left or right. And you were alone – it was up to you to master the situation. You did not know if you were flying in a cloud or not, and only by briefly switching on the navigation lights could one see the distant haloes at the wingtips that indicated you were flying through fog. You also had a pocket torch which could throw a sharp beam of light through a window to illuminate a wing to see if any ice had formed there.

And then your senses begin to play tricks with the movements of the aircraft. You suddenly feel the big machine is climbing directly into the sky, and your instinctive reactions take over – push the control column, get the aircraft down and level off – and then you are wide awake again: it was only an illusion. The artificial horizon and other instruments show clearly that the aircraft is flying correctly, but it requires all your will power to recognize it as a deception and avoid the wrong reactions.

All this happens because you are effectively blind – there is no horizon, no light to guide you in the darkness or fog. There are no criteria, nothing to indicate if your aircraft is turning, climbing, or going steeply down. Only the instruments give you information in your small enclosed world – and you have to trust them and absolutely believe what they are telling you. Your own 'seat of the pants' feeling that always distinguishes an especially good airman, is useless in clouds.

There is a game which we used to play as children that to some extent recreates – even if incompletely – what blind flying means to a pilot. In this game, the 'victim' has to sit blindfolded on a board, both ends of which are resting on chairs; his legs are not allowed to touch the ground. The sitter is then told that the board is being lifted up and carried away, while in fact it is only lifted up slightly and let back down again. Naturally, the board sways a bit while this is going on. The sitter is then told that the board is being lifted some more, almost to the ceiling, and moved up and down again. He is then asked to jump off. If he is brave, he will do so – and is most surprised to find that he was only a few inches off the ground. If, on the other hand, he is more prudent or scared, he will refuse to jump and even hang on to the board for dear life, to the great enjoyment of the spectators.

A pilot in blind flight is faced with a similar situation; if he relies on his own 'feel' he would do something wrong within a few seconds. As in the game, he is sitting blindfolded on a board that is hanging in the air, and can turn, rise or sink without giving him any fixed point. To be sure, he feels something – acceleration, motion in space and he also feels when such a movement suddenly stops. But what is there to tell him that what he 'feels' at any given moment is not exactly the opposite of what is really happening?

Back in the lone Ju 290 of KG 200 on the way to Iraq, after a while the observer's voice came on the pilot's intercom, reporting that the stars had disappeared – there was no longer any help from the night sky. From then on he had to try and fix his position according to radio stations.

The first and second pilots would alternatively leave their seats to stretch their legs. Even a well-padded seat would become uncomfortable when one had to sit strapped in it for hours on end. In addition to that, they were flying through bad weather which resulted in a rather 'bumpy ride'. There was snow in the clouds, and ice began to develop on the wings and fuselage.

All at once there was pale light ahead of them: the moon had risen just above the horizon dead ahead. The whole aircraft seemed to breathe a sigh of relief. Now it was possible to fly again without being tied to the instruments with one's eyes and brains. It had almost become relaxing. Below everything was pitch black but clear; had there been any clouds they would have looked like a white carpet in the moonlight.

The navigator pointed out the present position on the map. Assuming that his calculations were accurate, they had just flown over the Bulgarian-Greek border. A quick glance at the clock in the instrument panel indicated another six hours' flying time to their destination.

Then the crew could distinguish a coastline ahead, and a few minutes later it was possible to determine their exact position in relation to the contours below. A recheck of navigator's data showed that they had made better time than expected: a strong tailwind had developed on the way. A change of course brought them in the direction of a group of islands south-west of the Turkish coast. Ninety minutes later they spotted Rhodes; the island seemed like a dark leaf swimming on the water glistening like a pool of molten lead in the moonlight.

At 0130 hrs the pilot throttled back the engines. The extended descent towards their target area had begun. The bright moonlight helped orientation and they were soon over the Tigris, one of the two large waterways of the land of two rivers, once known as Mesopotamia. And there was the railway line, near which they had to deposit their cargoes!

The altimeter indicated just 1150 ft over the ground. The rear fuselage hatches were opened and everything prepared to jettison their cargo. The five Iraqis tried hard but in vain to hide their fear. And then came the signal from the pilot's cabin: – 'Attention! Get ready! Now!!'

In quick succession all five 'passengers' were despatched through the hatch, followed immediately by their equipment. A glance below, then report to the pilot: 'Task completed!!'

Gradually and carefully all four engines were set to climbing power and the navigator gave the pilot his new course. In a wide bank the large aircraft turned west over south and began to gain altitude. Thanks to the excellent visibility the crew could also observe that all parachutes had opened; they had completed their part of the operation to perfection.

The moon was now in the south, and their night flight became a sheer pleasure trip. It was four hours back to Rhodes and if the weather remained good, finding the island at the first attempt would be no problem. Rhodes flight control had already been notified of their expected arrival.

Exactly at 0510 hrs the Ju 290 flew over the island, although the crew had no idea exactly where the landing strip was situated. Suddenly several green flares rose into the sky from the darkness below – that must be the field! In a slight bank the crew recognised the provisional flare path, floated towards it, and landed at 0520 hrs.

After stopping the engines they were greeted by the crew of the other Ju 290 that had brought a supply of fuel. Everything had gone well this time and *Hauptmann* Braun began to relax – after a flight of nearly 13 hours it was great to feel the ground under one's feet again.

A group of officers and men of the island garrison gathered around to gaze in wonder at the two big aircraft and ask questions. It was quite unusual suddenly to have two Ju 290s on their landing strip; was something special in the wind? As well as they could, the crews found some answers. For them it was far more important to park their aircraft away from the landing strip so that they would be hidden from curious eyes before dawn. Soldiers from the island garrison willingly gave a hand, and soon the Ju 290s were out of the way.

But there was no time to rest as yet. With their machines seen to, the crews had to get down to other things. Their return flight was planned for the following night, and it was also intended to fly out about 30 sick soldiers who needed urgent treatment. The conditions on the island were truly catastrophic, the food shortage was so acute that the exchange price for one simple bread roll was about 1000 cigarettes! The KG 200 aircrews were really glad their stay on Rhodes was only in transit.

They took off on the return flight immediately after moonrise, with *Hptm* Braun leading. But this time things did not go as planned, he had to turn back and land only a few minutes after leaving the ground because one of the undercarriage wheels refused to retract. The mechanics did their best, but they could not discover any defects. *Hptm* Braun tried again, but the wheel stubbornly refused to cooperate. Now they were in a predicament: their aircraft had a technical defect they apparently could not fix themselves, and they had no way of getting in touch with their base at Vienna-Neustadt. The crew of the supply aircraft would probably report at home that *Hptm* Braun had taken off before them and had apparently gone missing on the way. But that was a minor problem. Things being what they were, it would not take long before the British would discover the presence of this giant aircraft on the island – and then it was only a matter of hours before the Ju 290 was destroyed.

Early next morning, even before it had become light, the crew were already hard at work, searching methodically for the elusive defect. It was then that the presence on board of an engineer came in very handy indeed, and *Lt* Pohl together with the available ground staff got busy dismantling and examining all the elements of the hydraulic system piece by piece. When finally they had checked and re-assembled everything they still had not found any defects, but the system was suddenly functioning again!

Hptm Braun's crew took off on the third night – right into another adventure. Shortly after becoming airborne the acrid smell of burning electrical cables pervaded the aircraft. There was a fire somewhere in the electrics, but it was impossible to detect it, and the result was that part of the system ceased to function, including the radio transmitter. This was serious: how were they going to find Vienna under these circumstances? And not only that: how were they going to announce their arrival, and inform the ground defences that theirs was a 'friendly' and not an enemy aircraft approaching the field?

Only the radio altimeter was still functioning, so that they could at least be certain of their height above the ground. After it had been established that the aircraft could be controlled in flight and they had finally succeeded in getting the electric compass going again, *Hptm* Braun decided to continue the flight. Soon they were over a closed cloud cover, navigating according to the moon and stars again. Less than five hours later they spotted the first Alpine peaks protruding through the clouds in the moonlight, and now it was a matter of identifying them to determine where they were. It took a while, but after consulting maps they felt certain they had recognised the peaks. The navigator computed a new course and estimated the time of arrival over the Graz basin – assuming they had identified the peaks correctly.

From then on it was a matter of nerves. In a gradual descent *Hptm* Braun let his Ju 290 glide into the clouds. Dead accurate blind flying was now essential and the direction, speed and rate of descent had to be held with the greatest precision. Also, something that no pilot likes now became a necessity, that the man sitting next to him should be talking out loud. *Lt* Pohl kept up a constant running commentary to his commander regarding the direction, altitude and speed so that he could concentrate solely on flying – not that *Hptm* Braun would let his eyes wander from the instruments himself.

They could only guess the lower cloud ceiling. The radio altimeter was still indicating a comfortable height over the ground, but what if the terrain below them suddenly began to rise again? What if they had made an error in identifying their initial point? There was no way back, they just had to get through now!

The whole crew knew exactly the situation they were in, only the 30 sick soldiers from Rhodes aboard had no idea. They were overjoyed to be on their way home to be nursed back to health again, and the crew were fully aware of their responsibility towards them.

Suddenly, they were through the clouds and *Hptm* Braun caught his first glimpse of the snow-covered ground. Despite the closed cloud cover the full moon was bright enough to distinguish details; the terrain was flat, but they could clearly see roads and villages. Every crew member strained his eyes to detect a familiar point of orientation – there! Was that the Neusiedler lake? Yes! They had made it!

The limping Ju 290 felt its way from the east towards the Vienna-Neustadt airfield. In this area they knew every nook and cranny; it was impossible to miss the field now. And then they were over the airfield boundary, fired the correct recognition flares – and were immediately shot at by the local Flak!

The crew had no other way of identifying themselves and, to avoid being shot down over their own base they had no choice but to turn away. The situation would have been comical if it was not so serious.

Hptm Braun now had to chose a landing manoeuvre that would leave only one alternative. He made a wide turn to the west so that the big Ju 290 was outside the vision of the field – it was fortunate that he knew all the orientation points on the ground in this area. Then he throttled back the engines and let down the undercarriage, followed by a slow bank towards the airfield. Holding back on the control column he then went down as low as possible, 'crawling' towards the airfield. With idling engines and wind-milling propellers the big machine floated over the boundary and touched down on the snow. Everyone aboard tensed in expectation of a crash: the whole airfield was covered with bomb craters, hastily filled in and levelled off only where it was absolutely essential. But nothing happened – the Ju 290 taxied peacefully to a standstill. They had landed furtively and unnoticed in the middle of the night at their own base, a place where they were not even expected. In fact, they had already been 'written off', posted as missing! And there they stood in the deep snow, cursing and at the same time glad and relieved.

Two of the crew hurried off in the direction of the flight control, and a short while later a small column of vehicles was approaching their machine. The casualties were transferred to ambulances, the tired aircrew piled into the cars and sped back to the warmth of the airfield buildings. Only the big deserted Ju 290 was left where it stood because it did not seem advisable to tow it at night over the cratered field; that could wait until dawn.

Another adventurous flight by a KG 200 crew had come to an end.

8. The Great Bluff

In surviving log books of some KG 200 pilots one can find a series of entries about supply flights that are marked solely by the code word *Rennstrecke* or 'Running Distance' (see facsimile reproduction in Appendix 16). The 'customer' for these flights was Army Group Centre, and the whole operation was under the tightest security wraps.

This especial secrecy covered the mission code-named 'Action Scherhorn'.

Early in October 1944 a radio agent left behind the Soviet lines suddenly got in touch with his control post in Germany to report that he had made contact with a large German combat group in the Berezino area, about 60 miles east of Minsk. The group numbered about 2000 men under the command of a certain *Oberst* Scherhorn. They had been cut off during the great retreat battles of summer 1944 and managed to draw together and hide until now in the immense forest and swamp area. The *Oberst* had declared his intention to attempt a break-through to the west and to this end he had formed two contingents: a strong advance force, sufficiently well armed to fight their way back again, and a smaller group that would march behind the advance 'battle group'. This smaller contingent consisted of wounded and sick and their attendant medical personnel. *Oberst* Scherhorn had no other means of keeping in touch with Army Group Centre as his scratch force possessed no radio sets or radio operators. He now requested urgent assistance from the Army Group to enable him to carry out his plan. To date, Soviet forces had not been encountered in the area. Above all, it was urgently necessary to fly in a doctor with all that was necessary to look after the wounded and sick soldiers.

Of course, at first this and the following radio messages met with some suspicion. They were evaluated and examined, and a series of 'control questions' sent to the *Oberst* via the agent contact. His answers left no doubt about the authenticity of this combat group deep inside enemy territory, although a measure of doubt remained.

To visualise the situation at that time, one has to keep in mind the enormous losses inflicted on the German forces by the Soviet offensive in the Central sector alone. As an example, and quite valid comparison, of the 71 generals in the German 4th and 9th Army and the 3rd Panzer Army areas alone no less than 47 were killed in action, 21 captured, two took their own lives, and one remains missing.

That *Oberst* Scherhorn's plan had a chance was shown by another commander, a General who, with the remnants of his division, managed to fight his way for over 310 miles back to the German lines in East Prussia. He arrived there with just 70 men.

In other words, Scherhorn's idea was by no means an impossibility. It was only a matter of what could be done to assist him.

Otto Skorzeny, the Waffen-SS daredevil – although not the most reliable of sources – has stated that he was called to the Führer's headquarters where *Gen. Oberst* Jodl reportedly told him: 'Unfortunately we don't know for sure where exactly in this vast and uncharted area the group is. Do you think it would be possible to find it and somehow help it? – Skorzeny is then supposed to have promised to try 'everything humanly possible – within the available means, of course'.

Under the code designation *Unternehmen Freischütz* (Operation Armed Insurgent) four reconnaissance troops made up of men proficient in the local language and with knowledge of the region were then supposed to have been dropped by parachute in the area.

It may seem rather puzzling to the present reader that the same mission was apparently pursued under different code names by different and possibly even rival organisations. To explain this, it has to be understood that after the attempt on Hitler's life on 20 July 1944 the military *Abwehr* was subordinated to Heinrich Himmler and integrated in the *Auslandsnachrichtendiest der SS* (Foreign Intelligence Service of the RSHA) under Walter Schellenberg. The military departments continued to work as before, but under a new direction. Otto Skorzeny, who had made his name as the 'Liberator of Mussolini', was at that time in charge of various training and operational units involved in sabotage, diversion and other special tasks, and he had under his command a sufficient number of agents proficient in languages and knowledgeable of the terrain for operations behind the enemy lines. In addition, to carry out such undertakings Skorzeny also had the power and resources of the RSHA behind him, and thus also the potential of KG 200 at his disposal. However, the *Geschwader* was never subordinated to Skorzeny, as has been portrayed in some accounts. KG 200 was a flying formation subordinated as such to *Luftflotte* 6 and decisions regarding the feasibility or otherwise of any flying tasks were solely in the hands of the KG 200 operations staff.

However, back to *Oberst* Scherhorn. Unfortunately it is no longer possible to completely reconstruct the fate of the four reconnaissance troops dropped in the area to establish contact with the German battle group. It is known that the eight volunteers came from *Jagdverband Ost I* (Raiding Detachment East I) and that one troop reported having got in touch with Scherhorn's force. A request was then forwarded to the Luftwaffe command to confirm the existence of this battle group by means of aerial reconnaissance. The Luftwaffe command ordered KG 200 to carry out this assignment – not least because later it would also have to organise the air supply action.

To begin with, it was a matter of setting down a reconnaissance officer who would also find suitable landing places for transport aircraft. It was agreed however that this officer should be flown out again to report in person because radio messages alone could not be taken as definite confirmation. Careful deliberations between Army Group Centre, *Luftflottenkommando 6* and KG 200 then led to the proposal that the first parachute drop should include a doctor, a pair of radio operators with full equipment, and a Luftwaffe officer. The latter would be responsible for the preparation of a landing place which could be temporarily used for transport flights in both directions, but principally to fly out the officer himself (see facsimile reproduction in Appendix No 2).

Everything went smoothly. In a single flight, a Ju 290 taking off at night from an airfield near Berlin transported and dropped by parachute the personnel and material in the exact area indicated by previously agreed Scherhorn's light signals. The make-shift and unreliable radio traffic via the agent was then replaced by the work of three well-trained Army radio operators equipped with powerful radio transceivers. One of the first reports came from *Fähnrich* (Officer cadet) Wild who had been landed by parachute to reconnoitre a suitable landing place.

However, the use of this landing strip had to wait because of the increasingly more urgent requests by Scherhorn for material support, fulfilled as well as possible by parachute cargo drops. In any case, experts who knew the area soon realized that a suitable landing strip could not be established so soon. It was already mid-October, the time when one could expect the start of the notorious rain and mud period – and that in a swampy area. It is certain that similar deliberations also took place among the High Command of the Luftwaffe and the Army Group Centre staffs. In any case, a teleprinter message from General Kreipe (OKL-*FüSt* = Operations Staff of the Luftwaffe High Command) ordering KG 200 to get in touch with *Oberst* Scherhorn and then start air supply operations, carries the following handwritten note added later: – 'According to consulation at 2330 hrs on 21 October Gen Kreipe has agreed to waive the condition re. return of the recce officer.' (see Appendix No 3).

In the meantime the He 111s and Ju 290s of KG 200 continued to carry out their parachute supply drop flights with irregular frequency. According to weather conditions, the aircraft would take off either from airfields in the Berlin area or from Stolp-Reitz in Pomerania near the Baltic Sea. This then was the *Rennstrecke*, the 'Running distance' for the KG 200 crews. In this way many tons of valuable material, medical supplies, provisions and even mail were deposited by parachute in the forests east of Minsk.

With the start of the winter weather, the clearing of a landing field, and consequently the return of the Luftwaffe reconnaissance officer was delayed even more. They had found the right place but apparently Scherhorn could not give an estimate for completion. The weeks passed, December arrived, but there was still no landing field. So another large-scale air supply action had to be mounted. The code word *Rennstrecke* really earned its meaning.

At Christmas 1944 *Oberst* Scherhorn was awarded the Knight's Cross, which was then dropped by parachute together with a cargo of luxury food and drink.

It was planned to spend the hard winter period there and start the return march in spring 1945 – supplied from the air by KG 200 of course. Eventually the whole affair dragged on until April, when the Luftwaffe reconnaissance officer at last reported the landing strip in the forests near Borodino was ready for use.

At KG 200, two twin-engined Ar 232A '*Tatzelwurm*' transports had long-since been held in readiness. Each of them could carry a load of four tons and was able to land and take off from rough ground. However, for various reasons the operation was postponed again and again, either because Scherhorn reported continuous bad weather in the target area or because the weather conditions did not permit flying from KG 200 bases. At long last on 20 April 1945 everything was just right, and confirmation was received by radio that all the necessary illuminations for night landings of the two Ar 232As were ready. The weather conditions were reasonable too. Reports from the landing strip itself stated that everything was prepared for unloading, and the badly wounded and sick soldiers were already eagerly waiting for their transport back home.

At the agreed time both aircraft took off on their way east, but then fate took a hand in the proceedings and, as often happens in flying, neither of the two machines reached their destination. The first Ar 232A had to break off its flight and return to base due to a technical fault, while the second was forced to turn back by the extremely bad weather encountered en route that made it impossible to continue the difficult night flight.

Of course, Scherhorn expressed deep disappointment when he was informed by radio about the hitch. There followed a series of bad weather reports from the area held by the battle group, and various other reasons that precluded the landing of transport aircraft, and these finally made the joint Army and Luftwaffe planners hesitate. The suspicion that Scherhorn deliberately wanted to delay the intended arrival of the transport aircraft began to grow – something was not quite what it seemed to be. From then on all radio traffic was checked especially carefully. Various innocuous control questions were included in the routine messages as well as certain tactical instructions that should have resulted in definite reactions. All this led to a gradual but notable change in Scherhorn's behaviour. Something was indeed wrong.

This side of the lines one could now assume with near certainty that the whole 'Action Scherhorn' was nothing but an enemy trick. When this point was reached, it needed only a few more tests to come to the uncomfortable conclusion that here was an elaborate enemy double-cross that had been successfully performed for a long period of time, perhaps as long as six months, and virtually everybody had been taken in by it.

A noticeable change in behaviour on the other side began when the two promised Ar 232A transports failed to arrive. Apparently those running the whole elaborate deception 'over there' had realised that the Germans had recognised their 'play' for what it was and reacted accordingly. This was the end of Scherhorn's phantom battle group.

In actual fact, *Oberst* Scherhorn with his troops had been captured in that area and he survived the war. He was released from Soviet captivity later than most and only then got to know how Soviet intelligence had aggravated the Luftwaffe with its dwindling resources by using his name even in the closing stages of the war.

Some readers may well wonder why this proverbial red herring was not spotted earlier by a few sensible and intelligent people who could have been in the position to end this nonsense. True enough – but try to stop a thing after it had grown to such proportions! Apart from that, the initiators were long since prisoners of their own wild schemes. If one should ask how it was possible that such bizarre operations could take place at all, probably the best answer has been given by one of the inner circle of Nazi leaders – Walter Schellenberg, the all-powerful Chief of the SS Secret Service.

Otto Skorzeny who, after the end of the war was headlined as 'the most dangerous man in Europe', states in his book *La Guerre Inconnue* how, in a discussion with Schellenberg, he had once described a plan suggested by the higher command as being utterly impossible, to which the Chief had replied: 'You had better pay attention to this! Perhaps I can give you a piece of good advice, a recipe from experience so to speak, that has proved its worth time and again: the more fantastic or absurd a plan from "above" may seem in your eyes, the more enthusiastic about it you have to be . . . pretending to recognise the genius in it! Then you can start preparations that might last for three or four months, and generally develop a suitable level of activity. The only trouble you might have is should you happen to generate too much interest in it, and cannot find anyone you can hang this on to. As a rule however those above have usually evolved some new fancy idea by that time and the other one is already forgotten. Like this, you will gradually gain the reputation as a man who is never held back by any difficulties, a man one can always rely on! . . .'

No wonder, then, that Schellenberg made such a career in Himmler's shadow, and that in the ensuing 'total war' it became more and more dangerous to show healthy scepticism towards the schemes and whims of the 'big names'.

It could also be dangerous to overestimate enemy capacity. In this respect the reconnaissance reports by Detachment *Olga* concerning the Allied preparations behind the Western Front could also have become a delicate matter because they had attracted attention 'higher up'.

In mid-December 1944 quite unexpectedly I was suddenly ordered to appear at the Headquarters of the Commander-in-Chief, Western Front, where I was immediately to report to a certain *Oberst* from the General Staff. The order did not mention anything else, but I suspected it had something to do with our reports about the enemy preparations as noted during the nocturnal flights. For that reason I decided to play safe and took my observer, *Oberfeldwebel* Hans Fecht with me. In more than five years of combat flying he had amassed an almost unique experience in appraising happenings on the ground. Apart from that he had an amazing memory I had never met in another person; it would seem that all visual impressions, including figures and geographical data were filed away in separate compartments in his brain, which he only had to open with his own special 'key' to immediately recall and reconstruct past events in detail. Although showing almost uncontrollable emotions when he disagreed with something, Fecht was imperturbably accurate and dependable when it was a matter of facts. After all, he was an engineer by trade and everything he thought and did was like a craftsman engineer, except when it had something to do with 'those above', not to mention the glittering 'Golden pheasants' of the Nazi party. In such cases Fecht could easily get himself and others into really dangerous situations by the way he could pass biting comments on the latest Dr Goebbels' articles in *Das Reich* or *Völkischer Beobachter**) without any concern about who might be listening. His vocal sentiments would fully qualify for an immediate 'entry card' into a concentration camp.

Things being what they were, the fighting men were now conversing 'in clear' among themselves. After all, we did not have to consider what effect such statements would have on our careers, as higher staffs had to; we were simply glad to have survived another day. Of course, there were also some ambitious characters among us who would have gladly sported another decoration or two on their uniforms, but by late 1944 such people were sown pretty thinly.

In short, to have my good but stubborn friend Fecht accompany me to the headquarters was not without certain problems. I pleaded with him to 'keep his trap shut' unless he was specifically asked something, and to keep his opinions to to himself if they were not needed for the business in hand. Grudgingly, he agreed.

Our destination was in Taunus, about 18 miles north of Frankfurt-am-Main, and very close to Usingen. I took another driver with me in my dented Mercedes 170V, not only because of the rather battered condition of the vehicle but also because constant all-round observation of the sky above while on the way along country roads had long

---

*Official periodicals of the State and the NSDAP (Nazi Party) respectively.

since become a dire necessity. The American P-51 Mustangs and P-47 Thunderbolts roamed at will in the skies over Germany and anything that seemed worth a hail of bullets from their heavy machine guns was shot at, especially anything that moved.

The atmosphere in Headquarters was already familiar to us from earlier visits to other such exalted places. However, here it seemed like another world, not just because life inside seemed to move at a peacetime pace but also because of the sheer size and complexity of the installation. After we had reported to the guardhouse and our identity and business there had been verified, we were handed over to an Army *Hauptmann* who requested us to follow him – not without first critically inspecting us in a superior manner. It was obvious that our external appearance did not quite meet with his approval, but nevertheless he accepted us without comment.

Quite unexpectedly we found ourselves in an underground labyrinth consisting of a maze of concreted tunnels. Their walls were rough and painted with white lime. The whole system extended over several levels, blasted and tunnelled with an unimaginable effort deep under and upwards into the mountain. The tunnels were so narrow that one had to press against a wall if somebody else was coming the other way. The concrete floor was laid with sisal mats. To the left and right, about two and a half yards apart, were narrow doors that led into small rooms which reminded one of 1st class railway sleeping car compartments; the size and fittings were very similar. As we followed our *Hauptmann* we could now and again glance into these rooms. Each of these compartments served one member of the HQ staff as an office, living quarters and bedroom. Along one longer wall was a writing desk topped by a document shelf; along the opposite wall was a bed that could be folded upwards in daytime. The whole warren was supplied with fresh air by means of large zink-plated ducts that stretched along the roofs of all the tunnels. We never forgot the noise made by air being forced through these pipes, it was an ever-present background hum in this ghostly enclosed world.

Naturally, there was no way of telling what time of the day it was in this underground complex, or if it was raining, snowing or sunny outside – not that it seemed to matter. Apart from that, the business activities of this giant headquarters and all that they involved did not differ from what we had already noticed in other higher staffs: wherever one looked, there were knife-sharp trouser creases, and conspicuously many and strikingly pretty signals girls. Only here they were no longer as 'normal' girls are, but rather aloof. We felt at least an inch smaller when they passed us by and simply seemed to look somewhere over our heads. Another thing that we had noticed before in such places, and met again here was that whoever happened to be facing us seemed in some way provoked by the decorations on our uniforms; we could find no other explanation for their behaviour.

Finally we had reached our destination at one of those narrow doors. On it was a small shield with an unintelligible combination of letters and numbers over the name of the General Staff *Oberst* we had been ordered to see. A brief military knock by our escort was met by a loud and evidently good natured 'Come in!' from the room.

We were faced by a handsome wiry officer I guessed to be just over 30 years old, about the same age as ourselves. A questioning look at my companion induced me to explain dutifully that I assumed we might be questioned about various points of our present operations, in which case my observer would be of certain help.

Our officer guide departed and the subsequent discussion of operational matters lasted about two hours. It was soon clear to us that our reports had indeed arrived at the Commander-in-Chief HQ and had also been read and considered carefully. There was also no doubt that the young *Oberst* knew his job inside out, judging by the expert questions he asked us accompanied by notes and markings on the maps, where Hans could be of some assistance.

In conclusion, and without any prompting on our part, he gave us a review of the current situation, interspersed with some careful remarks about intended counter-measures. Thus we could take home with us the knowledge – naturally under the seal of the strictest secrecy – that the German armed forces had by no means made its last throw, that the enormous Allied preparations for an advance did indeed require certain short-term military measures, but that preparations were also in full swing for the great German counterstroke.

There was also a Luftwaffe liaison officer present during part of our meeting, but they could have spared the trouble. He was nice looking, and that was about all.

When we took our leave from the *Oberst* the impression remained that we had met a clever and extremely understanding person. We were also naturally greatly impressed by what we had seen and heard, only we did not quite know what to make of it.

Were there really grounds to hope for a turn for the better at this stage?

9. The 'Self-sacrificers'

In 1944 there were all kinds of wild rumours going round about the operational use of manned V-1s. It was even said that the famous glider pilot Hanna Reitsch had been badly injured while testing such a device. How much truth was in all this?

To get the story in the right perspective it is necessary to go back a bit further, to the start of the German campaign in the West in May 1940. At that time a small group of glider pilots played a vital role in the capture of the supposedly impregnable Belgian fortress of Eben Emael. During the subsequent course of the war there were no other such decisive opportunities for glider pilots, quite the opposite in fact: they were employed for supply tasks, being towed across the Mediterranean where they became defenceless victims of enemy fighters.

As a result, one of the veterans of the Eben Emael operation asked himself, if we really are destined to perish like this, senselessly and without doing any damage to the enemy, is there not some possibility of giving us a weapon in hand with which we could perhaps make a decisive contribution to the destruction of installations vital to the enemy war effort? And so the conception of a 'total effort' (*Totaleinsatz*) weapon was born within a similarly-minded group who considered it justified in view of the increasingly critical general situation. One could compare it with the Kamikaze idea in Japan although their sacrifices did not become known in Germany until much later.

Hitler, who had always been strictly against the idea of total self-sacrifice by German soldiers, would have none of it at first, but was finally persuaded to give his reluctant approval for the formation of such a unit, retaining the personal sanction for its operational use.

Surprisingly, there were thousands of willing volunteers for 'special operations' although nobody had any idea what was involved. On instructions from General Korten, Chief of the Luftwaffe General Staff, a small group of about 70 volunteers were then selected, called up, and finally detailed to KG 200. After all, the technical means for such an operation still had to be developed and tried out.

The basic idea was a piloted glide bomb, and the selected group of volunteers began their training as glider pilots right away. After graduating on the Grunau Baby glider, the training was continued until they could safely fly and land the so-called 'Stummelhabicht' ('Stumped Hawk'). This glider was a special modification of the well-known Habicht glider which was often demonstrated in a masterly fashion by Hanna Reitsch. A fully aerobatic design, the Habicht could be dived at 300 km/h (186 mph), and was a joy to fly. The 'Stummelhabicht' was created by shortening the wings of this glider until literally only two stumps remained. Additional structural strengthening ensured that this short-span glider could reach the speed of a contemporary fighter aircraft in a dive, an amazing achievement. Naturally, its flying characteristics were no longer glider-like, but that had to be expected – and was in fact intentional. Once the volunteers had mastered point-landings with the 'Stummelhabicht' their gliding training was considered completed. But what of the actual device, the 'total effort' weapon?

The intended operational use could be either 'with' or 'without a chance' of survival. In the first instance, the pilot would dive with his flying bomb on the target, but could leave it at the last moment and save himself by parachute. The bomb could no longer miss the target, and the pilot could expect to fall into the enemy hands alive, or even land on his own side. 'Without a chance' meant just that. In this case there would only be the conscious knowledge of having accomplished a deed of possibly decisive importance to the war effort.

But all that was only theory; as yet there was still no suitable weapon to carry out such operations.

As the device was intended to be destroyed on its operational flight, the basic requirement was for an explosive charge of the greatest possible effect that could be controlled in flight like a glider. The training of pilots for these devices should be accomplished with the minimum expenditure of time and material and only go as far as mastering a simple gliding flight with this device, followed by a point-landing.

The requirements for such a manned glide bomb were set down in a top secret document (g.Kdos-Chefsache), a copy of which reached Prof Georgii, in charge of research for the R.d.L. and C-in-C Luftwaffe in Berlin on 10 March 1944. The transcript reads as follows:

Chef-Sache

Technical-tactical requirements for a manned glide-bomb

A) *Intended purpose of the glide-bomb*
   Certain destruction of prime enemy targets (eg. battleships, aircraft carriers, large cargo ships, dams, major power stations, vital key installations of the armament industry, etc.)

B) *Method of application*
   Transport to the target area by bomber. After release of the bomb it is guided onto the target by the 'total effort' pilot manning it

C) *Tactical requirements*
   1) Guaranteed destruction of the target (accuracy and effect)
   2) Quickest possible production
   3) Simplicity of service use (the possibility of wider utilization from the personnel point of view)
   4) Versatility in use (HE, mine-bomb)

D) *Technical requirements*
   1) External form
      a) Approximation to the aerodynamic character of a high-performance glider
      b) Aerodynamically advantageous glide-bomb chassis that would permit to attach various kinds of bomb devices (ie HE or mine-bombs acc. to target)
      c) Small wings
      d) Tailplane

   2) *Flying characteristics*
      a) Similar to those of a good glider
      b) Sufficient manoeuvrability to be able to follow evasive movements of the target
      c) High normal speed to quickly penetrate the anti-aircraft zone and evade enemy fighters
      d) The ability to commence independent gliding flight some distance from the target (reduced danger to the carrier aircraft)

3) *Transport of the glide-bomb*
   a) Rigid attachment under a suitable bomber
   or
   b) As *Mistel* on top of a suitable carrier aircraft

4) *Essential equipment*
   a) Suitable flight control device (enabling to keep normal flying position over water and in conditions of poorly visible horizon)
   b) Connection to the intercom system of the carrier aircraft to communicate the release point, target description, etc. (disconnected by the glide-bomb pilot)
   c) Armour protection for the prone position of the glide-bomb pilot to avoid the possibility of becoming a casualty during the approach flight (protection principally against anti-aircraft fire)
   d) A sighting installation for the approach glide to accurately determine the release point under any circumstances
   e) The possibility of adjustment in case of being too short or too far off the target to reach the best distance for accuracy
   f) Limitation of maximum speed by means of manually-operated air brakes (dive brakes or brake parachutes) to avoid reaching the critical zone of the speed of sound when it becomes necessary to glide at steeper angles of inclination
   g) A thrust device of controllable output to enable the glide-bomb to gain normal speed without prolonged sinking after release from the slower flying bomber-carrier. Other advantages: reduction of the glide angle, higher speed without negative effects on the glide angle, the possibility to independently achieve the right distance for the best target approach flight
   h) Parachute for the glide-bomb pilot (chance of survival in case of engine failure on the carrier aircraft, fighter attack or anti-aircraft artillery hit)

5) *Explosive charge*
   a) Sufficiently powerful explosive load (high-grade explosive)
   b) Guaranteed correct glide path when used in water against shipping targets (avoidance of rebound)
   c) Perfectly operating fuses with multiple safety features (to completely exclude duds)

d) Provision for fitting the correct fuses according to the type of target

e) Guarantee against deformation on hitting the water

f) High degree of safety while transporting the explosive charge

6) *Desirable technical installations and proposals regarding the progressive development of this device*

a) The possibility of occupying the pilot's seat in the glide-bomb from the bomber via a shaft, or by projecting the pilot's seat inside the bomber (avoidance of longer stay in the tiring prone position)

b) The fitting of a sighting device that would display the direct approach flight to the target to the glide-bomb pilot, although in the case of shipping targets the bomb has to enter the water to achieve the necessary mine explosive effect. (Display of the visual impression of the target approach flight is important from the psychological point of view!)

c) Diving capability at steeper flight path angles avoiding the critical maximum speeds and therefore enabling the device to carry out diving attacks

d) Catapult capability and a longer-effective thrust device. Advantages: Independence of the bomber at close-range targets (for instance, the invasion fleet). Eventually a sitting accommodation for the bomb pilot for better withstanding of acceleration

e) Progressive development of the device so that the man piloting the bomb has better chances of survival. (A practical proposal by *Lt* Eck is in hand)

E) *Training*

1) *Purpose of training*

Familiarisation of the bomb pilot with the device. In addition, the final trial and carrying out the necessary improvements based on that

2) *Training device*

A training model as similar as possible to the operational device

3) *Requirements for the training model*

a) The closest possible similarity with the operational device as regards the shape, flying performance, flying characteristics, and operation of all controls and equipment

b) Possibility to land the device without loss of human lives or material

c) Possibility of loading ballast (jettisonable before landing!) up to the operational weight so that the glide-bomb pilot can get used to higher speeds and the conditions that he could expect on operations

Heigl

Oberst and *Geschwader* CO

Distribution:
1 × G.L. *Obersting*. Hermann (Luftwaffe General Staff, Engineer-Colonel)
1 × *Lw.Füst* – Chef – (Chief of Lw Operations Staff)
1 × II/KG 200
1 × *z.d.A.* KG 200 (for internal service use only)
1 × KTB (*Kriegstagebuch* = War Diary)

Most probably Prof Georgii and his collaborators shook their heads: this was some development request indeed! And when was it expected to be ready? It was not possible a real airman had drawn up these specifications – the expression 'chassis' instead of 'airframe' would give toothache to anybody who had anything to do with aircraft, not to mention some other oddly worded points. Apparently they had based it on the assumption that somewhere among the various new developments and devices there was bound to be one that could 'fit' this dreamed-up weapon; one only has to recall the rocket motor powering the Henschel Hs 293 flying bomb that was lying on the scrap heap, so to speak, at that time. They probably also believed that with some fumbling about it would have been possible to assemble all such parts into one whole – after all, no characteristics had been forgotten in the requirement. But the remark about 'the possible wider utilization from the personnel point of view' makes it clear that in the meantime a wide gap had appeared between the thoughts of the initiators – such people as Hanna Reitsch herself and *Gen. Oberst* von Greim, C-in-C *Luftflotte* 6 – and the ideas of the SS 'experts', who were in on this as well.

Initially, so as not to lose any valuable time, a whole series of unrealistic ideas had been put forward to carry out the first operations with various devices already on hand flown by ordinary pilots, such as a Me 410 armed with a bomb-torpedo or a FW 190 carrying the heaviest bomb available. The drawback here was that this presumed the use of trained and experienced pilots, but hardly any volunteers had come forward from the Luftwaffe flying units – most of the candidates were young soldiers. They had all been promised training as glider pilots, and held out in prospect that they would then be equipped with special aircraft to carry out their unspecified 'special tasks' – no more, no less.

For that reason one should not be surprised by the large number of volunteers. Apart from everything else, this also presented a good opportunity for careful selection and tests regarding suitability. The fact that during the initial stages of recruitment the candidates were given only the vaguest description of their future tasks had probably more to do with an attempt to preserve secrecy than an intention to deliberately mislead. On the other hand, the initiated knew that it was a matter of flights 'of no return' and had affirmed their agreement to this in a special declaration.

However, there were doubts expressed among the older pilots regarding the value of massed basic training. In their opinion it corresponded to no more than that of a *Hitler-Jugend* youngster who had learnt to fly a glider and could land it more or less accurately. But that did not mean that such an S.O.* man would also be able to carry out a flight with a device equipped with an auxiliary power unit over longer distances. Apart from that, he probably would not be able to find his target either under combat conditions because he had not been sufficiently trained to do so. The few older hands among them could probably manage it, but none of the youngsters had ever been in an enemy defence zone and could not possibly even imagine how he should react to anti-aircraft fire or when intercepted by enemy fighters. Proof of this, if it was ever needed, was provided by the so-called 'final effort' of the Luftwaffe fighter arm when many of the young pilots never came back from their very first operational flight.

The possibility of surviving the first operation helped by the leadership and advice of experienced formation commanders did not apply to these 'self-sacrifice' men because their first operational flight would also be their last. Nobody doubts the brave intentions of these young men when they volunteered for this special and obviously very

*S.O.=*Selbst-Opferung* or 'self-sacrifice', the official term used to describe these volunteers.

hazardous task, for that is all they knew about it – but it is doubtful if any of them would have in fact found their targets, despite being released near them, or would not have fallen victim to enemy defences before reaching it.

This would certainly also have been the case if they had resurrected the BV 40 project that had been shelved earlier. This device was a heavily armoured and almost invulnerable combat glider armed with a fixed 30 mm cannon, initially intended to be towed to high altitudes then to dive into the American bomber formations.

Tests were also carried out with the Me 328, an aircraft that had been originally designed as a kind of towed fighter powered by two ramjet units of 300 kp (661 lb) thrust each, of the same type that powered the V-1. It was intended to be attached in so-called *Deichselschlepp* (pole-tow) to the He 177 or Me 264 to provide fighter defence on long-range flights. Later on, the Me 328 was to become a flying bomb, but subsequent flight tests had shown that the vibrations with power on were so violent that the airframe broke up in the air. Now the Me 328 was resurrected once more and, without its ramjet units, proposed as a suitable vehicle for the 'self-sacrifice' detachment.

The flight tests were taken over by Hanna Reitsch and Heinz Kensche from the RLM and took place at Hörsching near Linz. The basic Me 328 was a small aircraft with very short wings and could reach about 750 km/h (466 mph) at a glide angle of 1:5. For flight trials the Me 328 was carried aloft attached on top of a Do 217 to altitudes of from 3000 to 6000 m (9840 to 19,690 ft). The pilot would then release the coupling attachment whereby the small machine easily lifted off the carrier aircraft to start its gliding flight, as Hanna Reitsch herself has reported. These flight tests were completed in April 1944 and the Me 328 was ordered to go into series production soon afterwards, but for some reason did not get that far.

By then a manned version of the V-1 seemed the most promising solution. The Allied advance since D-Day had forced the V-1 launching sites further and further away from their intended targets so that the number of devices used were far less than planned. Apart from that, this weapon was already in production and required only 280 man-hours to manufacture.

Quite by chance, while visiting the 'House of Airmen' in Berlin, Hanna Reitsch met Otto Skorzeny who had already been told about the plan by Himmler. Skorzeny had similar ideas himself about operational use of special weapons, and so it happened that the SS too became involved in the affair. As a result, the 70 volunteers already under KG 200 wing were augmented by another 30 or so from Skorzeny's formations. From then on, Skorzeny began to handle the matter in his own characteristic way, in that he would simply let all the people concerned know that he held full authority and had to continually report about the state of things direct to Hitler.

In the German Research Institute for Gliding Flight (DFS) at Ainring near Bad Reichenhall the Fi 103 (the correct RLM designation of the V-1) was modified to accommodate a pilot and equipped with rudimentary controls within a few days. This project ran under the cover designation 'Reichenberg'. The initial version was powerless, fitted with landing flaps, and designed to land on a spring-loaded skid. For flight tests it was carried to release altitude under an He 111.

The development of the operational device, known under the cover-designation 'Reichenberg IV', went on in parallel. Its principal data were as follows:

Power plant 1 × Argus As 014 pulse jet developing 660 lb thrust at sea level

Pulse jet running time 32 mins.

Flying weight 2260 kg (4960 lb);

Weight of warhead approx 800 kg (1764 lb);

Range with power after release from carrier aircraft at 2500 m (8200 ft) altitude – 300 km (186 miles).

Flight tests of the unpowered V-1 airframe were carried out at Rechlin and were initially troublesome. On one occasion the pilot accidentally opened the small cockpit canopy, lost control of his machine and crashed. Another manned test airframe crashed when it lost the largest part of its sand ballast that was meant to represent the explosive charge. However, despite such setbacks, a reliable manually controllable flying bomb was developed in a very short time – not least because Hanna Reitsch herself had decisively joined the test programme. Later on it was said that Hanna Reitsch had been badly injured in a crash with a manned V-1. This was not true, but she was forced to make at least two crash-landings with the device. In fact, Hanna Reitsch was badly injured while testing the Me 163 rocket-powered interceptor. This revolutionary aircraft took off from a heavy jettisonable two-wheel dolly undercarriage and landed on a sprung skid like a glider. On one of her test flights the jettison equipment did not function and Hanna Reitsch had to glide in with all this additional weight. As it happened, she approached the airfield with height to

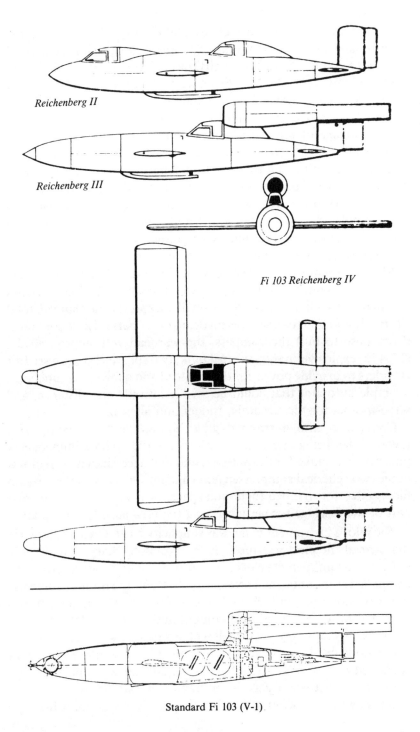

Reichenberg II

Reichenberg III

Fi 103 Reichenberg IV

Standard Fi 103 (V-1)

spare and then tried to correct the gliding angle by side-slipping. Unfortunately as soon as the aircraft was in a side-slip the control surfaces came into the turbulent airflow behind the take-off dolly and lost all effectiveness. The Me 163 stalled and hit the ground with great force – 'she came down like a piano thrown out of a third floor window,' as one eyewitness put it.

At this stage of tests with the powerless manned V-1, work was put in hand to build and prepare for service a training version powered by a pulse-jet unit and a two-seat trainer variant of this device. Both were closely based on the original and were fitted with a landing skid. The necessary flight tests were carried out as soon as the machines were completed, and so instruction and training went on unabated while the hangars at Prenzlau were gradually filling with the final version, the so-called 'sharp' operational devices.

After the completion of tests it would have required only relatively little work to convert the mass-produced unmanned Fi 103 airframes into manned versions fitted with a small cockpit for the planned 'total effort'. The Fi 103 fuselage was made up of six parts. These contained (from nose to tail) the compass, the warhead with approx 800 kg (1764 lb) explosive charge, the fuel tank, two spherical compressed air cylinders to provide power for the fuel feed and a few other functions, a simple autopilot that could be set for altitude and distance, and servo-motors for the elevators, rudder and ailerons.

Conversion into a manned glide bomb, the 'Reichenberg IV', involved the fitting of a small pilot's seat in the fuselage immediately under the air intake for the pulse-jet unit and necessitated the removal of the two spherical compressed air cylinders. Only one of these was in fact needed for manned flight and space for it was found in the rear part of the fuselage formerly carrying the now surplus auto-pilot.

The pilot's instrument panel was simplicity itself. On it was a switch that armed the electrical fuses of the explosive charge, an airspeed indicator, an altimeter, a clock, and an artificial horizon. A gyroscopic compass was mounted in a console on the floor. In addition, there was space for an accumulator and a transformer. The flight controls consisted of a normal control column and rudder pedals. The seat itself was a simple plywood shell with a small padded head support. The canopy of this small cockpit was one-piece and hinged along the starboard side to open. The frontal windscreen was made of thick laminated bullet-proof glass as on fighter aircraft. Several lines were painted on the side windows so that the pilot could compare his flight position with the horizon to estimate the correct gliding angle, and that was all. The wings had full-span ailerons along the whole trailing edge – there was no need for landing flaps of course.

An essential installation was the intercom connection that enabled the pilot to keep in touch with his carrier aircraft until the final glide.

This cramped and primitively-equipped cockpit, then, was intended to accommodate a man who had volunteered to glide this flying bomb onto a target and willingly sacrifice his own life doing so. Of course, he might be clinging to the idea of baling out at the last moment, but what in fact would have been his chances?

Before anything else one must bear in mind that the '*Reichenberg IV*' was a most unstable aircraft: it could not keep a straight flight path for more than 1000 m (3280 ft) without the pilot being forced to correct. This means that the glide bomb would most probably miss the target if the pilot baled out too soon. However, the only targets intended for this weapon were the so-called 'point targets', such as heavily armoured warships or a certain vital building of an armaments complex, or other such targets of great strategic importance where accuracy was essential. Apart from that, leaving the tiny cockpit with a parachute in a steeply inclined glide when the aircraft had reached about 800 km/h (497 mph) would have been extremely problematical. Opening and jettisoning the canopy alone required a number of manipulations that were bound to distract the pilot's attention from his target. Assuming he had managed to jettison the canopy and keep the target more or less in line, getting out of the cramped cockpit together with the hindering parachute would have been a masterly acrobatic and athletic performance indeed: at that speed, the slip-stream would crumple the human body like a piece of paper!

Taking everything into consideration, would the 'manned V-1' really have been of value as a 'total effort' weapon?

From the purely technical point of view, yes – it could be controlled in flight and directed onto a target with sufficient accuracy to ensure a direct hit. But, in cruising flight it was slower than enemy fighters. In other words, the manned glide bomb could be easily intercepted and shot down during its approach flight, not to mention the anti-aircraft artillery. This danger was increased still more by the glide-bomb being transported to near its target area at higher altitudes by a relatively slow carrier aircraft.

The second drawback lay in the comparatively limited effect of its explosive charge, which was far too small for an operation that would sacrifice human lives.

Over the long period of time that had gone by since the first fumbling experiments, compounded by the desperate situation facing Germany in spring 1945, the notions about the use of this weapon had also changed, particularly within the SS; Himmler was even thinking of using people who were depressed or despondent, sick or plain criminals!

The last Inspector of Bombers, *Gen Maj* Walter Storp, had different ideas. He wanted to expand the original concept to form a whole Luftwaffe 'Self-sacrifice Division' that would be known under the cover-name of *'Jägerdivision Hermann Göring'*. How unrealistic this idea was is shown, apart from everything else, by an entry in the OKL War Diary dated 24 February 1945, according to which 'the training of volunteers at KG 200 has to be suspended due to the shortage of fuel – except for 34 men whose training has already reached an advanced stage'.

Soon after that there was an angry confrontation in the presence of Göring between *Gen Maj* Storp and *Gen Maj* Dietrich Peltz on one side, and *Oberst* Siegfried Knemeyer, Chief of Aircraft Development, and *Oberstleutnant* Baumbach, the CO of KG 200, on the other. Baumbach considered an operational use of the glide-bomb as criminal under such circumstances, and did not mince his words. The day after, he discussed the whole matter with his friend Albert Speer, the Minister of Armaments. Speer 'took the bull by the horns', so to speak, and hauled Baumbach off with him to see Hitler. Never really convinced about the 'self-sacrifice' idea anyway, Hitler now rejected it once and for all, in no uncertain terms. On the same day Baumbach instructed *Major* Kuschke, commander of IV/KG 200, to disband the 'Total Effort' detachment forthwith. Kuschke acted quickly, and within hours the men were on their way back to their previous units or put at the disposal of the Personnel Branch.

All this happened just in time because the 'total effort' was going to be used operationally after all: Heinrich Himmler himself had taken over responsibility for this matter 'because one should no longer bother the Führer with such things . . .'

Fortunately what would have been a senseless massacre instead of a fulfilment of a highly idealistic idea was already stopped in its tracks before it could start.

10. The Pick-a-Back Aircraft

The British Home Fleet dominating the North sea had always been a thorn in the flesh for the German High Command. The *coup* at Scapa Flow of the U-boat captain Günter Prien* in 1939 remained a unique feat of arms, but now nobody could get at the ships by water.

At the same time, this British naval base was also outside the practical range of German bombers. It was the usual predicament, the longer the range, the less bomb load the aircraft could carry. And to destroy or at least seriously damage such heavily-armoured capital ships required enormous amounts of explosive. It just could not be done.

Then someone remembered the British Short-Mayo composite experiments of 1938 when a large four-engined flying boat had carried a smaller four-engined floatplane pick-a-back way out over the Atlantic before releasing it. With such assistance, the four-engined floatplane could fly all the way from Dundee, Scotland to the Orange River delta in South Africa, the first aircraft to do so non-stop. This pick-a-back combination had functioned without any problems, practically doubling the range of the floatplane. With the outbreak of World War II these promising trials with the Short-Mayo 'twins' were suspended, but the idea had been proved in practice.

Taking this a step further, it seemed possible to leave the lower, larger aircraft unmanned, load it full with explosives and fly it, controlled from the smaller upper aircraft to the target area. After release, this enormous 'flying bomb' could then be guided onto the target by the pilot of the smaller aircraft, who would then return to base. If this upper aircraft could be a fighter, so much the better: he could look after his own skin afterwards. In any case, the smaller aircraft would have saved fuel on the ingoing flight, and the lower component no longer needed any. Like this, the practical range would have been doubled – and that was what mattered!

As there was no practical experience with such 'composite aircraft' in Germany, the first flight trials attempted at DFS in 1942 involved a

*On 14 October, 1939 *Kpt.Ltn* Günter Prien with his *U.47* managed to penetrate unnoticed into Scapa Flow and sank the 31,200 ton battleship *Royal Oak* with the loss of 786 lives.

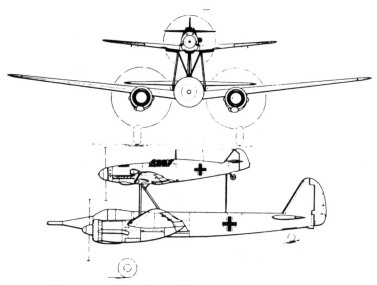

Mistel 1 (Ju 88A-4/Bf 109F)

lighter combination consisting of an DFS 230A glider and a Klemm
K1 35A two-seat sports aircraft. The small K1 35A was fastened
down on the glider's wings in such a way that the shock absorber legs
of its main undercarriage were compressed. At the moment of parting
the upper aircraft forcibly 'straightened up' a bit, so to speak, giving
itself a larger angle of incidence, and hence lifted off easily from the
glider. This K1 35A/DFS 230A combination had to be towed to
altitude by a Ju 52/3m, but it proved that, provided both pilots could
communicate with each other, flying in this way was quite possible.

The next experimental stage comprised a FW 56 Stösser fighter-
trainer and a DFS 230A, with a corresponding increase in speed,
followed by the final stage, a Bf 109 with extended main undercarriage
attached on top of another DFS 230 glider. This last trial combination
could already take off and even land on its own, without parting
company. Encouraged by these results, the former Junkers Chief test
pilot *Flugkapitän* Siegfried Holzbauer hit upon the idea of using old
Ju 88 bombers whose airframes and engines had reached their
maximum permissible service hours for one final operational flight as
'super flying bombs'. The realisation of this idea too had to be taken in
stages. To begin with, it was necessary to have a training version where
both aircraft were manned. The chosen combination comprised either
a Bf 109F or FW 190A as the 'controlling' aircraft, and a Ju 88A or

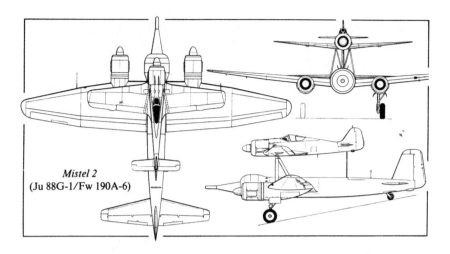

Mistel 2
(Ju 88G-1/Fw 190A-6)

Ju 88G as the 'carrier'. The upper machine was attached near its centre of gravity by means of support struts at two points to the main wing spar of the lower component, while the tail end of its fuselage was held in flight position by a 'buckle strut'. The separation in flight was achieved by first buckling the rear strut which gave the upper machine a greater angle of incidence so that in the moment of release it could immediately climb away from its carrier.

The operational training versions were all given the cover designation *'Mistel'* (Mistletoe) and involved the following combinations:

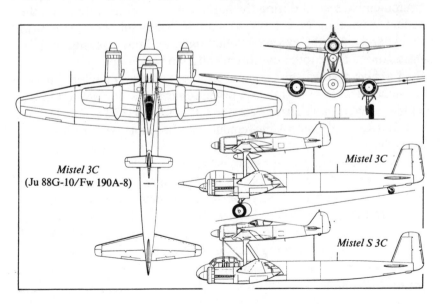

Mistel 3C
(Ju 88G-10/Fw 190A-8)

Mistel 3C

Mistel S 3C

113

Ju 88A/Bf 109F (*Mistel S 1*), Ju 88G/FW 190A-8 (*Mistel S 2*), and Ju 88G-6/FW 190A-6 (*Mistel S 3A*). The operational version comprised an unmanned rebuilt Ju 88A-4 fitted with a 3800 kg (8377 lb) hollow-charge explosive warhead in a special nose section, and a Bf 109F as its controlling aircraft. This combination was given the cover designation '*Beethoven-Gerät*', but the name *Mistel* had already been so well established that this version is better known as *Mistel 1*. Other combinations were:

Ju 88G-1/FW 190A-6 or F-8   (*Mistel 2*)
Ju 88A-4/FW 190A-8   (*Mistel 3a*)
Ju 88H-4/FW 190A-8   (*Mistel 3b*)
Ju 88G-10/FW 190A-8 or F-8 (*Mistel 3c*)

The special nose section with its hollow-charge explosive load and the protruding prong with the fuse components gave the Ju 88 a truly venomous appearance. The power of this hollow-charge warhead was awesome – it could penetrate 8 metres (26¼ ft) of steel or 20 metres (65¾ ft) of ferro-concrete! The nose section was attached to the fuselage bulkhead in place of the crew cabin by four large cap nuts.

In action this composite aircraft was controlled by the pilot of the upper fighter. He had to activate the small explosive charges that separated the aircraft at the very latest about 1500 m (4920 ft or 1640 yds) from the objective while the Ju 88 continued on its set course to hit the target with great accuracy. The following technical equipment was used during the approach flight until separation: the rudder servo-motors, the two-axis automatic flight control (vertical and lateral axis), the gyro-controlled sight, and the explosive jettison installation. The rudder control installation was fitted half way down the fuselage and was accessible from the outside. The pilot's rudder movements were sensed over a potentiometer and transferred to the rudder servo motor. There were two settings: 'take-off' and 'flight'. In the first case all control movements by the pilot were followed by immediate large and hard rudder deflections. In the second case the reactions were less pronounced and softer.

The control elements for the biaxial flight control mechanism in the pilot's cockpit consisted of a course-setting device for lateral movements at the control column and a spring-loaded switch for vertical movements (climb and sink) on the instrument panel. Both control devices were made to spring back to zero position when released. The pilot of the upper machine could not control the ailerons of the Ju 88, on the operational version they were locked.

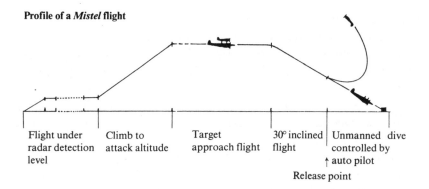

Profile of a *Mistel* flight

| Flight under radar detection level | Climb to attack altitude | Target approach flight | 30° inclined flight | Unmanned dive controlled by auto pilot |

Release point

The gyro-controlled sight did not differ externally from the well known *Revi* (reflex gun sight). It had switches for two settings: 'Gyro locked' and 'Gyro free'. When using the first setting the sight was fixed, ie it acted as a normal gun sight with a fixed focus firing ring. In the second setting the sight became 'alive' and reacted to all vertical and lateral changes, indicating them as so much lead in the sight display. During any movement of the aircraft the indicating sign wandered off centre.

The upper controlling aircraft was attached to its lower component with electrically detonated explosive ball joint locks, at three points. The gap between the two aircraft was just high enough for the propeller of the controlling fighter to turn freely over the Ju 88 on both the operational and training versions. On the *Mistel* trainers the propeller blades rotated only about 10 cm (4 inches) above the Ju 88 cockpit, just above the instructor-pilot's head.

As already mentioned, the rear support strut was made to buckle and the toggle joint in the middle of this support carried an additional explosive charge. In the moment of separation this charge ignited a split second before the other three, the 'knee joint' bent forward shortening the strut, which pulled down the tail end of the controlling aircraft. The remaining three explosive ball joints were timed to detonate at this moment. The controlling aircraft was now free, and pointing slightly upwards. This was intentional, the buckling rear joint was specially designed to prevent the smaller aircraft from 'sinking back' again even if the pilot failed to react by immediately pulling away.

The separating explosive charges were detonated via a flick switch that was normally set to 'safe'. In case of a failure the pilot could use a second, 'emergency' switch which immediately ignited the three ball joint charges but without the 'buckling strut' effect.

Although compared to a multi-engined bomber, the instrumentation and equipment carried by a fighter were almost spartanly simple, the pilot had very little room in his small cockpit because it now also had to accommodate all the additional instruments and levers necessary to control the Ju 88. Thus, instead of a single throttle lever there were three, all indicators for oil and coolant temperatures were in triplicate, and the same applied for the rev counters, engine boost, oil and fuel tankage. Additional switches and instruments were necessary for the complete electrical system and the fuel flow pump installation – not forgetting the control devices and instruments for the complicated fuse system of the 3·8-ton 'superbomb'. The problem of transmitting the numerous operational data for the transfer of the control and other signals was solved by installing thick strands of cables more or less provisionally between the two aircraft, the only mechanical connection were the throttle rods for the Ju 88. The rest, such as the propeller pitch and radiator gill settings, undercarriage and landing flaps were activated via an electro-hydraulic system, while the elevators and rudder responded to the servo motors as mentioned above. Only one otherwise essential control was missing on the operational Ju 88, the undercarriage wheel brakes. They were considered, but the necessary installation would have demanded too much constructive effort for the intended use. This meant that the operational combination could not be braked, but that risk was acceptable; after all, brakes were only needed while taxiing for take-off. As a result, all operational *Mistels* were towed to their take-off points while all transfer flights were carried out with the normal crew cabin in place instead of the special warhead that was attached only before an operational flight. In other words if for some reason such as a technical defect the pilot had to land, he had to activate the separating detonators – the Ju 88 with its hollow-charge warhead was lost, but the controlling pilot could save himself and his aircraft.

Of course, there was also the question of weight. While a normal loaded Ju 88 had a maximum loaded weight of 13,000 kg (28,660 lb), a fully tanked *Mistel*, including its warhead, weighed over 20 tons. To land with this weight would have required a completely new undercarriage which of necessity had to have larger diameter tyres or even twin wheels – for which there was no space in the existing wheel wells. Indeed, the undercarriage was the weakest point of this composite aircraft. Each take off was a high-risk undertaking with the

116

question foremost on everybody's mind: will the tyres hold, or will one of them burst? To minimize this risk, the ground crews would often sweep the hardstands and concrete runways before operations so that even the smallest stones that could possibly damage tyres were removed.

It was a different matter with the *Mistel* trainers. Lacking the heavy warhead they had a comparatively normal weight, and for local circuits the fuel tanks did not have to be full up. In fact, a training *Mistel* Ju 88 with its upper fighter component weighed about the same as a fully loaded Ju 88 with full tanks. The basic prerequisite for retraining flights with this composite aircraft was that the pilot could safely fly both machines on their own. The lower component was externally the same as a normal bomber with the standard frontal cabin, but with the fittings altered for use as a 'double' aircraft, ie controlled from the upper aircraft. However, the instructor-pilot in the lower component could always take a hand when the trainee made an error, and he was also the one to land the composite aircraft.

Another point that had to be taken into consideration was that all control surface movements were 'remotely controlled' so to speak, being transferred via an auto-pilot and consequently the *Mistel* reacted relatively sluggishly compared to an ordinary Ju 88. For this reason it was impossible to fly the *Mistels* in a tight formation which required constant and quick corrections to keep close to the neighbouring aircraft. But not only that; this 'delayed reaction' was a particular and even dangerous drawback during take-off.

Even a normal Ju 88 needed watching during its take-off run: at a certain point only a quick reaction by the pilot would prevent it from a sudden swing to port. Flying a *Mistel* demanded the greatest attention and concentration from its pilot if he did not want to veer off the concrete runway and end up with a 'bent' undercarriage on the uneven grass field. The whole procedure was not made any easier by the pilot's field of vision being restricted by the bulky engine of the FW 190, and the fact that being on stilts as it were some fifteen feet above the ground the upper component would pitch and toss as the aircraft gathered speed, knocking the pilot's head against the cockpit glazing.

This increased tendency to swing to port was not due solely to the delayed rudder action – the upper machine was quite a distance above the aerodynamic centre of the composite aircraft, and its heavy propeller created an additional turning moment, especially when the tail end of the Ju 88 had just lifted off the ground.

These negative characteristics of the *Mistel* combination resulted in several accidents during conversion training. In one case a young *Oberfähnrich* (Senior officer cadet) lost his life together with his instructor in the Ju 88 when neither succeeded in preventing their *Mistel* from developing a swing. Another two pilots lost their lives during night training when their *Mistel* came in too hard and the supporting struts holding the FW 190 were rammed into the Ju 88.

And of course everyone, and particularly the pilots had great respect for the explosive charge carried by the *Mistel*. True enough, the more experienced airmen had long since grown used to handling all kinds of ammunition, bombs and explosives, but this hollow-charge 'super bomb' of nearly four tons was something different! But even then, they really knew very little. All details that did not concern the actual operational use of the warhead were secret and 'not available'. The only people in the operational *Staffel* who knew more were the special armourers. It was their task to fit the seven fuses in the protruding pointed 'trunk' and another seven electric and acoustic fuses in the rear part of the warhead. A thick armour plate was then fitted between the warhead and the remaining empty space left by the removed crew cabin to prevent the highly dangerous explosive from detonating if the *Mistel* was attacked from behind.

One who would know these technical and flying problems better than anybody else was the Technical Officer of the unit. He also knew that the *Mistel* had undergone only a minimum of testing and that many components were only improvised. A good example were the many electric cables between the two aircraft which were fastened to the connecting struts in quite primitive fashion by strips of adhesive tape.

It was part of his usual 'understatement' to assert that he had overcome his great fear once he had managed to reach the cockpit of the upper aircraft. Climbing up those fire brigade ladders always made his knees tremble.

The Technical Officer was also decisively involved in the preparation of the so-called 'survival kit' for the *Mistel* pilots. It consisted of emergency rations, some medicaments, bandages, a pistol with ammunition, compass, maps, some additional clothing, a folding hunting rifle and other essentials, including matches in a watertight packing. All these items were strapped to the pilot's body and, in case he had to bale out, were to help him survive in enemy-held territory and eventually break through to his own lines.

The former *Mistel* pilot *Leutnant* Eckard Dittmann recalls the following interesting details:

'Before each operational take-off a proper "timetable" was hung around the pilot's neck to remind him of the correct sequence, which was:

1) Trim the Ju 88 to "Zero"
2) Trim the FW 190 to "Zero"
3) Set Ju 88 landing flaps for take-off
4) Set FW 190 landing flaps for take-off
5) Set Ju 88 propellers to 12 o'clock*
6) Set FW 190 propeller to "automatic"
7) Rudder servo motor flick switch to "Take-off"
8) Hollow charge fuse switch to "Unprimed"
9) Set directional gyroscope to departure course
10) Undercarriage locking switch "Up"
11) Check the transfer function of the rudder servo-motor on the Ju 88 rudder.'

It may be nearly forty years hence, but occasionally he still thinks back to those anxious seconds when he was tossed and pitched in his FW 190 high above the speeding Ju 88, and the ever-present worry of keeping the whole contraption on the runway until the tail lifted, one could see straight ahead, and the *Mistel* left the ground. It was a very special kind of flying indeed!

---

*Propeller pitch settings in German aircraft were indicated on a clock-like dial on the instrument panel.

11. 'Plan Eisenhammer'

The first *Mistels* were delivered to 2./KG 101, a unit that was supposed to attack the British Home Fleet at Scapa Flow, in May 1944. In the meantime two other plans to use this weapon, raids on Gibraltar and on Soviet warships at Kronshtadt had been abandoned.

However, before 2./KG 101 could deploy to its operational base in Denmark, the Allies invaded Normandy and the *Staffel* was transferred to the West. Using all five available *Mistel 1s* the unit made its first operational flight against shipping targets in the Seine Bay on the night of 24/25 June 1944. One *Mistel* pilot was forced to jettison his 'bomber' on the way, but the other four reached their target area and sank several blockships. All five Bf 109 pilots returned to base.

In August 1944 this *Staffel* formed the nucleus of the first *Mistel Gruppe*, III/KG 66. Early in November this unit was redesignated II/KG 200 and comprised three *Staffeln* – 5.(Bel)/KG 200, equipped with Ju 88S, Ju 188A and Ju 188E, was the 'target illuminator' unit for the *Mistel 1s* and *Mistel 3s* of 6./KG 200, while 7./KG 200 functioned as the replacement and training *Staffel* for the entire *Gruppe*.

Another plan to attack the British Home Fleet was being prepared at this time, and a *Mistel* formation was again deployed to Denmark. Then, on 11 November 1944, the British finally succeeded in sinking the German battleship *Tirpitz* in Norwegian waters and the situation changed once again. The menace of the *Tirpitz* had tied down a sizeable part of the British Home Fleet by her presence alone, but once she was gone, several warships were moved away from Scapa Flow and there was nothing really worthwhile left for the *Mistels* to raid.

By that time the remaining *Mistel* formations – I and II/KG 30 – were operationally subordinated to KG 200 and combined into *Gefechtsverband* (Task Force) Helbig, named after its commander *Oberst* Joachim Helbig*. Now that the Scapa Flow operation had been abandoned the command had dug up the 1943 *'Plan Eisen-*

---

*Known as 'Captain Fit' to his Luftwaffe comrades, Helbig had gained fame by his extremely successful dive-bombing attacks/with Ju 88s on British warships in the Mediterranean in 1941 before being promoted to lead larger formations.

6./KG 200 symbol was the 'Father and Son' cartoon motif.

hammer' again that had much more going for it than sinking some warships.

The original *'Plan Eisenhammer'* had been based on recommendations made by Prof Steinmann of the RLM. A clever, thorough and modest person, he had pointed out the great strategic importance of various centres vital to the Soviet war effort and suggested raiding them as selected point targets. (In fact, he had vainly protested against the senseless and wasteful bombing of British towns and cities in 1940, trying to persuade the Luftwaffe command to pay more attention to, and attack with concentrated force the nerve centres of an industrialised nation, the power stations, instead.) He argued that the manufacture of a steam or water turbine used for generating electricity demanded the highest precision and technical capacity and could not be done quickly. For instance, it took about one and a half years to complete just one turbine. Apart from that, the Soviets still could not manufacture their own turbines, and their only turbine repair works at Leningrad was damaged and out of action. And there were no 'spares' – nowhere in the world were turbines manufactured for stock. The important point was that nobody could afford to suddenly 'lose' such highly sensitive installations, particularly the Russians. For them it was literally a matter of survival, a direct threat to life. They had no integrated grid only separate centres, of which only two smaller ones were intact in the Urals and the Far East. The most important power centre was near Moscow which supplied 75 per cent of the armament industry. The stark fact was that if only two thirds of the turbines were out of action this vital industrial region was practically paralyzed. No other targets could be more important.

Next in the line of such sensitive targets were power transformers and overland power lines, and of course the dams associated with hydro-electric power stations.

Basically, the revised *'Plan Eisenhammer'* visualised attacks on important Soviet power stations in the Moscow and Gorky areas. These point target raids were to be carried out by two *Gruppen* of KG 30 with Ju 88A-4, five *Gruppen* of KG 4 and KG 55 with He 111H-6 and H-16, and III/KG 100 with Do 217s carrying the FX 1400 guided bombs, while I/KG 66 would act as pathfinders. Some other units, probably with the He 177 and Ju 290 'heavies' were also supposed to join the attacking force. In addition to the FX 1400, it was also planned to use the 'S-Bo', the so-called *'Sägebombe'* ('Saw Bomb') to help cut the overland power lines.*

However, the whole operation had to be postponed again and again because the Soviet 1944 summer offensive had overrun the intended German take-off bases, until finally the distance to the targets was greater than the range of the available aircraft.

It was at this stage that KG 200 was called in to carry out this operation with its *Mistels*. By that time it was already February 1945, and the only remaining suitable take-off bases were some airfields around Berlin and near the Baltic coast.

A surviving eyewitness from II/KG 30, Eckard Dittman, recalls:

'The higher command based its evaluation of the situation and drew the strategic consequences from the following: the Soviet forces have been exhausted by their continuous advance, and their offensive power has been consumed. At the given moment, all replenished SS divisions, equipped with modern weapons, will attack from Western Hungary in a wide sweeping pincer movement in the northerly direction, break through to the Baltic Sea and cut off the Soviet armies. At the same time the Luftwaffe paralyzes the Soviet armament industry. After this has been achieved, Germany can make a separate peace with the Western powers and Central Europe would remain outside the Soviet grip.

---

*SBO 53 or *Sägebombe* was evolved from the anti-aircraft 'cable bomb' and intended to destroy high tension electric cables. It consisted of a spherical weight attached to a 400 m (1312 ft) long twisted steel cable wound on a reel fitted inside the aircraft. Various test flights using a Ju 88 were carried out in summer 1942; the device justified itself but demanded high flying skills. It is known that the SBO 53 was subsequently used for service trials, but its operational use in the intended role cannot be confirmed.

The following were needed to fulfil the operational tasks allocated to the Luftwaffe: 100 selected *Mistel* pilots from LG 1, KG 6, KG 30 and KG 200 plus 150 pathfinders on the Ju 88s, and a mixed force of He 111s, Ju 188s, Do 217s, Ju 90s and Ju 290s of KG 66, KG 200 and other such long-range units. The targets were about twelve steam and hydro-electric power stations in a circle east of Moscow, including Tula, Stalinogorsk, Gorky and the giant reservoir at Rybinsk north-east of Moscow. The take-off was to be at night, at 2130 hrs, the attack itself at 0700 hrs on the following morning. This meant a flying time of about $9\frac{1}{2}$ to 10 hours, plus the return flight by each pilot on his own with the "released" FW 190s of some $4\frac{1}{2}$ to 5 hours across Soviet territory. The returning fighters were to land in the Courland bridgehead in Latvia, the most easterly area still held by the German forces. The intended take-off bases were Oranienburg, Rostock, Peenemünde, Rechlin-Lärz and another three or four smaller airfields.

To begin with, the *Mistels* were to fly a feint northwards, to Bornholm, then change course eastwards over the Baltic Sea, making a landfall north of Königsberg. After crossing East Prussia and the old Soviet border the next stage was a flight along the great highway from north of Minsk to Smolensk, where the force would divide. A number of *Mistels* would turn south-east for the targets at Stalinogorsk and Tula while the rest would continue eastwards in the direction of Gorky. At a predetermined distance north-west of Moscow the remaining group of *Mistels* would turn off towards Rybinsk. From Bornholm in the Baltic to the first branching off at Smolensk the pilots needed to make only two minor corrections of their flight path.

The task of the pathfinders was to mark all flight path points, turns and points of orientation at half an hour intervals by continuous 30 minute illuminations. The final point of orientation and target marking would be taken over by the Ju 90 and Ju 290 crews who were more experienced in long-distance flights.

The *Mistel* pilots had to fly exactly according to the time-table and keep to the predetermined flight path and turning points. These were clearly marked on their flight maps, as were the illuminations by the pathfinders at the same regular intervals. In other words, the *Mistel* pilots did not have to worry about navigation: all they had to do was keep exactly to the marked flight path, watch out for sky markers and correct their course when necessary.

To have the necessary range all FW 190s were fitted with special supplementary fuel tanks of 1200 litre (264 Imp gal) capacity. These looked like fat aerial torpedoes and theoretically would ensure the return flight to Courland.

Special attention was also paid to the engines. All the BMW 801 radials of the FW 190 controlling aircraft were carefully checked for "service life" and all those that had not reached 30-40 hours were taken out and replaced by others that had from different aircraft. Specialists then set these engines for the most economical fuel consumption, and all pilots were given a third clock and an engine time-table. According to this, they had to interrupt their economical cruising flight every half hour for three minutes to clear the spark plugs by giving slightly more than normal throttle. Until separation and their solo flight the FW 190s were of course using fuel from the Ju 88 tanks.

The target briefing was quite unique. Each *Mistel* pilot was given a folder with excellent aerial photographs, even including oblique shots, taken under various weather conditions, and detailed technical, navigational and other information. It was also seen to that he had enough time to study this material. Each target was also represented by a scale model surrounded by summer or winter landscape painted on by artists according to aerial photographs so that all pilots could have a realistic idea what to expect.

The separate "target groups" were then formed, without regard for former *Geschwader* membership. The most important group was the one selected to attack Rybinsk because they had to destroy the giant dam and the turbine installations. If successful, this would have raised the water level of the river Volga by five metres even at its estuary at Astrakhan, and the entire Volga basin would have been flooded. At least, that was what the experts had asserted.

We were even given a practical instruction at the Spandau power station. The poor emaciated fellows working there could not understand what we really wanted, and we could not tell them, but they tried to help nevertheless. In the end we shared out all our cigarettes and sandwiches among them.

Then a veteran fighter ace instructed us about the types and characteristics of Soviet aircraft we might encounter and the superior points of our FW 190s – which had to be unarmed to save weight.

In case some of us were shot down, a botanist gave us practical advice how to survive on various tree barks, lichen, mosses, berries, herbs and wild animals. Next on the agenda were language experts who taught us the most essential Russian idioms and distributed pocket dictionaries. Other experts gave us lectures on how to use our parachutes as emergency shelters, about partisan areas, and how best to obtain food locally. Each of us was then given a packet of Roubles (they were supposed to have been forgeries), emergency provisions, including 25 cigars with golden bands in a tin, and a briefing about Russian weather conditions.

Finally everything was ready and carrying the "Most Secret" target folders and the scale models with their painted summer and winter "carpets" for last-minute rehashing, we climbed aboard a bus and left for our take-off base, "Target Group Stalinogorsk" – at Oranienburg.

By that time each pilot knew 'his' target really well. He had learned his task at the "sand model", as it were, including the approach speed, gliding angle and release point. He knew he would be assisted by his autopilot which would transmit the final independent course settings to the Ju 88, and the BZA, the *Bomben-Ziel-Automatik* (automatic bombing run device) that would calculate these data automatically and display them in his reflex sight. And he knew that all the calculations had to be correct until this point, the approach to attack, for the mission to have any success.

After that it was every man for himself, truly a matter of "to be or not to be" for the lonely pilots in their unarmed aircraft, who had to cover a distance of some 1600 km (994 miles) on the way back over enemy territory. And that had to be achieved somehow with an aircraft that normally did not have half that range – not to mention the long tiring flight before that.

The *Mistel* pilots who had the most easterly targets in particular could calculate that they needed a strong tailwind if they wanted to reach German-held territory at all. The only other chance was to fly on until the fuel tanks were dry and then bale out, hoping to avoid an immediate capture by the Soviets. All being well, one could then always try to sneak through to one's own lines. They had discussed this often enough during the long weeks of preparations, and each of them had also asked himself – if not the others: why do you want to take part in this operation at all? After all, in this case you were deliberately risking your own life at the proverbial five minutes to midnight!

It was a good question – but none of the *Mistel* pilots reported being unable to carry out his task. To an outsider, this may be difficult to understand, but it was so nevertheless. None of these young men were suicidal types or stubborn and stupid fanatics, they were intelligent, sensible and experienced pilots who had survived the war so far.

There was this young *Leutnant* who had been allocated the most distant target. Like most young men, he had everything to live for, but still he had decided to be a *Mistel* pilot, knowing full well the great risks involved. And this was to be it. He calculated again and again – the distance, his fuel supply, the fuel consumption under the various conditions, weather, his own speed there and back – all the factors that determined his chances of getting back home again, or at least somewhere near German-held territory, but the stark figures were clearly against him. Try as he might, it did not work out. His only chance was a strong tailwind on the way in, and a strong tailwind on the way out, that would just about take him to Courland in Latvia. But he was also fully aware that a weather situation where there would be a strong westerly wind and then, exactly nine hours later, an equally strong easterly wind, could only happen once in a hundred years.

Nevertheless, this young officer – and an experienced airman and fighter – did not report to his *Staffel* commander that his task was impossible to carry out, that he had no chance of returning back home again. He knew only too well that his comrades flying the other *Mistels* faced the same predicament, even if their targets were not so deep in Soviet territory. Apart from that, his *Staffel* commander was quite aware of this himself – after all, he was flying another *Mistel* on this operation. They were both standing with their backs to the wall. He just had to sort this out in his own way – and, like all airmen before a dangerous operation, he knew deep inside him that, whatever happened, *he* would make it back. It was a hope and conviction that helped to sustain many in those days.

Also, they were all aware that this was not just an ordinary operation, and these were not ordinary times any more. Each operation was now important if it offered a chance to hinder or weaken the enemy in the East, to give a bit more breathing space to the troops fighting desperately to hold back the onstorming masses – and perhaps a bit more time for their families at home. There was also that silent hope that this would indirectly help the Western allies to advance further across the Elbe and towards Berlin. Many fighting men had this in mind, especially those whose homes were in the way of the advancing Red Army – and of course nobody knew, or would have believed if told, that the German Reich had already long since been divided among the victors!

Now it was only a matter of waiting for the right weather conditions – but then fate once again turned the tables. An American daylight

126

bombing raid on Rechlin-Lärz destroyed 18 *Mistels*, the main force. Some of the composite aircraft were totally consumed by flames, and the crews watched in amazement as their "super warheads" failed to explode but slowly burned out.

And with that, the operation had to be postponed once again, although the tension remained – until one day an order simply announced "Eisenhammer cancelled", without any explanation.'

12. With the *Mistel* against Bridges

By February 1945 the advancing Soviet troops had reached the river Oder and this difficult obstacle gave the exhausted retreating German troops a temporary respite.

In the course of their retreat they had naturally tried to blow up all the bridges, but had not always succeeded. In fact, only twelve bridges had been so completely destroyed that they could not be repaired until March, but some 120 railway and road traffic bridges fell almost undamaged into enemy hands. Nevertheless, even these available crossing points could not take the immense advancing Soviet army with all its equipment, thousands of tanks and guns, and enormous material supplies across the Oder in the necessary mass and time, therefore the Red Army pioneers also built a number of auxiliary bridges across the river.

Of course, none of us suspected that the Americans would make a halt at the Elbe and leave everything east of that line, including Berlin, to the Russians. Quite the opposite. Rumours that talks were already taking place with the Western powers persisted obstinately and they all carried the same basic message: there would be a separate armistice, so that Germany could mount a counter offensive in the East with all available forces.

When it became obvious that the measures taken to date would not hold up the Soviet forces crossing the Oder and now advancing towards Berlin, the supreme commander tried to master the situation in his own way. In Hitler's opinion, the responsible commanders and army formations had failed him, and so he appointed a special 'Plenipotentiary for combatting the Oder and Neisse crossings'. The obvious choice for this important post would have been a particularly experienced and competent troop commander who would then be endowed with all the necessary powers of authority, but that was not Hitler's idea. Instead, he appointed an airman.

The *'Führerbefehl'* of 1 March 1945 reads: – 'I empower *Oberstleutnant* Baumbach, *Kommodore* of KG 200, to combat all enemy crossings over the Oder and Neisse rivers. To this end, *OTL* Baumbach has to coordinate and bring into operation every suitable means from all sections of the armed forces, the armaments industry and economy.

He is subordinated to the C-in-C Luftwaffe and will operate in the area controlled by *Luftflottenkommando* 6. The stipulations for the execution of his task will be issued by the C-in-C Luftwaffe in agreement with the Chief of the Supreme Command of the Armed Forces (OKW).'

These orders came through from *Luftflottenkommando* 6 the very next day and did not leave much to be desired (see facsimile reproduction in Appendices No 3 and 4).

It is easy to explain, if rather difficult to understand, how and why Baumbach came to be entrusted with this critically decisive task.

Werner Baumbach was the most successful bomber pilot of the Luftwaffe. In addition to that, during his service in various command positions he had also made a name for himself as an ingenious and fearless leader. And more – he also looked the 'Germanic hero' type – tall, blond and intelligent, and was the complete opposite to a career officer. Thanks to the news media and radio, he was known to all for his achievements as an airman and most successful dive bomber pilot, helped by his Siegfried-like appearance. During the war years he had been summoned to see Hitler several times, and the Führer already knew him well personally. In Hitler's opinion, only such a man as Baumbach could now be able to mobilize the last reserves of forces when it was a matter of mastering desperate situations.

And it was in this way, through the person of Baumbach, that KG 200 was given a task that was outside the normal operations of a flying unit. It was also the beginning of confusion of command authorities that sometimes made one wonder who in this *Geschwader* and its subordinated formations was really responsible for what. There could be no doubt that Baumbach was invested with all possible powers – but there could also be no doubt that, at this stage of the war, he had to expect resistance from all those authorities in the Army, Navy, Luftwaffe and the Nazi party who felt 'passed over' by his appointment.

There were various accepted ways of destroying bridges, such as the devices used by the Army pioneers, but there were also a number of more unusual weapons available to the Navy and the Luftwaffe. For instance, there were the so-called *Kugeltreibminen* (spherical drift mines) that carried a relatively small explosive charge of 12 kg (26.5 lb). Originally, these mines were intended to be dropped into the water from boats upstream from the bridge and were to drift under the water surface till they hit the bridge supports and detonated.

However, although the operational use of these drift mines was ordered on a large scale it was decided not to proceed. The reason for this was that it would have required an enormous effort to achieve even a modest success: as it was no longer possible to use boats on the Oder these mines would have to be dropped from aircraft – which did not have the necessary release mechanisms. A provisional jettison method had been evolved in great hurry, whereby the mines would be released from a He 111 via a kind of sliding chute, but the pilots rightly commented that one might as well attack the bridges with ordinary bombs. Apart from that these small mines were practically useless against solid structures, and tests had shown that a pontoon of an auxiliary bridge needed several hits by such mines before it would sink. This did not seem at all hopeful as one had to succeed in destroying at least five to six pontoons to effectively disable a pontoon bridge.

There were a number of other negative points regarding dropping these drift mines from aircraft – low accuracy, unknown water currents, and river bends upstream from the target, to mention only a few.

Of course, the most effective way of pushing back the Oder crossings and Soviet bridgeheads would have been 'rolling' bombing attacks by larger Luftwaffe formations composed of all types of aircraft – bombers, fighter-bombers, Stukas, close-support aircraft and fighters – but there were simply no aircraft and, most important of all, there was no fuel.

It was evident that, despite the bombastic listing of ways and means in the *'Führerbefehl'* Baumbach's task could hardly be accomplished from the material point of view alone, not to mention the almost complete enemy superiority on land and already partly in the air as well.

Another weapon that was available in larger numbers was the Hs 293 guided bomb, which had been ready for operational use since spring 1943. It had the effect of a 1102 lb bomb and had been successfully used against shipping and other targets. Basically, the Hs 293 was a small, remotely controlled aircraft that could be guided onto the target by radio impulses. After release from the carrier aircraft, the Hs 293 was accelerated by its rocket motor and came into the observer's field of vision, who was then able to remotely guide it by means of a small control stick towards the target. Although quite successful, the obvious drawback of this system was that the radio impulses could be intercepted and jammed. To avoid this, it was later intended to modify the Hs 293 for wire guidance, whereby the electric control impulses would be sent via a thin wire that would unwind simultaneously from spools inside the missile and its controlling aircraft. This arrangement could not be jammed or interfered with.

Without doubt the Hs 293 was one of the most advanced developments of weapon technology at that time representing the first of what later became known as 'stand-off' bombs. It could be released up to 13 km (8 miles) from the target and guided on its way from practically any flight position. All the observers in the carried aircraft had to do was to 'fly' the missile with his control stick, keeping the brightly burning flare fitted in the tail end of the bomb in vision until impact. The results of tests and training launches had indicated that one could expect a target accuracy of about 40 per cent, and the Hs 293 was accepted into service. The planned production and operational rate was set at 1000 units per month.

Of course, the device was kept under the strictest secrecy wraps so that even the commanders of regional *Luftflotten* did not know about the presence of these bombs in their area. Then came the crash 'Fighter Programme' with its priorities which soon stopped all production and hence operational use of this novel bomb. In fact, a large number of these unique weapons were even scrapped! In addition there was a lack of suitable carrier aircraft. The He 177 originally intended as a launch platform was plagued by frequent engine fires and remained only conditionally operational. A provisional solution was then found by modifying a number of He 111H bombers, but these machines were soon commandered to fly supplies to Stalingrad where most of them were lost. When some improvement to the problems besetting the He 177 was at last in sight, series production of it was also stopped in favour of the 'Fighter Programme'.

A unit specifically to use this guided bomb, II/KG 100, was then formed with Do 217 bombers, and began operations in the Mediterranean against Allied merchantmen and warships. Although the limited range of the Do 217s was a drawback, the successes achieved by this unit proved that, provided the Hs 293 was used in sufficient numbers by well-trained crews flying suitable carrier aircraft, it could have a most destructive effect against point-targets.

From his earlier function as General of Bombers, Baumbach knew this weapon quite well, and in his time had requested a more widespread operational use. After his appointment as the Special Plenipotentiary for the Oder Bridges he immediately thought of the Hs 293. No other weapon could have been better suited for this task under the given tactical conditions. But the word about this novel weapon had spread.

Already in autumn 1944 a senior SS officer from the RSHA called on Werner Baumbach. It was known, he said, that KG 200 had control of the available stock of the Hs 293 bombs, and the RSHA had plans to use this weapon against Britain in quite a novel way.

The idea was for KG 200 to drop agents by parachute over the British Isles, who would then install small radio transmitters at selected targets that would enable the bombs to be automatically guided towards them by means of a simple radio direction-finding method. The officer was also informed that such experiments had already been carried out on the island of Usedom in the Baltic.

This was another typical task for KG 200, only nothing came of it. Not that the *Geschwader* lacked the necessary means, but simply because the highest Luftwaffe command, the 'court party' around Göring, would not give this idea their support.

It may sound almost unbelievable, but the Luftwaffe Operations Staff to which Baumbach was directly subordinated, tried even now to hinder the use of this weapon by referring to Göring's strict standing orders. The *Herr Reichsmarschall* had to be asked first to change his previous strict order that, to preserve its secrecy, this guided bomb should not be used against land targets!

Imagine the situation – a developed weapon is readily available and stored in secret arsenals, a weapon that has a proven 40 per cent accuracy against point-targets, in addition to which it has the advantage that it can be released from the carrier aircraft outside the range of enemy anti-aircraft guns – and yet its operational use in this desperate situation is held up because of some previous 'higher' restriction that no longer applied under the circumstances. Granted, this weapon was originally intended only for use against shipping targets to avoid it falling into enemy hands – but by spring 1945 the Luftwaffe had practically no strategic targets within its reach. Instead, the situation at all fronts literally cried out for more tactical support by the Luftwaffe, and here were people in responsible positions arguing about proper command procedures and competences.

It was only after Baumbach had been given those extraordinary powers that he succeeded in acquiring some Hs 293s to launch against the Oder bridges.

The following technical details apply to Hs 293A-1

Length	3818 mm (150·3 in)
Span	3100 mm (122·05 in)
Height overall	1100 mm (43·3 in)
Tailplane span	1102 mm (43·4 in)
Bomb casing diameter	470 mm (18·5 in)
Total weight	975 kg (2150 lb)
Power unit	HWK 109-507B bi-fuel rocket motor
Fuel	66 kg (145·5 lb)
incl. *T-Stoff**	60 kg (132·3 lb)
*Z-Stoff***	3.4 kg (7·5 lb)
Compressed air	2.6 kg (5·7 lb)
Thrust	600 kp (1323 lb/static)
Burning time	12 secs
Max speed	205 m/sec (673 ft/sec)

The Hs 293A could be released at distances from 3·5 to 18 km (2·1 to 8 miles) and at altitudes between 400 and 4000 m (1312 to 13,123 ft). Even when released 12 km (7·45 miles) from the target its accuracy factor was still 40 per cent. Total production amounted to 1900 missiles.

In his search for other effective means to carry out his task, Baumbach activated all kinds of people and organisations from whom he could expect help and support and the operation was given the cover name *Wasserballon* (Water Balloon).

After it had become evident that the intended use of small drift mines did not seem very promising the logical development was to use larger drift mines of higher explosive power. However, no such mines were available, and a provisional solution had to be found hence *Wasserballon*, that covered a programme that involved producing improvised mines which could be dropped with greater accuracy from aircraft. Apart from their more powerful explosive force they were to function in the same way as the smaller drift mines: they were to be dropped upstream from the bridge and would float under the water surface towards the target. The detonators were designed to become

---

T-Stoff = Cover name for 80 per cent hydrogen peroxyde + oxyquinoline or phosphate as stabilizer.
**Z-Stoff* = Aqueous solution of calcium permanganate.

sensitive only a few seconds after dropping into the water.

However, the development work involved in fashioning drift mines from ordinary bomb shells required so much time that *Wasserballon* had to be discounted for the operation in hand. According to surviving documents, the Flam C 250 was expected to be ready by mid-April and the Flam C 500 – only by early June 1945, assuming trouble-free development. A curious point was that although *Flam* stood for *Flammenbombe* (Incendiary bomb), these shells were to be filled with explosives instead of the petrol-oil mixture until they just floated in the water. There were also problems regarding the necessary depth of water, which had to be 3·8 to 4 m (12·5 to 13 ft).

A report by the *Führungsstab* of the Luftwaffe dated 1 March 1945 concludes as follows:

'At this time the water level hardly permits the use (of the larger bomb-mines) anywhere else but in the Rhine and part of the Danube. This situation demands the use of already available means. These are, beside the drift mine, the FK (for *Flugkörper* or guided missiles/bombs) Hs 293 and FX 1400. In view of the fuel situation and the available missiles the more expensive effort with the guided bombs commends itself in particular because of the higher target accuracy.

On orders from *Herr Reichsmarschall*, the guided bombs are however to be used first and foremost by KG 200 against the Vistula bridges.'

By that time the realisation that bombing attacks against the bridges would not work because of lack of the essential prerequisites, namely a sufficient number of aircraft and at least a temporary aerial superiority over the target areas led to the decision to prepare and use the *Mistels* for this task. Nevertheless, the Chief of the Luftwaffe General Staff, General Koller, still held back 56 of the available 82 *Mistels* exclusively for the *Eisenhammer* operation which had now been finally scheduled to start on 28 March. Once again it was a matter of priorities as seen by different authorities with the inevitable tug-of-war for the available resources; there just was not enough for both undertakings.

By early March 1945 the organisational and command relationships were already somewhat confused:

Baumbach was *Kommodore* of KG 200, and also the 'Special Plenipotentiary for Bridges'. In the first capacity he was subordinated operationally to *Luftflotte* 6, in the second – personally and directly to the C-in-C Luftwaffe, Göring, and had special powers regarding all three branches of the armed forces.

134

– I/KG 200 with its various detachments led its own life far removed from the HQ and received its orders from the RSHA;

– II/KG 200 with pathfinders, radar jamming aircraft, bombers and *Mistels*, together with other *Mistels* and some special units formed the 'Task Force Helbig' assembled especially for Operation *Eisenhammer*, and was operationally subordinated to *Luftflotte* 6;

– III/KG 200(BT), originally intended to use FW 190s armed with bomb-torpedoes, existed only as so much personnel and had no operational aircraft because the development of this weapon had run into difficulties;

– IV/KG 200 was the training and replacement *Gruppe*, which had also been responsible for the S.O. (self-sacrifice) men;

– The Operational Detachment 200(FK) with nine He 111H and one Do 217 equipped with the Hs 293 flying bombs was also subordinated to 'Task Force Helbig';

– *Oberst* Helbig, commander of the named Task Force, had been appointed as OTL Baumbach's deputy 'Special Plenipotentiary for Bridges'.

– In addition to that, there was also the HQ staff of KG 200 and the staff of *Fliegerführer 200*, which in fact had nothing to do any more.

On 1 March *Oberstleutnant* and *Geschwaderkommodore* Werner Baumbach signed the first order regarding the operational use of the *Mistels* (see facsimile reproduction in Appendix No 6). This order covered the use of *Mistels* to attack bridges over the Vistula at Warsaw, Deblin and Sandomierz. The task force was commanded by *Oberleutnant* Pilz and comprised six *Mistel 1* and eight *Mistel 3* composite aircraft of 6./KG 200, together with a weather reconnaissance aircraft, nine 'target indicators', and three reserve aircraft. 6./KG 200 was stationed at Burg near Magdeburg and its *Staffel* symbol was the well-known 'Father and Son' based on the cartoon series by the artist E. O. Plauen.

On 6 March, an He 111 of 'Task Force Helbig' attacked the Oder bridge at Göritz and achieved a hit with its Hs 293 guided bomb. The first *Mistel* attack on the Oder bridges took place on 8 March, also at Göritz, with a force comprising four *Mistels* with five Ju 188s and two Ju 88s as escorts. The formation left the ground between 0900 and 0920 hrs, and it took some time before the different aircraft types assembled in the air. The Ju 88s and Ju 188s had to attack simultaneously with the *Mistels*, bombing anti-aircraft sites near the bridges to make it easier for the composite aircraft to approach the bridges.

The formation approached the target area at about 1000 hrs. North and south of Göritz the Soviets had erected no less than seven auxiliary bridges and several rope ferries across the river. Their intentions were clear – they were preparing to establish a bridgehead west of the Oder. as a jumping-off base for the advance on Berlin. Many more bridges were erected or in preparation also on both sides of Küstrin – all the signs of preliminaries for a major offensive.

There was strict radio silence between the aircraft. The crews were fully aware that they had to fly into a murderous anti-aircraft fire of all calibres. A surprise attack from a greater altitude and at higher speed was out of the question because of the low cloud base of only 9840 ft.

The four *Mistel* pilots in their confined Bf 109 cockpits were now as lonely as a human being can be. They knew that everything was up to them, that the eyes of their escorts and the thoughts of people back at the base were with them. None of them had flown an operational *Mistel* before – under the circumstances it was impossible to carry out training target approach flights, not to mention releasing a Ju 88 with a dummy warhead that could be guided into an assumed target. Their first air-to-ground release and final test was now, in action.

The pilots also knew of course that 'those above' were also expecting results, and that there was no way they could get out of this now.

Well, they made it – or three of them did. The fourth *Mistel* pilot was forced to release his Ju 88 because of defective hydraulics on the way.

On landing back at the base the returning pilots were congratulated from all sides and received an elated welcome at their command post. The crews of the escorting aircraft and the *Mistel* pilots themselves had observed that at least two bridges had been destroyed. One *Mistel* had only narrowly missed its target and slammed into the western bank between two bridges, leaving an enormous crater in the ground.

The bombing raid of the seven escorting aircraft had not only created an effective diversion during the attack and dispersed the ground defences but had even managed partly to silence the anti-aircraft guns. The only loss was a Ju 188 that received a direct hit by an AA shell, although the crew managed to bale out. The combat report covering this *Mistel* raid has survived (see facsimile reproduction in Appendix No 7). Nothing could be more concise.

But what did this *Mistel* raid really achieve in the way of holding up the Soviet forces crossing the Oder? Successful it may have been, but at the end of the day one has to admit that it probably did not achieve

136

much at all. Two secondary military bridges were made impassable for a few hours, and a few AA sites temporarily knocked out, that was about all. It could also be that for a short while the enemy had been given a mighty shock, but he would soon recover from that – especially when it became obvious that the operational use of these terrible weapons was limited to a few individual cases.

Another successful *Mistel* raid took place on 31 March against the Steinau railway bridge.

When the order to attack this bridge was received the KG 200, or rather the 'Task Force Helbig' staff immediately began planning the new operation. How many *Mistels* were needed? At what time of the day, and in what kind of weather should this attack take place? How many escort aircraft with what tasks should accompany the *Mistels*? What would be the organisation and number of the fighter escort? And of course, the routes to and from the target – everything had to be determined and synchronised.

It was decided to use six *Mistel 1s* that were deployed at Burg near Magdeburg. From there, the distance to Steinau was more than 186 miles, not counting possible diversions to pick up the fighter escort.* Operational discussions with the fighter command resulted in allocation of six sections of fighters based at Schweidnitz in Silesia. Accordingly, the *Mistel* formation with its two Ju 88 and two Ju 188 escorts routed its way from Burg to Waldenburg in Silesia where they were to pick up the fighters. From Waldenburg they were to fly directly north towards their target, about 44 miles away.

It was quite an event for late March 1945 – a close formation of six composite aircraft, four bombers and 24 fighters. One would have had to search long and far to recall seeing such a large group of Luftwaffe aircraft in the skies at that time.

Everything was planned to the smallest detail, from the flight time to an as accurate as possible estimate of the required amount of fuel for the fighter escort. This last point was of especial importance at the time when the Luftwaffe had to economise with each ton of aviation fuel. There were already orders regulating the warming-up and power-testing of aircraft engines to save fuel, and here and there aircraft were being towed by tractors on the runways and to and from their parking places. And many aircraft did not get to fly at all, for the same reason.

Another important part of planning was the search for emergency

---

*see facsimile reproduction of the requirement for this fighter escort in Appendix No 8

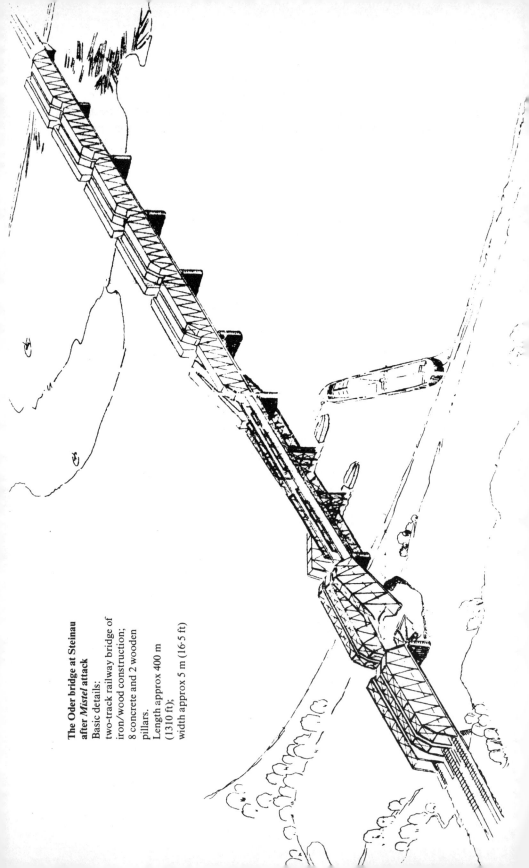

**The Oder bridge at Steinau
after *Mistel* attack**
Basic details:
two-track railway bridge of
iron/wood construction;
8 concrete and 2 wooden
pillars.
Length approx 400 m
(1310 ft);
width approx 5 m (16·5 ft)

landing places, no longer such an easy matter on account of the constant enemy bombing raids.

The four escorts were to fly ahead of the *Mistels* as guides and, at the target, divert the enemy defences by attacking the AA sites and the nearby railway station, as well as to act as rearguards in case of enemy fighter interception.

The fighter escort was picked up by sending ahead a Ju 188 that would orbit the Schweidnitz airfield and fire the agreed recognition flares for an immediate take-off of the waiting fighters. In the meantime the rest of the formation was to fly a left-handed circuit over Waldenburg. When the fighter commander was ready to proceed towards the target he would approach the leading bomber and waggle his wings. The radio silence was to be absolute.

All that was needed now was the right kind of weather – and waiting for that took days. In between there were new operational orders that were recalled after wearisome preparations had already been initiated. After all, on receiving each new order the aircraft had to be tanked up for the intended operation and loaded with the required amount and type of bombs and ammunition – not to mention all the detailed route planning and other staff work. The people who suffered most of course were the six chosen *Mistel* pilots. For them, these operations that never got off the ground were a terrible ordeal of nerves. No wonder that everyone became more and more irritated. Even the specialists of the technical personnel – usually the most steady of men – began to lose their nerve because of the constantly changing preparatory work that turned out to be only so much wasted effort. Quite a few of them hissed some abusive aside at 'their' *Mistel* pilot when he appeared again and again to check if his 'carriage' was functioning perfectly for the planned new operation. The tension was very high.

Finally, on 30 March, everything fell into place. The weather forecast for the following day looked promising for an operation in the Steinau area and the airfield at Burg now became a hive of activity. The take-off time was fixed at between 0700 and 0800 hrs, and the fighter escort at Schweidnitz was informed accordingly. The chosen six *Mistel* pilots were named, and the rest looked visibly relieved – although the orders stated: 'The remaining *Mistel* pilots are in reserve'. This thrice-cursed eternal 'readiness for action'!

The final pre-flight briefing took place the same evening when the operations officer explained the situation in the target area according to the latest aerial reconnaissance photographs. There was the double-track railway bridge that spanned the stream. This side of the river, the railway lines made a wide curve directly into the big Steinau station – a target for the escorting bombers. The station and Steinau itself were already in Soviet hands.

Naturally, this extremely important bridgehead was packed full with defensive weapons against attacks from the air and the ground, and the aerial photographs clearly showed numerous light and heavy AA gun sites.

For the time being all thoughts about the fire they were to fly into were put aside as the crews were briefed for the forthcoming operation. The attack plan was defined down to the last detail both for the *Mistels* and the escorting bombers. Just as important were arrangements with the fighters whose task was to screen the *Mistels* and their escorting bombers against enemy fighter attacks so completely that the formation could reach the target with the least delay and losses. And that was not all that easy because the differences in speed of the various aircraft types was quite considerable. Apart from that this kind of close cover was against the mentality of all fighter pilots who preferred to have wide-ranging freedom of movement in action. They only real freedom they had was that, depending on conditions in the target area after the *Mistel* attack, they could also shoot up ground targets.

On the evening before 31 March 1945, peace and quiet came early in the billets occupied by the flying crews of II/KG 200 at Burg near Magdeburg. The pilots of the six *Mistels* and the crews of the four escorting bombers had completed their preparations for this operation, but most of them had a troubled sleep. Time and again, the same thoughts crossed their minds – what will the weather really be like? Will the engines and other vital parts of their equipment function the way they should? Would the fighters appear on time? The only consolation was that this flight did not take them deep into enemy territory but over their own land all the way.

When the duty NCO walked into their rooms to wake them at 0500 hrs, most of the men were already wide awake and waited nervously and impatiently to be called. Bleary-eyed and tired looking, they now gathered for the final pre-flight briefing at 0600 hrs.

The weather outside was gloomy and unfriendly – was this really the last day of March? The 'weather frog'* appeared, carrying a folder

---

Wetterfrosche = 'weather frogs', colloquial Luftwaffe term for meteorological experts.

with the latest reports. The situation looked promising between 0700 and 1100 hrs: the western part of the target area was covered by broken clouds with a base at about 8200 ft. However, the clouds broke up even further east and the sky over Steinau was expected to be completely clear. This meant that the fighter escort had to function particularly well in the target area as there would be no clouds to offer an escape in case of an enemy fighter attack.

The final orders were quickly formulated and distributed, and the fighter command post at Schweidnitz informed regarding the estimated time of meeting of the two formations over Waldenburg. An 'oldtimer', an *Oberfeldwebel* with more than 200 operational flights with the Ju 88 under his belt was then chosen as leader of the *Mistel* group. He would give the signal to attack, and dive first onto the target. An *Oberleutnant* of the younger generation flying one of the escorting Ju 188s was to function as leader of the whole combined force. The take-off time was set at 0715 hrs.

The aircrews shivered as they climbed into the rickety old bus that would take them to their aircraft. From the direction of the runway they could hear the sound of engines being run up, and then they were there. The leading mechanics reported their aircraft clear for operations, the crews climbed into their machines and quickly rechecked the controls and instruments. The hands on the instrument panel clock were nearing the take-off time, and the cockpits were closed. The *Mistel* pilots kept looking up into the sky trying to gauge the weather by observing the clouds and wind direction.

They would have their hands full on the way out. Each one of them also mentally went through the whole attack procedure for the umpteenth time – after all, this was their first real live operation.

The pilots and aircrews became restless and impatient. Although the agreed take-off time had come and gone, there was still no signal to get moving. What was going on? Was this intended operation too being cancelled or postponed at the last moment? All eyes were on the leading Ju 188 because of the complete radio silence. At long last, its propellers began to turn – the sign for all other aircraft to start up their engines.

After that, the take-off itself was routine. Soon they were in the air and the tension eased: the first stage had gone smoothly.

The *Mistels* followed the leading bombers in a wide swarm. On reaching Waldenburg there were only five of them orbiting to pick up the fighter escort – what had happened to the sixth? Another *Mistel* sheared out of the formation and disappeared westwards soon after the whole group had set course towards the target. Now there were only four of them.

The pilots had carefully noted the estimated times, and a quick glance showed there were only thirteen minutes left before the attack. Somehow they all had a feeling that the worst was already over despite the fact that they had not even seen the target yet, not to mention the expected furious AA fire. The Soviet fighters based on the other side of the Oder were probably also being scrambled – nobody could miss this German formation moving northwards parallel to the front line!

But all that did not matter: it was quite some time since the aircrews had been accompanied by such a big bunch of their own fighters, and that gave them all a great feeling of confidence.

Generally speaking, it was a peculiarity of operational flying that the excitement and fear were greatest before the take-off. When, during the subsequent flight everything functioned as it should in the aircraft, the weather showed promising development, the chosen tactics had proved to be the correct ones, and no special difficulties were expected on the way back, this seemed to eliminate so many problems and imponderables of an operational flight that the really difficult and dangerous part, the actual attack, remained as the only source of fear. One felt somehow free, and could concentrate on the tasks at the target.

As an attacker, one then had a feeling of superiority, which perhaps could be explained by this notion that the worst was over before actual contact with the enemy. It was a kind of self-delusion, but it helped.

Now only a few minutes remained before the attack, and the sky had cleared up as promised. Obliquely to the right the great Oder bend at Maltsch came in view – it was less than 18 miles to go.

The escorting fighters tried hard to keep still closer contact with the *Mistels* and bombers – a Soviet fighter attack could be expected at any time. Only three *Mistels* now remained in the air – whatever had happened to the others? On the way, the formation had come under fire from their own light AA guns – could that have caused some casualties. This gave cause for some unrest in the formation and in the remaining aircraft the crews were again naturally cursing their comrades. Half the *Mistel* strength lost even before reaching the enemy! It would indeed be an irony if this was booked as 'success' by their own AA guns. The strict radio silence only contributed to the suspense.

And then from their 8200 ft altitude they began to make out Steinau on the horizon.

The remaining three *Mistel* pilots did not bother to compare the landscape below them with the map, they relied on the escorting bombers. After all, they all had four men aboard and could navigate accurately.

Everything was unusually quiet, and the pilots felt uneasy. Although the river was only a few miles away parallel to their course, not a single shot from heavy Soviet AA guns had come their way. Were they still asleep? Or was that a sign that their fighters were already in the air? They were committed now, and preparations for the attack went ahead – the sights were switched on and regulated for brightness, the weapons were cocked, and the power circuits for the electric fuses of the hollow-charge warheads were activated. The harness straps were tightened, and then another quick look around – still no sign of any Soviet fighters, and no bursting AA shells either.

One could now sense nervousness in the formation more than perceive it with one's eyes. Each individual pilot began to search for some position that seemed to offer better advantages for his own attack and promised more safety at the same time. While doing so, their minds were already on how best to get away from the target and out of the enemy defensive fire after the attack.

The airspeed indicators climbed forward a few notches – quite unconsciously all pilots had given a bit more throttle.

The leading Ju 188 then turned eastwards and the others fell in behind. The target was now clearly visible – the large railway bridge, a road traffic bridge and some pontoon bridges. As agreed, the bombers turned directly towards the target area while the *Mistels* swung out a bit sideways. The fighter escort too formed themselves according to plan. While part of them continued to keep close contact with their charges, the rest sped ahead to be first over the target.

The Soviet AA guns opened up, but their fire was weak and badly laid. The *Mistels* remained untouched, a sign that the diversion flown by the bombers was effective at least for the time being. Then came the first flashes of exploding bombs in the target area, indicating some hits on the station and the Soviet AA sites both sides of the river. The dance had begun.

The *Mistels* were already in inclined flight and their airspeed indicator needles hovered around the 600 km/h (373 mph) mark. The leading *Oberfeldwebel* turned into his final target approach from south and went into an even steeper flight, increasing his speed even more. He had to trim to equalize the changed forces acting on his controls, but the target remained steady in his reflex sight.

This was the most important part of the whole procedure, to keep the composite aircraft rock-steady in the final target approach flight – even the slightest correction with controls immediately affected the accurate working of the autopilot's gyroscopic mechanism. 'Flying on your nerves', the pilots would say when they discussed such flights into well-defended enemy targets on the ground but now, in action, there was no time to contemplate. What's the altitude? Distance to the target? Airspeed? – these points were more important and immediate.

The ideal distance for release was about 3300 ft from the target. They had been taught that the 'flying bomb' could then no longer miss the target. But that was also the right range for the light AA guns if the gunners were on their toes!

The airspeed indicator had climbed to 650 km/h (404 mph), but the *Mistel* was in a steady high-speed dive correctly trimmed and free of any acceleration. The autopilot was functioning perfectly, and the whole contraption could be flown hands off if necessary. Where was the dreaded AA fire? Where were the other aircraft?

The bridge could now be made out clearly in every detail. It was an iron structure resting on solid masonry pillars. To achieve decisive destruction a *Mistel* bomb would have to hit one of these pillars, demanding utmost precision and a fair bit of luck. Could they make it?

The sight showed the bridge section on the left bank. A final fine correction, and in the sight the illuminated graticule pointed exactly on the supporting pillar closest to the bank. Now! A slight pressure on the release button, the muffled sounds of light detonations, and the controlling fighter was free again – what a relief! A steep bank to the west, a quick look behind, and right where the pilot had aimed his *Mistel* an enormous fountain was climbing upwards, impossible to tell whether it was water, mud or parts of the bridge. The Soviet AA guns were firing like mad, and a great cloud of smoke began to cover both river banks near the bridge, blotting out all details.

Suddenly another Bf 109 appeared alongside. The initial cold shock that it could have been an enemy fighter changed to joyous relief having a comrade for company. Both pilots held their thumbs up, indicating that everything was in order. They grinned at each other happily and continued flying west, not caring exactly where they were. Out of habit, both had pressed the buttons of their stopwatches and relied upon spotting a railway line, a town, an *Autobahn* or some other notable point of reference to help them orientate. Both pilots were 'old foxes' and navigation in good weather and over their own homeland was no problem to them. In low level, the two Bf 109s were racing home across the countryside. They had successfully flown their first live *Mistel* operation.

The first general picture of their attack emerged during the following hour at the command post. As it was later confirmed by photographic reconnaissance, a bridge support pillar near the western bank had received a direct hit leaving a large crater into which the destroyed bridge structure had collapsed. This meant that no rail transports could cross into the Steinau bridgehead at least for several days, giving some relief to the hard-pressed defenders.

The sober language of the official combat report however hardly gives an indication of the drama behind this operation:

Combat Report
Concerning the attack on Steinau railway bridge on 31 March 1945:

1) Task Force Helbig with operationally subordinated II/KG 200 with 6 'Pick-a-back' aircraft against the Steinau railway bridge; 2 Ju 88 and 2 Ju 188 (as pilot aircraft and rearguards) to attack the bridge and, for diversion, the Steinau railway station.
Escort: 24 Bf 109 from JG 52.

2) *Take-off*: 0723-0735 hrs

3) *Landing*: 1025-1038 hrs

4) *Attack time*: 0905-0912 hrs

5) *Attack altitude*: gliding attack from 2500 to 200 m (8200 to 656 ft) for 'Pick-a-back' aircraft. Attack altitude for Ju 88 and Ju 188 around 2500 m (8200 ft).

6) *Successes*:
   a) One 'Pick-a-back' attack at 0905 hrs against the central part of the railway bridge. Good release, but failure of the auto-pilot. Effect not observed. Followed by low-level attack with the Bf 109 against identified infantry positions.
   b) One 'Pick-a-back' hit hard next to the bridge in eastern part.

c) One 'Pick-a-back' attack, normal release, probable hit, but without observed effect. Aiming point centre, good release.

d) Two Ju 88 and two Ju 188 with 8 SC 1000 Trialen* and 30 SD 70 bombs

7) *Withdrawn from action*: Three 'Pick-a-back' aircraft
Reasons:

a) One 'Pick-a-back' released unfused from 70 m altitude shortly after take-off at 0736 hrs due to defective hydraulics (undercarriage not retracted). Hit the ground near Genthin.

b) One 'Pick-a-back' flown normally until meeting the fighter escort over Waldenburg, when the Bf 109 had engine failure. Attempts to restart engine unsuccessful. Subsequently return flight to Burg on two remaining engines. After 80 mins of vibration of the Ju 88 port engine the 'pick-a-back' released near Trettin/Torgau. 'Sharp' hit in a field east of Trettin; explosion observed, presumably without causing damage.
   Bf 109 force-landed with dead engine west of Trettin, total loss. Pilot suffered broken left shin bone.

c) One 'Pick-a-back' released during outward flight in Lauben area with direction east (see No 14). Reason: Bf 109 engine failure. Bf 109 belly-landed at 0835 hrs at Görlitz; 60% loss.

8) *Amount of bombs*:
Six 'Pick-a-back' (*Mistel 1*)
Eight SC 1000 Trialen
Thirty SD 70

9) *Losses*:
One Bf 109 60%
One Bf 109 99%

10) *Enemy defences*:
Little heavy AA, badly directed; moderate light AA.
Fighters not observed.

---

*Trialen = explosive filling used in German aerial bombs consisting of 70% TNT + 15% RDX + 15% Aluminum

11) *Other remarks*:
Bridge covered by artificial smoke screen 0912-0915 hrs.
Station fully occupied.

12) *Weather*:
During outward flight 6/10 cloud cover at 2000 m (6560 ft).
From Schweidnitz to over the target clear, visibility 10 km
(6·2 miles).

13) *Fuel consumption*:
33 m³ (7259 Imp gal) incl. fighter escort.

14) *Special occurrences*:
At 08.45 hrs light AA fire over Görlitz, no damage. AA fire
opened with about 40 rounds despite clearly visible German
insignia after the detonation of a released 'Pick-a-back' in this area
on the assumption it was a disguised enemy formation.

15) *Experiences*:

   a) Technical failures at 50% are very high. Although this concerned old aircraft (*Mistel 1*) one has to reckon with similar
   shortfalls on future operations because it is known from
   experience that defects could occur in uncontrollable measure
   in aircraft held in long storage even after good maintenance.
   The intended longer distances to the target would be compen-
   sated by (using) better aircraft. For that reason the allocation of
   six 'Pick-a-back' aircraft for one bridge target must until
   further experience be taken as minimum to ensure sufficient
   prospects of success.

   b) Fighter escort must be laid on relatively strong in daytime
   because for flying reasons no 'formation flight' will be possible
   with 'Pick-a-back' aircraft (spread-out flying on sight). In the
   above case the fighter protection for 'Pick-a-back' aircraft can
   be described as good. Fighter pilots report considerably more
   difficult fulfilment of their task due to extended gaps between
   aircraft.
   For reasons of fuel economy as well as safety it would be
   desirable to make operational flights without fighter escort
   (outward flight on clear nights – by moonlight – or by sufficient
   cloud cover against enemy main points of defence.)

147

c) Post-attack target photographs confirm good effect with 'Pick-a-back' aircraft against the railway bridge despite very limited target dimensions, which however sets high demands on the abilities of the aircrews.

> For the Luftwaffe Command
> Chief of the General Staff
> (pp) Mahlke
> > *Oberstleutnant* in General Staff

Another *Mistel* attack with five composite aircraft was flown against the Vistula bridges at Warsaw on 8 April 1945. All five pilots returned safely with their FW 190 controlling aircraft to Rechlin-Lärz. This time, because of the strong AA defences in the target area, it had not been easy to fly an accurate final target approach flight. Although the pilots had observed *Mistel* detonations they were unable to give any details as to the achieved effect.

On 16 April began the last major Soviet offensive. A day later, a secret teleprinter message from *Luftflottenkommando 6* reached the HQ of Task Force Helbig (see facsimile reproduction in Appendix No 9):

1) Lfl.Kdo.6 requests soonest possible destruction of the now repaired single-track railway bridge at Steinau by 'Pick-a-back' operation.

2) Notice of the intended time of attack as well as request regarding fighter escort to Ia Flieg. (Operations Officer Flying).

3) Advance notification by telephone.

> Lfl.Kdo.6
> Chief of the General Staff
> (signed)
> Kless
> *Oberst* in General Staff

The destruction achieved by *Mistel*s on 31 March had not lasted very long.

In fact, the *Mistel*s had become the proverbial straws grasped by the desperate leadership.

148

Ju 290A-0 (Ju 90 V7) J4 + CH of LTS 5 at Riga-Spilve airfield, Latvia, in March 1944.

This illustration shows to advantage the novel so-called *Trapoklappe*. This hydraulically-operated loading ramp lifted the tail end of the fuselage enabling vehicles to drive straight into or out of the cargo compartment.

Ju 290A-1 transport. Note the differences in cabin glazing, ventral nose gun gondola and aerial arrangement. The Ju 290s formed the nucleus of KG 200 long-range transport capacity.

One of the five Ju 290A-3 long-range reconnaissance aircraft completed before delivery to FAGr.5 at Mont de Marsant, France. The machine is already equipped with FuG 200 *Hohentwiel* ASV radar. From summer 1944 onwards all FAGr.5 aircraft came under KG 200 control.

The great size of the Ju 290A undercarriage is evident from this view of a KG 200 aircrew member posing at the twin-tyre main wheel.

The first prototype of the six-engined Ju 390 very long-range transport (GH + UK) was also at KG 200 disposal. The aircraft is shown here at Prague-Rusyne airfield in spring 1945.

An RAF reconnaissance photograph of the Frankfurt-Main airfield, base of Detachment *Olga*, 24 hours after the US 8AF daylight raid of 24 December 1944. The bomb pattern potholed and made unserviceable two-fifths of the north-eastern part of the landing ground, apart from other damage to buildings and installations; it also killed 16 men from Detachment *Olga* who had continued working on maintenance tasks despite the air raid alarm.

At least 22 aircraft are visible on this print, two of which are damaged. Other aircraft are seen dispersed in the woods.

The piloted Fi 103 (V1) missile code-named *Reichenberg* was a make-shift solution intended for the so-called S.O. or 'Self-Sacrifice' volunteers but was never used operationally. The illustrations show (top) a *Reichenberg IV* found after the capitulation in Germany, and (below) another example displayed at the German Aircraft Exhibition at RAE Farnborough in November 1945, the only genuine Re IV brought to the UK.

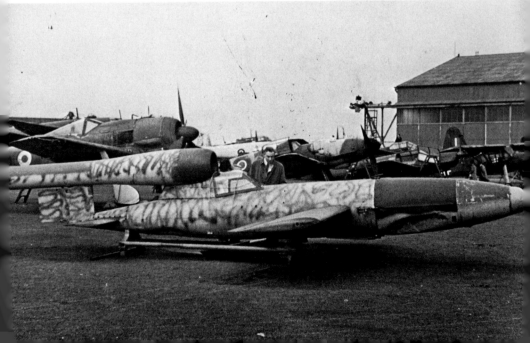

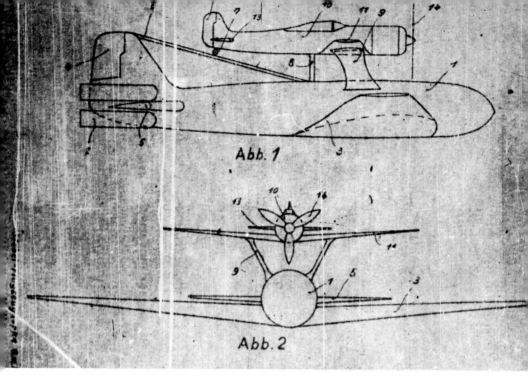

Abb. 1

Abb. 2

Among the many and varied *Mistel* combinations proposed by several German aircraft firms in 1944 was this project by the Siebel Flugzeugwerke, Halle.

In this case, the lower component is a large cargo glider guided by a FW 190. The necessary acceleration for take-off was to be provided by four solid-fuel rockets attached to the glider's tail that would force the composite aircraft up the special take-off ramp. A similar idea now in use is the 'ski jump' ramp for Sea Harriers mounted aboard two Royal Navy aircraft carriers.

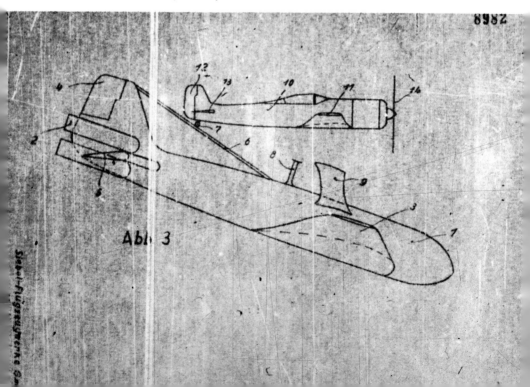

Abb. 3

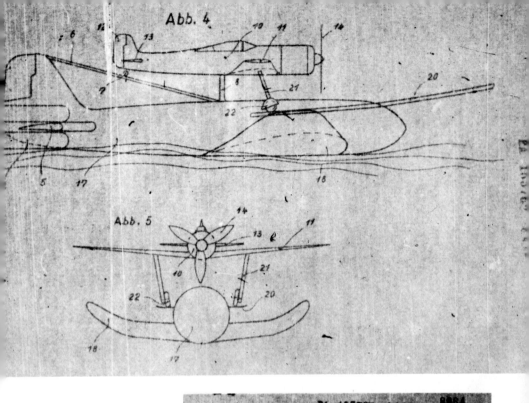

Abb. 4

Abb. 5

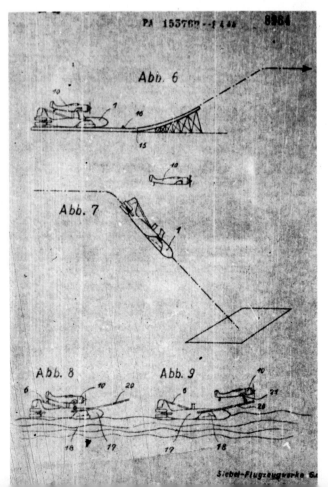

Abb. 6

Abb. 7

Abb. 8   Abb. 9

Siebel-Flugzeugwerke Sa

Operational *Mistel 1* composite aircraft of 6./KG 200 on a Danish airfield late in 1944.

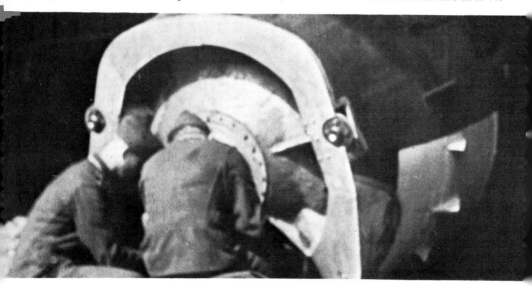

Armourers fitting the rear fuses in the 3.8-ton hollow-charge *Mistel* warhead. The upper two of the four large cap nuts that attached the warhead to the airframe are clearly visible.

Right: Additional instrumentation and controls carried by a FW 190 *Mistel* control aircraft.

Clearly visible is the additional instrument panel bolted over the central console. It contains (centre) the two Ju 88 propeller pitch dials with (left) the landing-flap flick-switch ('Down' for take-off; 'Up' for cruising flight). On the left next to it, the two control lights for electrics and hydraulics; left over it, the two switches activating the release detonators ('Right'–normal; 'Left–emergency release). On the right next to it, the control light for detonator installation. To the right of the Ju 88 propeller pitch dials is the spring-loaded flick-switch regulating rudder control effectiveness ('Down' for take-off = hard reaction; 'Up' for cruising flight = soft reaction). On the right next to it, the special switch for arming the warhead fuses. Over the propeller pitch dials: spring-loaded flick-switches for climbing/sinking flight ('Up' for nosing down; 'Down' for climbing). To the right next to the control panel: fuel transfer switch (from the Ju 88 to FW 190).

Under the propeller pitch dials are the two combined multi-display instruments for the Ju 88 engines: boost, revs, oil pressure and oil temperature. Left above behind the control column: course indicator for the rudder servo motors (directional changes to

port/starboard). To the left, under the left pedal: the two Ju 88 throttle levers. Above, centre: the gyro-stabilised reflex sight. Under it (left) the flick-switch for manual control override of the servo motors for the target approach flight by means of the course indicator (lateral and vertical axis). The switch is shown to the left–controls 'In'. Flick-switch for the gyro sight: left–'gyro free'; right–'gyro locked'.

Two variants of the Hs 293A rocket-propelled guided stand-off bomb. This missile represented a great advance in weapon technology but was not used in any numbers until the closing stages of the war.

Reconnaissance photograph by 2.(F)/100 of the Oder bridges at Steinau after the first *Mistel* attack. The subsequent evaluation notes indicate the North bridge (57) as destroyed, and the Central and South bridges as repaired. Fig 5 marks assembled construction/repair material.

Later enlargement of the target area clearly showing *Mistel* hits on the Steinau railway bridge and close to it on the bank, revealing some collapsed framework. Three large craters caused by *Mistels* that missed the target are visible on the bank between the railway and road bridges.

Despite clearly visible Luftwaffe markings this converted B-24 Liberator was fired on by German Flak during a ferry flight on 6 April 1945 and had to make a forced landing near Aschersleben. In this case it was all smiles afterwards, but such 'mistakes' were the greatest fear of all Luftwaffe aircrews flying captured enemy aircraft by day or night. Note the faired-in nose section of this converted B-24J.

During take-off from Hildesheim on 13 April 1945 this B-24 Liberator operated by KG 200 ran into some soft ground and suffered a collapsed nose wheel. The aircraft immediately nosed over and caught fire, but the crew managed to escape in time.

Tragedy strikes KG 200. In March 1945, shortly after a night take-off from Echterdingen near Stuttgart, a B-17 piloted by *Oberfeldwebel* Knappenschneider carrying a full crew and ten members of the French Vichy government in exile crashed and burned out on an open field killing all aboard except the tail gunner.

The machine was to fly its VIP passengers to a certain spot near the French-Spanish border where they were to land by parachute.

The illustrations show (top) the author in his capacity as commander of Detachment *Olga* laying a wreath during the funeral at Echterdingen, and (below) the graves of the unfortunate Frenchmen, still well looked after today.

An abandoned *Mistel 2* on the Junkers works airfield at Merseburg. About 50 *Mistels* in varied condition were found by the US forces on five airfields near Bernburg and Merseburg in May 1945.

A 'Mistletoe' made in England. No *Mistels* were flown after the end of hostilities, but to complete the collection one 'mock-up' was assembled by RAE technicians for the German Aircraft Exhibition at Farnborough in October-November 1945. It comprised a Ju 88A-6 (ex-Air Min 77) and FW 190A-8/R6 (ex-Air Min 75).

The then *Leutnant* Eckard Dittmann remembers clearly the last *Mistel* operations which he flew as a leader:

'We were supposed to attack the Oder bridge at Küstrin with seven *Mistels* on 26 April 1945. Three Ju 188 pathfinders and a whole *Gruppe* of fighters were made available to take over navigation and protection tasks.

The take-off was fixed for 1545 hrs and the attack was to take place at 1700 hrs. Seven *Mistels* stood nicely lined up behind each other at the end of the runway, right on the centre line. Unfortunately we already had two "flat feet" while towing the machines from their revetments to the take-off runway. We also learned that two take-offs from other fields had failed. *Hptm* Nolte as leader of an operation had taken off first and got away clear from the concrete runway. Immediately afterwards, his *Mistel* had broken up and his FW 190, ripped away from its supports, had hit the ground a hundred yards further on and burned out. The pilot was extremely lucky because he managed to free himself and run away from the wreck, aflame from head to toe. Although he did not succeed in putting out the flames by rolling on the ground, the fire service crew were on the spot within minutes and covered "Pitt" Nolte, his FW 190 and the Ju 88 with a mountain of foam.

The take-off was cancelled after *Feldwebel* Lukaschek's *Mistel* swung off the runway, crashed into a revetment and the pilot died an airman's death in his exploding aircraft.

The main problem was and remained to keep the *Mistel* straight on the runway until the Ju 88 lifted its tail. Until that moment, the view ahead was miserable and a sector of 40 per cent was completely blocked by the bulky engine of the FW 190. The second essential point was that the formation leader had a smooth take-off, otherwise the rest of the pilots might not be individually up to the additional mental and nervous strain.

Can anyone even imagine what it means to take off past or, worse still, over another crew burning to death in their crashed aircraft? In such cases one really had to "grab himself by the scruff of the neck", so to speak, to force oneself back into the normal state of mind.

Courage is nothing else but the overcoming of fear. In such situations it was best to give unimportant instructions to one's crew, at the same time displaying what we used to call "beer calmness" and complete control of yourself to all intents and purposes. So, after climbing out of the bus that had taken us to the machines, I said in a

149

more lighthearted way: "Well, make it good, comrades, I wish you what, and show me what you can do with your joysticks when I look down again!" – The commander was in the same mood: "Everything is clear, there is nothing more to be said. I wish you 'neck and legs'*" – and then, no longer in service manner, he poked me in the ribs while turning away: "Make it good, tall one, and see that you get up there into your lofty swing!"

And so I climbed up the wobbly five-yard long ladder and let myself slide into the lightly swaying FW 190. The First mechanic followed and helped me to put on the back and parachute straps. Contrary to the technical conception, I flew the FW 190 with a seat-type and not a back parachute as I found the latter too uncomfortable.

The First mechanic leaned over once more, wished me the usual, and then climbed down. The control people then checked the functioning of the electrical control cables from the FW 190 to the Ju 88 for the last time and indicated that everything was in order. So be it! I started the FW 190 engine, while the engines down below were activated by the mechanics. Then a brief check of all the instruments and manipulation of the necessary switches and levers according to the check list I had hanging around my neck, and I was ready. The take-off officer passed on my hand signal to the leading mechanic, who pulled away the wheel brake blocks. *Oberleutnant* von Male lifted his hand again and I pushed the FW 190 throttle and then the Ju 88 throttles to full power. The "double decker" began to move forward, swaying all the way, and I banged my head against the cockpit cover several times. But I got off the ground in good order.

Now, adjust the Ju 88 prop pitch for better climb, throttle back, retract the landing flaps one after another, set the rudder control to "Flight", trim a little and tune the engines, and I was on my way.

I made a circuit around the field. The other *Mistels* took off one after another – there were no problems. The three Ju 188s followed, making a fine formation take-off. Down below they must have given the "all clear" as I could see some movement around the place again – before the take-off, as a precaution, there was an air raid alert and everybody had to get into the bunkers. One never knew with the *Mistels*.

Then we hanged ourselves behind the trio of Ju 188s, still flying in a

---

*Hals und Bein = Hals und Beinbruch! (Broken neck and legs!), a colloquial Luftwaffe send-off before take-off. To wish 'good luck' was unthinkable – the pilots were a very superstitious crowd.

150

clean formation, if a bit loosened up. Our aircraft were alternatively falling and climbing slightly in a wavy fashion caused by the delay factor in the electrically-operated remote controls. To an observer, this must have looked a most unusual flying cavalcade – I wondered what the people down there really made of all this. At long last our "secret weapons" are going into action? Perhaps.

We flew a course south-south east towards Berlin and climbed to 9840 ft, our attack altitude. We then picked up our fighter escort over Strausberg as agreed – a complete *Gruppe* of FW 190s. It happened very suddenly. One moment I had looked for them sideways and downwards, and there they were, beside and above us, as if appearing from nowhere.

Now we turned eastwards. The three Ju 188s spread out and went into inclined flight, disappearing in the haze. The visibility worsened, caused by hazy high-pressure atmospheric conditions and wherever one looked below there were fires and smoke streaming upwards.

Shortly afterwards we flew over the combat zone. In this area the Soviets had captured the Oder bridges intact and bludgeoned out a strong bridgehead this side of Küstrin almost to Seelow. All our dive bomber and close support aviation attacks had been shot to pieces in their massive screen of anti-aircraft fire, and now we were to achieve what they could not.

The smoke was now so bad that we could no longer see anything, or distinguish any details on the ground but we must have been somewhere near our release point. Their medium-calibre AA guns began to heat up the air around us and increased visibly. My fellow pilots became restless, I could feel it almost physically, and I loosened the formation by wagging my wings to indicate individual attacks. We had no radio contact, but being 'old hands' they understood at once.

However, to carry out our diving attack we first needed ground visibility and that was a bit of a problem here. The attack glide had been planned to commence about 6·2 miles from the target, in good visibility, but the conditions just did not match the weather forecast. The air was thick with smoke, and so we split up and began to lose altitude in soft spirals, each on his own. This helped to disperse the AA fire, and their concentration point began to wander all over the place as comrade after comrade disappeared into the fiery smog. Soon I could smell smoke in my cockpit. Although the Soviet AA guns must have been firing blindly, their shells seemed to be attracted to me personally. By then I had gone down to about 2300 ft, and still could not see anything. There was nothing for it but to keep on turning and losing altitude till I could.

Suddenly, a river bend shimmered through the haze – the Oder! I had memorised the map of this area and recognised at once that I was a few miles too far south. Right – another 270 degree bank, and that should lead me to the railway line and the bridges at the end of it! The smoke closed in and all ground detail disappeared once more. My *Mistel* was now way below 3280 ft and must have been clearly visible to the Ivans* – they were blazing away at me like mad.

The rest happened very quickly. The ground features appeared shadowy from the smoky haze, and then there was a darker line – the railway. I had flown over it aslant. Next moment I could see a bridge, then several – the target! I banked tightly to starboard, switched on the steering controls, released the gyro, made a quick correction, there was no time for more, no time for a really "clean job", and then it was high time to release the Ju 88!

There was a bang, and I could feel a blow from below. My FW 190 suddenly turned several rolls to port and for a moment I thought they had "cooked my goose", but the crate just needed re-trimming and in a few seconds I had her again. In all that tracer and smoke I could not tell for a while where was up and where was down, but then things fell into place. I turned into the lighter, redder part of the sky – that must have been the low-lying sun. The AA fire followed me all the way.

Once I had my bearings again I pressed the FW 190 closer to the ground and a while later I was hopping over some meadows, fields and pine trees until I suddenly chanced upon a group of tanks parked in readiness next to some woods. Somebody jumped from a tank – they were probably Russians. Somewhere there I also saw someone waving at me, I believe – where exactly was I?

Very carefully, I pulled my machine higher and then saw some buildings appearing from the haze, the first suburbs of Berlin. I must have been over our own territory long since. And that there must be the Müggel lake. I flew on westwards past Strausberg and soon found Werneuchen where I had to land after this operation.

I was anxious to find out what the others had to say. I was not really satisfied with my own performance this time and hoped that the others had done better. Very steady and carefully I let out my landing flaps and wheels, and everything was in order. I soared in and landed from

---

*Ivan = colloquial German front-line soldier's term for the Russians

the west, taxied to the right, braked and switched off the engine.

The next machine to follow me down was a Ju 87G with two 37 mm cannon under the wings. The Ju landed skipping and lurching and rolled to a stop. An ambulance came alongside and they lifted out the pilot. Badly wounded, he had flown his machine home with the last ounce of strength.

Then came a FW 190, levelled off near the runway and landed on its belly. It was *Oberfähnrich* Gutsche from our *Mistel* formation. His aircraft had been hit several times and he could no longer lower the undercarriage, but at least he was back safe. He too had wandered around in the same smog and released his Ju 88 at the last moment, without being able to observe any results.

And that was that. Nobody else came back. I phoned the fighters at Strausberg, but they did not know anything either. We were the balance, the only two survivors from seven *Mistels* sent out on this operation. Until this day I have no idea what happened to our other five comrades, their fate remains unknown.

On the fifth day I flew my somewhat peppered but still completely airworthy FW 190 to Peenemünde. The situation there was already precarious as well. The big and until then highly secret rocket test and manufacturing area had already been evacuated and I could look at everything without being disturbed by anybody – it was quite spooky. Some of the installations had been badly damaged in bombing raids, others destroyed. In one place there was a big heap of dismantled and scrapped Hs 293 remotely-controlled glide bombs. Where were they when we needed them?

The next operation came on 30 April when the remaining four *Mistels* were to attack the Oder bridge east of Prenzlau near Tantow. The Soviets had crossed the river in great force and built up a strong bridgehead on the western bank already extending half way to Prenzlau.

The attack was to take place at 0900 hrs, the fighter escort had to be picked up over Pasewalk at 0845 hrs, and our landing base was to be the Heinkel works airfield at Rostock-Marienehe.

Once again, the compulsory air raid warning on the field blared as all four *Mistels* were lined up at the end of the runway, with *Hptm* René, our commander, a bit to one side. In between there was *Oberleutnant* von Male, running forwards and backwards as usual.

It was a good, clean take-off and we all got off the ground according to book. One after another I took them with me into the waiting circuit off the field with a friendly wave and nod, but the fourth failed to appear. As I found out later, he had been forced to release his Ju 88 component due to a technical fault into the Baltic off Peenemünde a few minutes after becoming airborne. So there were only three of us now.

After two circuits around our agreed meeting point at Pasewalk, the fighters appeared on the scene – two sections of Bf 109s. We straightened out and set course south-west to our initial point. I intended to turn east from there and attack the bridge in one go.

The aerial activity over the bridgehead was lively up above, on the middle floor and down below, and I was quite pleased to join what I thought was an obvious major effort by our Luftwaffe. It did not take long however before an optimistic fool had to learn differently! We were flying at about 8900 ft altitude, and over the bridgehead there was an intermediate cloud layer at about 2000 ft, thickening towards the Oder. Our easterly course must have taken us near the front line when things began to change. All at once I realised that something was being cooked for us – those machines down there were Soviet low-level ground attackers, now clearly visible in between the cloud patches. And whatever was flitting above and between them were Soviet fighters – all the way up to 23,000 ft altitude!

Yes indeed, the Russians had learned a thing or two. They had hermetically sealed off their bridgehead, and down below their *Shturmoviks* were roaring around undisturbed, shooting at every German soldier in sight. Poor devils, what hell they had to suffer now – and how they must have cursed their own Luftwaffe for forsaking them!

A quick glance over my shoulder showed two banking Bf 109s behind me. We were now right over the bridgehead west-south west from the target, and the dance was already in full swing. Up to this point our fighters had covered our backs, from here on they could no longer manage to do so. We were on our own.

The target was still about six or so miles half-left ahead of us. The gaps between the clouds were clear of any movement for the time being – this was our chance. *Uffz* Seitz had closed in with me, while *Ofw* Braun on the right pointed to the Soviet fighter to the left above me and then turned his hand half-way to the right. I understood right away, and *Uffz* Seitz apparently as well. What Braun had in mind was for us to fly along on the right and attack from the south. I waggled my wings making the agreed sign to break formation and prepare to attack individually.

From now on each of us was on his own. In any case, we could not defend each other with our unarmed and unwieldy contraptions. At best, we would only hinder each other.

Immediately afterwards *Uffz* Seitz began closing in towards me far too fast from the left and I had to press down. He pulled away over me and then hung left next to Braun who was banking away to the right. The way Braun – and probably Seitz as well wanted to attack was quite logical under the circumstances, from a right turn. I had the same thing in mind, but when I realised what was brewing against us from the left I knew what had to be done – attack at once, right through the milling Soviet fighters!

I pushed the throttle levers to full power and "took the tops back" for combat performance. The engines roared up and the aircraft began to shake and rattle. There was no time to tune the engines. I pushed the nose down a bit and flew towards the target at about 298 mph, which I assumed to be ahead of me behind those cloud tatters.

The pirouette began, opened by two Yak-9s of the top cover attacking in diving spirals. I let them calmly shoot past me down- wards. To hit me they should have had a four radii deflection on their reflex sights, but their aiming point was already through the engine after one and a half radii, I knew that much from my fighter training. And so it was – both of them dived past on the way down without chipping anything off me. At least I had those two off my neck.

And then something happened that has puzzled me to this day. Two Yak-9s came towards me from the left and turned to fly close alongside. Both pilots then looked at me full of curiousity, slowed down to keep pace with me, then began turning in and pulled away upwards past my *Mistel* so close that I could have almost grasped them with my hands. I can still clearly recall the wide open eyes and tense faces of both pilots under their greenish-yellow flying helmets as they gave me a close once-over. Why didn't they shoot me down there and then? And what happened to them? A quick glance behind answered that one – they were turning in behind me, and there was a whole bunch of other hungry Soviet fighters coming up fast. It was high time to get out.

I had started my gliding attack automatically. The Oder was clearly visible, and my target, the bridge, was at the end of the highway leading eastwards. Controls on, turn towards the target, gunsight gyro "off", a correction upwards and sideways in my sight – ready! The AA fire began to hammer and grew in intensity. I recall noticing that with some surprise because only the fighters and the bridge had existed for me at that time – it was a race between them and me.

I expected to be "collected" by the fighters at any moment, my intention being to immediately detonate the release points and then sell my life as dearly as possible.

Why didn't they roast me? It was only then that I noticed the thick curtain of steel thrown up by the ground defences between my lumbering *Mistel* and the pursuing fighters. Most of it was now behind me and was keeping the fighters at a distance. At the same time I also noticed the visibly increasing number of holes appearing in my Ju 88 and scraps of metal mushrooming upwards from it. Their ground fire was registering alright. And then I noticed something else and swore aloud – the bridge, my target, was already destroyed! Damn!! Then I made out another flatter bridge a few hundred metres upstream, probably a pontoon bridge, and reacted at once: gyro locked, a correction on the controls, and gyro free again. The gliding angle was now too flat, and the Russians were banging away like crazy. They must have been firing with everything they had, it was impossible to tell where all that tracer was coming from.

This was it! I bent forward and made the final target corrections. Suddenly there was a bang in my cockpit and I could smell something. Quick – detonate the release points! Another, more distant bang, a blow, and my FW 190 swung into a violent roll to port. I made a few involuntary rolls like this, the aircraft was so much out of trim. Only one thought was in my mind – avoid hitting the released Ju 88 at all costs! While upside down in one of these rolls I pushed the control stick forward and tried to pull out to port from the transverse position – this unwanted rolling was going on far too long for my liking! Next moment I had my FW 190 once again in hand. I had to keep the control stick forward and slanting to the right to hold the untrimmed machine straight.

There, fighters from the left! I had probably flown a semicircle while doing those involuntary rolls. Throttle hammer in, and up. I pulled the FW 190 in a steep climbing spiral and glanced behind me. A big cloud of smoke was mushrooming at the river, but I had no time to observe any details. I wanted to get into the protecting clouds above, but I did not make it. Suddenly there was no pressure on the controls – I had stalled the aircraft! The machine fell away outwards and I found myself in a pretty flat spin. That's all I needed now! I had only a few hours on the FW 190 and was not very familiar with her, but I knew that when heavy machines go into a spin more often than not one cannot get them out again, and one cannot bale out either. And now it was happening to me!

I kept on turning towards the earth below and tried desperately to regain control, first with opposite rudder and full throttle, and then with all possible control settings. Throttle forward, throttle back . . . whatever you do, don't give up! Oh, shit! And then, all at once, I felt two hefty blows in the wings and I had her in hand again. Phew!! I was right close to the ground now, but I was flying again, what a relief. It felt like being born again!

Where was I? The Oder was behind me to the left, so I was still over the bridgehead. Right, down to the ground and in the lowest possible flight – nobody was going to cook my goose now. My FW 190 leaped forward and I was away. Somehow everything seemed ever so peaceful here, no AA fire, what had happened? A quick glance behind – no fighters either! That was funny. And then a glance at my still swaying compass: East! What a shock! I was flying in the opposite direction, and I also realised why: the sun was behind the clouds.

I really had enough now and did not want to take any more risks. About turn, down to the ground again and back to the Oder as quickly as I could.

Suddenly, there were aircraft in front of me and coming towards me at about ten to twenty metres above the ground. My reflex sight was still switched on and that made me feel almost belligerent. I will show them! I continued flying straight ahead and whizzed through the oncoming aircraft. They were Soviet assaulters, the Il-2s, returning home having shot themselves empty, and flying in a messy looking gaggle. Then came the next bunch of the same kind, two of which pulled outwards as I raced towards them. I took one of them full in my sights and pressed my firing button – he would have had it, but of course my guns had been removed. It made me feel a bit better though – at least I had made some of them sweat blood. And so I just shot past them, flew under the following returning untidy group of Il-2s, and another. A few AA shots were fired at me, but the trajectory was so flat that they just shot at themselves.

Another quick glance behind me while banking lightly to port and starboard. Everything was clear. Then a Yak-9 was coming towards me in inclined flight and opened fire, and kept on firing when I was already past, before pulling up. I think the pilot had not even seen me

157

and was attacking some target on the ground.

Another burst of AA fire from the left, and this time the shells were well placed. I made a quick avoiding turn to starboard, but collected a hit in my upturned port wing: suddenly there was a hole like a cabbage head with the fringe. The double-row BMW 801 engine continued to run smoothly with its characteristic hard knocking sound, and that was what mattered. A few more pearly chains of AA tracer, and then no more.

I continued skidding low over the ground westwards and kept making sure my back was free, that there were no fighters behind me. By then I must have been over our own territory, and began carefully to lift my nose. Ahead of me was a town which I immediately recognised as Prenzlau. I flew close past it and had a look at the airfield. A few aircraft were standing around, but there was nothing flying.

Next, I came past the Lychener lakes and could not resist the temptation to make a brief "compassionate visit" to my mother. I saw her last from above.

Soon after that I was at Rostock-Marienehe, the Heinkel works airfield. For some reason contrary to my usual habit first to "buzz" a field, I made my approach from the east, over Warnow, as soon as I could see the landing cross. It was quite by chance, but most fortunate because as soon as I began to soar in my engine turned sour. I found out later that it had been hit several times, and would no longer react to throttle. Against my natural inclination I put the nose down and did not try to hold on "on an empty stomach". I had not forgotten the experience one of my comrades had with his shot-up FW 190 coming in to land at Prague-Rusyne. I set down my warhorse immediately next to the banks of Warnow, between stacks of bombs and air-raid trenches, and pulled up about 300 ft behind the landing cross. They fired three red flares from the business end of the field before my comrades realised my predicament. A tractor rolled over and they towed my lame FW 190 across to the other end to park it next to a line of brand-new He 162 jet fighters.

Now I had a chance to look over my brave bird, and what a sight she was. The FW 190 had suffered quite a bit. One AA shell had bashed in a cylinder and ripped off two ignition cables. Another shell had gone clean through the cockpit from the left behind, leaving a hole the size of a fist on the right. The shot had gone past the armour plate exactly where my head would have been when I had bent forward to make the final target corrections just before releasing the Ju 88. It was one of those things that make you stop and think. I think I had rather refrain from listing all the other hits – after all, I was not the only one being shot at and punctured that day.

I met *Ofw* Braun at the Flight control. He had just reported back to the *Geschwader* HQ. His Ju 88 had been shot aflame by fighters immediately after we had separated to commence individual attacks, but he had managed to release the burning lower component at the last moment and then fight his way back home again. We never heard anything about our comrade *Uffz* Seitz and his fate remains unknown.

I made my report back to the *Geschwader* and then we both set off on foot in our leather flying suits to the *Gruppe* HQ at Warnemünde. A group of our comrades drove towards us in a consumer-gas powered lorry and shouted. They were on their way to fight as infantrymen.

I followed them with the rest of our *Gruppe* three days later . . .'

13. *Olga*'s Last Missions

The war for *Olga* in the West had gone on in the same way. New flights behind the Allied lines were prepared daily, 'Operation XY' or even 'Special operations', but the winter weather had hindered the planned take-offs time and again. Now the Western Front had also begun to crumble, and the Americans had crossed the Rhine.

However, this did not seem to matter to those 'higher up'. New operational orders and repeats of those not carried out arrived constantly and with almost mindless punctuality.

The conditions became more desperate daily and our *V-Leute* quarters were bursting at the seams. In the meantime the Allied troops were advancing south, and the American air raids on our airfields were happening almost daily and finally made our further stay in Frankfurt impossible. We could actually predict the time when all our aircraft and technical equipment would be destroyed on the ground. And not only that. The Detachment lost sixteen men, including our *Oberwerkmeister* (workshop chief) and my observer Hans Fecht during a heavy American air raid on Christmas Eve 1944. It was a great personal loss and even more tragic because this disaster could have been avoided.

As it happened, the air raid warning had been given early and we had made sure that all personnel were in bomb-proof shelters outside the airfield in good time. Unfortunately a group of men took a lorry and drove back to the field again to complete their technical tasks as quickly as possible because of our Christmas festivities prepared for early that evening. They had simply driven off without reporting in the proper service manner – something that would have been unthinkable before. Perhaps they had wanted to save me an uncomfortable decision. Be that as it may, a bomb carpet fell right on the spot where they were working. That was our Christmas Eve, 1944.

The funeral in a nearby cemetery affected us all very deeply, particularly as the relatives of the dead men were also present. What could I say in my funeral speech? Should I talk about heroism and bravery, use all those 'big words' again in view of this now senseless sacrifice? It was very hard indeed. Deliberately, I decided to forgo the

160

usual military ritual with a guard of honour and the last salvo by the graveside. I had to read the names of our dead comrades from a list so that I would not leave somebody out, there were that many.

The loss of my observer and friend Hans Fecht hit me especially hard. We had begun to fly the Ju 88 together in 1939 and since then had participated in nearly 300 operational flights on almost every front and over the sea. The mood remained depressed – how could one even think of Christmas cheer under such circumstances?

Things took a considerable turn for the worse early in 1945. The weather forecasts became increasingly less reliable, and the navigational aids that still could be used decreased in number. To add to our problems, the number of other available airfields suitable for all-weather landings was very limited.

The flying performance of the aircrews also began to sink, caused by slack morale, and the sick reports began to pile up. It became so bad that flights were abandoned for the most trivial reasons. For example – a Ju 188 took off on an operational flight with the task of dropping a PAG with three Frenchmen in western France. The pilot was an *Oberfeldwebel* whose flying capabilities I had judged to be good. Three and a half hours later the machine was approaching the airfield again and the pilot asked for the usual assistance for his night landing. Something had obviously gone wrong, because the flight should have taken at least six hours. The mystery was solved after landing, the PAG was still hanging under the wings with the parachute cap missing together with the three parachutes. The three French agents inside the container were half frozen and had to be lifted out carefully and immediately delivered into the care of our doctor. The crew then told me a story I considered pure invention.

Some time after take-off they suddenly realised they were flying east, despite the fact that the compass and their auto-pilot were set for westerly direction. 'Luckily' they then managed to establish their true position by taking bearings from several radio stations – they turned out to be somewhere over Slovakia. In the meantime the aircraft had climbed into some clouds and developed heavy icing. The thick ripcord attached to the parachute cap must have been heavily iced as well, only that would explain why it was ripped off. The three agents could consider themselves extremely lucky not to have frozen to death in the Arctic cold at high altitude. After determining their true position the only thing left to do was to get back home as quickly as they could.

161

I could not prove or disprove how true this story really was, but it sounded somewhat suspect. Our technical check of the compass installation the following day gave a clean ticket – it was working perfectly. I ordered the pilot to report to me and told him that I had to express doubts regarding the truth of his story. However, as I could not see any way of proving that he had submitted a falsified report I could not do anything else but to have him transferred away at once.

The increasingly more critical situation then forced us to pack up everything and move from Frankfurt to Stuttgart-Echterdingen, but this transfer was preceded by an almost unbelievable turn of events – nobody was willing to have us. All the airfields in southern Germany were choked with surviving remnants of the Luftwaffe. Although on paper Detachment *Olga* had priority over all other Luftwaffe formations that did not make any difference when it was a matter of putting up a new operational base for it. I could not expect any help from the *Geschwader* staff in far-away Berlin, and so once again I was left to my own devices. To make things even more difficult the teleprinter connections were no longer functioning reliably and higher command posts declared themselves unable to help me.

My solution to the problem was to jump into a Ju 188 and make flying visits to all possible places until I succeeded in finding an understanding airfield commander at Echterdingen who was willing to take my detachment. I immediately sent an advance party to his field and was greatly relieved when they finally reported back that everything was ready. They had done very well. Parking places for all our aircraft had been prepared a safe distance away from the airfield, a certain target for enemy bombers. Quarters for officers and men had been found in nearby billets, and a tavern had been earmarked as a command post. And not only that – telephone lines had also been laid and connected, a technical basis for repairs and maintenance work had been established, and fuel supplies organised – as far as it was still possible to arrange such a thing more or less reliably in those days.

A particular problem was the food supply, but our efficient *Leutnant* Schiessl had managed to rent a temporarily closed guest-house and engage the landlady as our 'chef' at the same time.

As a residence for our motley crew of *V-Leute* and their controllers our advance party had found a castle about 12 miles from the airfield, and a high school in the nearby village was taken over as a store room for their quite substantial equipment.

However, the transfer of aircraft and the road transport of the

162

complete technical personnel and material that would normally take at the most only two days, lasted longer than a week. And then one could not really call it an orderly transfer, it was more like a hurried rush from one place to another.

The situation being what it was, I could only advise my 'hangers-on', the leaders of the *V-Leute* and their Dutch, French, Arab and British male and female personnel to look after themselves and make their own way. And in fact they eventually arrived in dribs and drabs at their new home near Stuttgart.

I left Frankfurt very much as the last *Olga* representative nursing a sick Ju 188. This machine had a defective hydraulic system so that I had to fly with the wheels down and operate the landing flaps via a manual emergency pump. The complete radio installation too was dead, so I had to be on my toes all the time. We took off in the evening dusk and landed in Echterdingen at night. To my mind, the risk involved flying such a sick bird at night was still less than trying to dodge roaming American fighters by day with a good aircraft.

As mentioned previously, for transport tasks involving heavy loads and very long distances our detachment could always request the use of large four-engined aircraft, including captured American B-17s and B-24s. These former enemy bombers were selected from those that had made forced landings in German territory and were only slightly damaged. Very often it was only a matter of some bent propellers and a few dents in the fuselage, damage that did not require much effort to repair and make these ex-enemy bombers airworthy again. They were then rebuilt and refitted internally for our purposes and, as far as necessary, equipped with German instruments, radio sets and navigational devices.

However, these aircraft were not available in such large numbers as two hundred or so, as has been asserted on the Allied side. That figure is a complete invention: at the most, there could have been no more than about 20 such ex-enemy aircraft in our service at any one time.

Another point that has to be made is that these machines were not used for deception purposes as has been suggested, or that they were better than available German types. For instance, in the Ju 290 we had an excellent four-engined transport aircraft that possessed even better flying and performance characteristics than these American bombers. The drawback was that there were only a handful of these machines, and it was no longer possible to produce them in the required numbers as we lacked the necessary materials, production capacity and means of transport. Also, by 1944 the military situation demanded that every effort should be concentrated on producing the largest possible number of fighters.

To come back to the first point. As stated above, it has been repeatedly asserted that the Luftwaffe used these captured bombers for deception purposes, often even with Allied markings. That simply is not true. First of all, we flew at night when 'all cats are black' anyway, as they say, and secondly, these captured bombers were on principle always flown with German insignia. Apart from everything else, this fact is clearly proven by surviving logbooks (see Appendix No 14).

It happens to be a simple fact that a breach of international law – as flying in enemy colours would have been – could not have brought us any benefit, except possible damage by our own AA guns or fighters. Apart from that, in case of capture their crews would have been dealt with as spies and not as ordinary airmen. Personally I have not heard of a single case where this legend of 'German aircraft in Allied markings' has been substantiated.

Perhaps the reason this story refuses to lie down is that the British themselves did not think much of using a He 115 with German markings in the Mediterranean. Thus 'camouflaged', this floatplane was successfully flown on various 'special missions' between Malta and North Africa. (The aircraft was a Heinkel He 115A-2 export version, six of which were sold to Norway and ten to Sweden before the war. At least one of the Norwegian aircraft got to Britain in 1940.)

In addition to that, R. E. Gillman tells us in his book *The Shiphunters** on p.169: – 'At one point, a slipway crossed the road and disappeared into the water, but at the top of the slope was a large and mysterious shed. Some two weeks previously, a crew had been walking back from the village rather later than usual when they came upon a great deal of muted activity by the slip. They were surrounded immediately by armed soldiers who materialised out of the darkness. Their identity cards were scrutinised by torchlight, they were searched and then ordered to stand facing the wall with their hands above their heads. However, Maxie, by squinting under his arm, managed to keep the shed in view and was astonished when a large black seaplane bearing German markings was trundled out and down the slip. Immediately it hit the water, the engine was started and it taxied off into the darkness.

*Publ. by John Murray, London, 1976.

The soldiers with their rifles at the ready, then ordered the crew to walk towards the shed where they were taken to an officer for further interrogation. He warned them to forget anything they might have seen and above all to mention it to nobody, not even to servicemen. They felt, not unreasonably, that they had been left in a dilemma; if this was a British intelligence activity, then fair and good. But what if it was something else? Shouldn't someone be told about it, or at least a check made?

They approached the intelligence officer at the airfield the next day and told him what they had seen. He showed no surprise, but taking them into his office and closing the door, he told them that the machine was, indeed, a captured German seaplane, a Blohm und Voss, and that it was used for intelligence purposes, landing off the coast of Sicily at night to drop off, and pick up, agents.'

Next to the legend of captured bombers used by KG 200 with Allied markings there is another that apparently just cannot be rooted out – the cyanide capsules. Time and again one reads or hears stories that KG 200 aircrew had carried poison capsules on their flights to commit suicide in case of capture. There is not a grain of truth in this either, but once started, such fairy tales seem to gain credence by repetition and are very hard to stamp out.

Our operational activities from our new base at Echterdingen were even more limited than previously, again mainly because of the bad weather during the early weeks of 1945. Another reason was of course that it was becoming increasingly more difficult to prepare and carry out night flights. During the daylight hours marauding Allied aircraft made all technical service on our machines so difficult that even the smallest repairs and maintenance tasks that normally would have been completed within hours now took several days. Another problem were the spare parts which had to be collected and brought back by special couriers because the normal rail/road communications had already broken down.

For example, once I had to send an NCO to the KG 200 technical base at Finow, near Berlin, to collect certain small but important parts. He arrived back after two weeks without any material, wounded, and just about able to walk. On the way back he had run into an air raid and lost everything he had so laboriously acquired.

Another important reason for our reduced operational activities was the growing realisation that further sacrifices seemed futile. Eventually we only flew operations that were absolutely essential, such as setting down an agent or two or some vitally needed supplies. By then, it was up to our 'customers' to convince us of this, although the final decision remained in our hands. As time went by we also began to fob off the still keen agent controllers with various excuses and white lies. Fortunately there were people among them who had insight and understanding, although there were also some diehard Nazis.

At the very end, our detachment suffered a grievous tragedy when a B-17 'Flying Fortress' crashed and burned out immediately after take-off. Only one man survived of the eleven-man crew and ten passengers, the tail gunner, who was just about to get into his position when the machine crashed. The tail end was ripped off and remained outside the exploding fireball.

As it happened, I witnessed this crash from my Ju 188 parked on the runway behind the B-17. I was to take off next on an operational flight over southern France. I saw the navigation lights of the doomed aircraft slowly gaining height towards Echterdingen village when suddenly they began turning away to right. Before I could grasp what was happening the lights disappeared behind some ground obstacles. Next moment there was an enormous jet of flame that coloured the whole western horizon red.

I abandoned the take-off and taxied my Ju 188 as quickly as I could in the darkness and over the half-destroyed tarmac back to the starting point. A car was already waiting for me and we immediately set off towards the crash area.

A gruesome sight met our eyes. The big aircraft had come down on an open field the other side of the village and must have hit the ground at a very flat angle: the track from the initial point of impact to the last bits of wreckage stretched for at least 400 metres. Flames were licking everywhere, bits of wreckage, the ground – and smashed bodies. Some civilians, mainly women, stood in shocked silence nearby in the darkness. A rescue team from the airfield was also on the spot and began searching for survivors. We all joined in and were soon covered from head to foot in blood, dirt and oil. We did not leave the gruesome place until after we had made certain that nobody else but the tail gunner had survived in the wreckage. Only an airfield fire service detachment, a guard detail and some officials from the local NSDAP remained behind.

On the way back to the base I was still unable to think clearly. It was fortunate that *Leutnant* Schiessl was with me because his trained judical mind was now urgently needed. As I found out, the ten dead passengers were nothing less than prominent members of the Vichy French Petain/Laval 'exile government'!

In view of the developing total German collapse these people should have been, or had wanted to be set down by parachute somewhere in the French-Spanish border area. And now this!

During the night we drew up the preliminary reports about this fatal accident, as far as it was possible to do so in the following confusion. An advance report by telephone to Berlin took hours, and was evidently only half understood the other end.

It was impossible even to think of sleep. Next morning, dirty and tired as we were, we had to receive a judge-advocate from the Stuttgart air district command who had been empowered to carry out the preliminary judical inquiry. He was obviously already informed about the identity of the prominent passengers. An uniformed engineer arrived at the same time and declared himself responsible for the technical investigation. Contrary to his colleague he had already made up his mind about the cause of this accident even before he had a look at the crash scene. 'Sabotage, naturally!'

He began his investigation accordingly – instead of looking for possible technical causes he wanted to find out if the fated aircraft had been sufficiently closely guarded and secured before the flight. He was also quick to push the responsibility for guarding the aircraft into my shoes, although he should have known that such tasks were the responsibility of the station commander. Fortunately the judge-advocate was on my side from the start, otherwise this business could have had some unpleasant consequences for me. The judge immediately declared his suspicions that the engineer had been given strict instructions to 'find' evidence of sabotage, that would have made it easier to overcome the sensitive political aspects of this case.

The subsequent interrogations and investigations went on for days. Total strangers of all ranks and arms of services kept coming and going until we almost lost track of what was happening.

The result of all this activity was a 'preliminary report of investigation' which stated among other things that the cause of this crash could not be determined with any certainty and that, 'for the time being', no direct guilt could be proved against me, the officer responsible for the aircraft.

In between we took part in the solemn funeral which in view of the prominent dead had to take place with all then still possible pomp and ceremony. Despite the pressures of my other duties I had to take charge of all this as well, and also make the funeral speech 'on account of my competence'.

There was another epilogue to this tragedy when for quite a few days afterwards local people would bring in bundles and loose amounts of paper currency of various denominations which they had found in the area. Part of the cargo carried by the fated B-17, these banknotes had been scattered far and wide by the winds, and possibly the heat and flames as well. We took charge of this foreign currency, and in the end burned it together with all other documents.

The official investigation was one thing, but we ourselves were also puzzled as to the actual cause of this crash. The first pilot was a particularly experienced *Oberfeldwebel*, a former civilian test pilot. He had a lot of experience on four-engined American aircraft and therefore could not possibly be blamed for this disaster. There was also nothing wrong with the engines, as attested by many eye-witnesses. Although the night was very dark, one could not blame the weather either. It was calm, with good 'fire visibility', as we used to say. We could only make guesses, no more. In the event, the cause of this fatal crash was never established.

On 7 April 1945 we were forced to move again: the advancing American and French troops were fast closing in on Stuttgart.

By that time one could no longer rely on the daily High Command reports on the radio. To be informed about the situation it was far better to ask the more or less orderly retreating troops of German soldiers who now started filling the roads in increasing numbers. But where could we go? In the whole of southern Germany there did not seem to be a single reasonably large airfield left that would accommodate us with our big aircraft. Wherever I tried I was brusquely turned down by pointing out that they were already overcrowded, or that the airfield was no longer usable because of enemy action, or because there was no fuel left, or for a thousand other reasons they were just not suitable to accommodate an operational unit such as Detachment *Olga*.

To avoid falling into American or French hands at Echterdingen I quickly ordered all to prepare for a move to Fürstenfeldbruck near Munich. I knew that at least the runway there was still in order.

Once again we were faced with the problem of how to move our quite extensive technical and other material by road transport to Bavaria. All we had on hand were three medium lorries of which two had been converted to consumer gas. This meant that they could only carry light loads, otherwise they would not be able to negotiate the rather steep roads of the Swabian mountains. Our remaining PAG containers alone took up the available load space, but what of the rest, the technical and office equipment, radio installations, tools, parachutes and all the other paraphernalia? It was obvious that we would have to make several trips on consecutive nights to avoid being shot up by Allied fighter-bombers.

Even so, we could only take the most essential items and had to leave everything else behind. This led to the grotesque situation when no military or other official establishment at Echterdingen would accept responsibility for storing this in part quite valuable (and under any other circumstances most desirable) equipment. There was nothing for it but to pile everything into a big heap in a half-destroyed hangar – it must have been at least two wagon loads – and be on our way. What a situation!

Quite by chance we then got to know that somewhere at the Daimler-Benz works in Untertürkheim there were two brand-new lorries 'superintended' by some military department or other. In a quick action under the cover of darkness our efficient workshop chief with a few volunteers managed to 'organise' a beautiful 7-tonner complete with a new trailer, and things began to look up. We had plenty of diesel fuel on the airfield and thus the transport problem was solved to some extent. After all, the complete ground personnel too had to be moved, and nobody could tell how far, where and how often the railways were still operating.

When everything was ready for our departure and I was just about to report accordingly to the station commander, a frankly macabre episode took place. An elegant BMW sports car pulled up outside the office, and an athletic-looking general climbed out, followed by a remarkable female companion dressed in an extravagant fur coat. He introduced himself as 'General for Evacuation and Destruction', something we had never heard of before. After a quick look around he found everything 'prepared in the best possible way', only 'the air was a bit dry', to which the upright station commander replied apologetically that he could only oblige with a small *Schnapps*, which was graciously accepted. A few minutes later the uniformed gentleman with his lady companion was gone, only her perfume still lingered for a while in the room.

The station commander, an *Oberst*, shook his head and looked at me silently. We were both speechless.

In a streaming rain I then climbed into my trusty Ju 188 where the rest of the crew were already waiting impatiently, as well as the leading mechanic and a few of his technicians who were to leave the place last and follow in my car.

'Fortunately the weather is foul,' I commented, 'otherwise we would have to fly at night – and I am certain that nobody at Fürstenfeldbruck would bother to switch on the airfield lighting.'

After becoming airborne and even before we had reached the airfield boundary the aircraft was enveloped in streaky clouds and underneath everything turned dark, almost black. We had to fly blind, climbing all the while to reach a safe altitude for crossing the nearby mountains of the Schwäbischen Alb. Soon, the rain turned into snow, announced by that characteristic hissing sound one only gets when flying into snow. I switched on the de-icing installation – better safe than sorry!

We all kept busy trying to forget that we were now flying towards the end of the war and an uncertain fate, but it was not easy.

The seconds were ticking away on the stopwatch in the control column horn. Except for that and the compass there were no other navigational aids for us any more, it was all dead reckoning. After the previously estimated time had elapsed I had to start carefully feeling my way downwards, keeping an eye on the radio altimeter all the while. Assuming the wind direction and strength on which we had based our calculations had been correct, we had to get a glimpse of the ground a few kilometres from our destination.

For a short while my thoughts were with the other crews who had taken off before me. I hoped that they had managed to get down alright under these conditions, and that some mad Flak commander had not gone completely berserk and shot at our aircraft while they were approaching to land. It would not have been the first time.

We tightened our harnesses. The engines were throttled back, radiator gills closed, supplementary fuel pumps switched on and the propeller pitch changed – we were ready.

I went into a flat sinking flight and kept a very close check on the airspeed, otherwise all our calculations would have been in vain. The airspeed indicator needle hovered around the 236 mph mark and then underneath everything became darker, a certain sign that we were getting closer to the ground. The snow was as thick as before – keep looking – there! Our first sight of the ground! We were flying through scattered clouds just 160 ft above it, but the snow was so bad that we could hardly see anything ahead of us. Then suddenly we were over a railway line, some parked aircraft – the airfield. We had made it by our own devices.

I pulled a tight turn close to the ground and touched down immediately the green signal lamps showed me that the wheels were locked down. In one corner of the airfield I recognized the dark shapes of my two B-17s and taxied over that way. We had hardly climbed down when we were surrounded by our crews who made it clear that all hell had broken loose here. I was to appear before 'the General' right away.

I had expected something like that and shrugged my shoulders: 'He cannot do any more than chase us away again!' – And even that only if he knows of another airfield that could take us and would be suitable for us to continue our operations, I thought.

While waiting outside his office for my 'summons' I checked once more that I had the red piece of paper on me which attested to the fact that I was engaged in carrying out secret and urgent tasks and requested all military and Party authorities to give me all the necessary assistance.

The general was quite young, but with grey hair. The Knights Cross around his neck he had probably earned himself, at least he gave that impression. And then I recognised him. During the long wartime years we had met several times on different airfields. He was a fighter pilot, and I was a bomber man. And so the expected thunderclap did not materialise.

"That's all I need! . . . And you can take that red scrap of paper with your 'urgency' bit and rub it into your hair if you like. At least, as long as you are here.'

I had to explain to him how and why we had left Echterdingen, pointing out that it was only a matter of days before the airfield was occupied by the enemy.

'Have you still got some fuel in your machines?'

'Yes, some.'

'Well, then see that you disappear from here as quickly as you can. I cannot help you any more than that. Perhaps you could move to Oberpfaffenhofen. Granted, it is the Dornier works airfield, but perhaps your red paper will help you there."

And I was free to go. Naturally, Oberpfaffenhofen wanted to avoid taking us in, just like all the other airfields had done before that, but in the end I managed to get landing permission by referring to KG 200, that still seemed to pull some weight.

It did not take long to have our machines ready for take-off again and after only a few minutes of low-level flying we touched down on the concrete runway at Oberpfaffenhofen.

It was impossible to notify the *Geschwader* staff in Berlin regarding our new base, there were no communication lines any more. Once again, we were left to our own devices and had to make the best of this situation. It did not seem that we would be carrying out any more operational flights because, apart from everything else, it was doubtful if our 'baggage train' of agents would now find us at all. That being so, we taxied our aircraft into safety as far as possible outside the airfield perimeter and moved ourselves into some barracks nearby. *Lt* Schiessl with the lorry caught us up next morning and we could establish ourselves more properly.

Soon afterwards, and quite by chance, I discovered that the KG 200 staff had managed to get out of Berlin at the last minute and were now settled near the airfield at Holzkirchen. This was a heaven-sent opportunity to arrange for an official order that would regulate the future fate of Detachment *Olga*. After all, seeing that we no longer could fly operationally it was obvious that there was no justification for us to remain as a unit in the present form. I had to act quickly, and fate stepped in to help me.

In a wood near the airfield my men had come across a seemingly abandoned but airworthy Fi 156 Storch, which I now took over without bothering to find out who the rightful owners were. I felt fully justified in so doing. I had to get to the *Geschwader* staff as quickly as possible, and I could no longer make it by car. The roads were full of retreating troops and my vehicle would most probably have been 'impounded' by some general who was on his way on foot to the imaginary 'Alpine Redoubt'.

In short, it had to be an aircraft. The only problem was that I did not know Holzkirchen and knew only approximately where it was. But it had to be done.

When the evening dusk began to blur the shadows, my men quietly prepared the Storch for its nocturnal flight. We made sure that nobody would notice anything. While some men remained with our commandeered machine, others pumped enough fuel from our own aircraft to fill up the fuel tanks of the Storch to the brim.

I did not dare to taxi the Storch the long way from the clearing to the big Oberpfaffenhofen runway, the noise would have attracted some attention. The take-off had to be from where it stood. To complicate matters, that very evening I was invited to meet the airfield commander, but managed to take my leave as quickly and as politely as possible.

Although I was familiar with the Storch from some harmless 'fine weather' flights, this experience was not enough for me to know how pilot and aircraft would respond when faced with a more difficult situation such as take-off from a meadow surrounded by tall trees, followed by a flight at night assisted by rather meagre instrumentation, search in darkness for an unknown airfield – which would certainly also be camouflaged – and possibly a night landing on some field I had assumed to be the airfield.

My observer climbed with me into the unfamiliar cabin and we quickly settled in our places. The necessary maps, torches and notes for our stealthy flight we had stowed into our knee pockets. Fortunately the night was clear, although the moon had not risen yet.

In addition to the usual flight instruments the Storch was only equipped with a rather primitive turn-and-bank indicator and a small emergency compass for flights in bad visibility – and here I was, preparing for a proper night ride.

Before I started the small 250 hp engine however I first had to 'search and find' all the levers, switch buttons and instruments again so that I would know instinctively where they were.

The machine was parked at the far end of the glade. The engine had been run warm, all the instruments were functioning as they should, and I was ready. At the other end of the forest clearing we had posted a soldier with a torch who was to indicate the direction. Right, here goes!

I gave a brief signal with my landing searchlight and the torch was lit up the other end. Full throttle, let go of the wheel brakes, and we were on our way.

Not being so familiar with the aircraft I had to wait and see how the Storch would behave so that I could react accordingly. As a pilot of bigger aircraft, one always felt somehow helpless in a smaller and less familiar machine because there seemed so little one could do to control it. Once you have given full throttle, all you could really do was to wait and see if the take-off would be what you expected it to be.

And so my Storch was stumbling forwards, gaining speed. Ahead I could see some tall pine trees, but could not tell how far away they were. Our stumbling run seemed endless until suddenly the knocks in the wheels became less noticeable and I could feel that we were airborne. I looked for the airspeed indicator but could not find it right away on the unfamiliar instrument panel. To be on the safe side, I dipped the nose a bit to gain more speed and then, 'by feel', gradually pulled the control column towards me until I could see the stars in the night sky.

I was quite pleased about the primitive turn-and-bank indicator, without which I would not have been able to keep the aircraft straight and level. There is nothing like some solid blind flying experience to back you up in cases like this!

Once I had gained a bit of altitude I turned towards the northern end of the Starnberger lake. The night was still dark, although the rising moon already announced its arrival with a lighter streak on the eastern horizon. I could see the lake quite clearly and needed only a minor correction to turn us towards Holzkirchen. The stopwatch was ticking away while we kept a sharp lookout for the *Autobahn* which made a distinct sharp bend near Holzkirchen. The airfield was due west from there – if we could find it in the darkness.

Our nerves were really tense during this nocturnal flight with the small unfamiliar single-engined aircraft. Finally, after about 20 minutes, I spotted an open space on the ground. During my first pass I switched on our small landing searchlight to have a closer look – the field seemed free of obstacles and – hopefully – also level, so that it would have to do. I made another turn, throttled the engine and began my landing approach in the spooky moonlight. Slower, still slower, landing flaps full out until the aircraft was literally 'hanging on its propeller' – and then we were down. The long shock-absorber legs of the Storch bent softly at the knees and I braked so hard that we nearly stood on our nose. It would have been silly to keep on rolling somewhere in the darkness. As soon as we stopped I let the engine howl up a couple of times to attract the attention of possible listeners and then switched off. Everything was dead quiet. We were just about to climb out to search on foot when my observer drew my attention to a small green light flashing in the distance away to our left.

The man behind the flashing light turned out to be an *Obergefreiter* (Senior lance corporal) from the Holzkirchen flight control and spoke to us in plain soldier's language – our officers uniforms were not recognizable under the flying suits:

'Are you crazy? What do you want here in the middle of the night?' –

174

but everything was quickly sorted out. He then led us to a barrack which housed the airfield flight control where he was on night duty all by himself. Unfortunately the good man could not help us regarding the whereabouts of KG 200 headquarters, he simply had no idea. After prolonged enquiries we found out that during the last few days a tented camp had been set up on a wooded hill a few kilometres south of here, and that it 'simply teemed with Luftwaffe people'.

Next morning – it was 27 April, 1945 – at about 0530 hrs with the first light of dawn we climbed back into our Storch to search for this camp from the air. Hardly ten minutes later we had spotted the badly camouflaged tents and set down our stalky bird on a meadow near some woods.

Apparently nobody had noticed our arrival, but after a short while somebody came along and we found out that the entire KG 200 headquarters staff had indeed hidden themselves here among these tents. We also heard that the CO himself, Werner Baumbach, had remained in Berlin and that a *Major* von Harnier had been authorised to represent him.

We were then led into his tent.

'Man alive, Pietro, where in the world do you come from?'

We had known each other since the beginning of the war, and later on Adolf von Harnier had been my CO during some particularly hard months in Sicily and Sardinia. The two of us now belonged to the handful of survivors from KG 30 who had been in action on the nastiest fronts without a break since the beginning of hostilities. Probably no other friendship could be tighter welded than one that had grown together under such demanding circumstances.

He pulled me into his tent which he shared with two other officers.

'Breakfast will follow later – but for now let's crack my last good bottle which I had actually saved for the final victory!'

I then had to tell him what had happened to *Olga*. Apparently the last that our *Geschwader* knew about us was the B-17 crash at Echterdingen. They had been greatly worried about our detachment, but had been unable to help in any way. Also, since 25 April the *Geschwader* had been officially disbanded in all its forms, and looking at things from that point of view he no longer had any power of authority over me. It follows that nobody could order Detachment *Olga* to disband either – it was entirely up to us.

Now that I had been briefed on the situation we agreed that I should bring my men over here as quickly as possible so that we could await the inevitable end together.

I was already leaving when Adolf von Harnier called me back again:
'Have you still got juice in your aircraft?'

'Of course I have – thousands of litres in fact!'

'Well, we urgently need some juice here. We happen to have a large number of cars but nothing in their tanks. And we reckon that we might have a small chance when we have finally been collared by the Americans that they might let us drive home in our own cars, sporty and fair as they are!' – He was indeed an optimist!

I must admit it was not an easy decision to order another transfer for our aircraft simply because of the fuel in their tanks. The day promised to have a clear sky, and that meant total domination of the air space by the American fighters. The only time we could feel reasonably safe in the air with our 'big bluebottles' was after the 'knocking-off time', during those few minutes between the evening dusk and nightfall. Despite this I promised to try and bring my aircraft to Holzkirchen, provided the grass airfield there was suitable for landing our big machines.

That sorted out, I flew back my Storch to Oberpfaffenhofen, hedge-hopping all the way, landing in the same remote woodland glade. Nobody seemed to have even noticed that the Storch had been in the air.

After briefing the assembled personnel of *Olga* about the situation, I told them that there was a chance to await the arrival of the American forces together with the *Geschwader* headquarters personnel at Holzkirchen, and then to try somehow to avoid captivity. Any operational activities or continuation of hostilities had now become meaningless.

Then we all got down to making the necessary preparations for our final move to the woods south of Holzkirchen. It took us two days to acquire by already proven means the tents, equipment, provisions and money – and also some civilian clothing.

On 29 April everything was ready. At dawn, before the American low-level fighter-bombers were in the air, our big aircraft took off for the last short hop to Holzkirchen. I followed them in my Storch. Once on the ground, we immediately took care of our faithful machines and before the first Americans had appeared in the sky over Holzkirchen they were all hidden among the trees and carefully camouflaged. We had achieved our objective without enemy interference and could now pump all spare fuel from our aircraft and transfer it as quickly as possible to the fuel tanks of the various KG 200 vehicles, and we also stored some of it in safe hiding places.

Afterwards, we found billets in the villages and scattered farms in the vicinity of the woodland camp. The people who put us up were all ordinary farmers and looked after us as well as they could under the circumstances. They did more than that, they also advised us how best to prepare hideouts in the forest, if need be.

In the evenings, we met in smaller or larger groups to discuss our plans for the immediate future, how best to avoid captivity, and how we might manage to reach our homes again in the inevitable turmoil. It was a tragic and yet uplifting time when true comradeship proved its meaning. We exchanged addresses and offered to help each other, not knowing how we would fare ourselves:

'If you cannot get any further, here is where you can find me!'

It was of course much harder for those of our comrades who came from the eastern areas: we had all read reports about the inhuman excesses of the Soviets. Now suddenly these men were homeless and most of them did not have any news of their families either. It was indeed a very trying time for us all.

All our surplus equipment we gave away to the local farmers, including several hundred parachutes – which, despite their grey-green camouflage patterns, were in great demand as material for silken underwear and other things. Then there were all kinds of tools, a small crane, various other odds and ends – in fact, the complete technical equipment of a flying unit.

We knew it would be put to good use.

14. The End

In those final days our thoughts went out to our other comrades of KG 200. Where were they now? What would be their fate?

It was only later that we found out what had happened, although many details were lost forever.

Thus, II/KG 200 at Burg near Magdeburg had to transfer all its airworthy machines – the 'illuminators' of 5./KG 200 – to I/KG 66. The 50 *Mistels* they had at Burg could no longer be flown out and remained there, while the flying and ground personnel were impressed for ground defence duties near the base.

III/KG 200(BT), the bomb-torpedo unit, was subordinated operationally to Luftflotte Reich, but was fated never to be fully organised or equipped.

Einsatzkommando 200(FK) (Operational Detachment/glide bombs) with nine He 111s and one Do 217 remained with *Gefechtsverband Helbig* which embraced all Luftwaffe formations used against bridges: *Stab* and II/LG 1. KG(J) 30, remainder of II/KG 200, *Einsatzkommando* 200(FK), II/KG 4 and I/KG 66.

3./KG 200 with its considerable transport capacity was based at Rügen and then on Baumbach's orders concentrated at Flensburg. The giant BV 222 flying boats were also based there, and were being prepared to fly out 'a large group of people' – obviously meaning government high-ups – to some hidden spot near the coast of Greenland. Once there, and completely cut off from everything, it would have been possible to survive for quite some time and then somehow try to attempt to 'come back to life' undisturbed. At least, that is what they intended. It was an adventurous plan that reveals more boy scout imagination than common sense, and was never carried out.

Then there is the question of Werner Baumbach, the last commander of KG 200, and his role in all this.

At the end of April 1945 he was still supposed to have been appointed *Chef der Regierungsstaffel* (Commander of Government Flight), whatever that may mean. It is possible that Baumbach had accepted this post to have the freedom of movement which seemed necessary to him in that critical phase.

It is known that quite a few higher Luftwaffe command staffs were unable to get hold of Baumbach in those days, as shown for example by a note on a report by *2.Abteilung des Generalstabs der Luftwaffe* (2nd Section/Luftwaffe General Staff) dated 17 April 1945 (*see* facsimile reproduction in Appendix No 10). The reproachful tone of this note is probably unjustified because at that time Baumbach was travelling a lot on service matters, even if they only concerned KG 200 marginally. After all, he knew that the primary task, the destruction of the Oder bridges, was in good hands with *Oberst* Helbig.

Baumbach did not hide either, although the collapse of most means of communications made everything worse. And he certainly was not cowardly. In those last weeks, together with his friend Albert Speer, the Reich Minister of Armaments, he had attempted to use his influence behind the scenes to prevent further senseless destruction. One also has to remember that he did that in the then hyperneurotic atmosphere when such actions could easily have had the most unpleasant consequences. We can also read some of this in Baumbach's own book *Zu spät?* (English title: *Broken Swastika*, London 1960).

In April 1945, 1./KG 200 consisted of Detachment *Olga* and several smaller detachments in Austria. One of these, transferred to Hörsching near Linz, was commanded by *Hptm* Braun. In the last few days of April *Hptm* Braun suddenly received a visit from *Major i.G.* (General Staff) Bellmann who brought him secret oral instructions to prepare for a flight to Spain, where the aircraft and its crew would remain after fulfilling their task. Their passengers would consist of a group of ex-Vichy French VIPs from their government in exile who had until recently domiciled in the Hohenzollern town of Sigmaringen in Württemberg and now in view of the German collapse wanted to avoid falling into the hands of the victors. This highly secret oral instruction to *Hptm* Braun has been set down in a written protocol that was also formulated to serve as an official Flight Order (*see* facsimile reproduction in Appendix No 12).

Dated 30 April 1945, this document states that *Hptm* Braun and his 10 men crew are ordered to fly the Ju 290 identity markings PJ + PS carrying a certain group of persons to Barcelona as soon as the weather conditions permitted. If it was impossible to make the return flight and the crew had to be interned in Spain, *Hptm* Braun had to report this to the German air attache in Madrid. The aircraft would

179

then be offered for sale to the Spanish.

This is followed by an instruction that all (interned) soldiers were still bound by the military regulations, and a specific reminder that they were all under an obligation to preserve the strictest secrecy. This specific obligation had to be attested by *Hptm* Braun with his signature.

It is of interest to note that even in those circumstances specific instructions were attached to this document to the effect that 'No attempt should be made to respray the aircraft or use some kind of camouflage. The crew had to fly in ordinary uniform as on an operational flight.' (*see* facsimile reproduction in Appendix No 13).

As it happened, this flight never took place: the French VIPs got stuck somewhere in the chaotic traffic on the roads and never arrived in Hörsching.

On the other hand, during the confusion of the last few days of the hostilities this written secret Flight Order became practically a 'letter of safe conduct' to *Hptm* Braun and protected him from being ordered to carry out other senseless flights.

Near the end he was then forced to move with his big Ju 290 once more and came via Königgrätz to Munich, where he landed on the last day of the war.

While in Königgrätz *Hptm* Braun met *GenOberst* von Greim who, in his capacity as commander of *Luftflotte* 6, asked Braun to see his flight orders and was shown the precious 'letter of safe conduct'. When von Greim heard why Braun still had not flown to Spain and safety, he immediately cancelled the original order and gave *Hptm* Braun his permission to 'fly to Spain even without the French government'.

However, *Hptm* Braun preferred to help 70 German soldiers by flying them home to Germany, where they all landed in American captivity in Munich.

For us at *Olga* these last few days before the sudden total collapse were most depressing and full of worries about our relatives at home and the immediate future.

I had parked my Storch next to the farmhouse which was my last billet. On the other side of the meadow was a highway leading to the Tegern lake and the mountains. Day and night, this highway was filled with an uninterrupted mass of soldiers moving jerkily like a giant worm southwards. It was an army in flight, on foot, and in a motley collection of vehicles, a depressing sight.

All kinds of rumours were flying about, the most common one being the same old hoary tale about 'secret talks with the Western Allies' that would lead to an armistice and eventual common front against the Soviets, the true enemies of Europe with their plans for world revolution. And so on. What amazed me was that there were quite a few people around in those days who clung to this fantasy and were prepared and willing to start all over again to chase the Bolsheviks out of their homeland.

However, things happened quicker than we we had expected. To be better informed about the situation I would make a daily early morning 'scouting flight' with my Storch in northerly direction to see how far the Americans had advanced. Even in daytime, the weather was on my side because the clouds were so low that no American fighter pilot would risk being in the air. On the other hand, bad visibility, low clouds and hefty downpours were no problem for the Storch.

My usual route was close to the highway. Whenever possible, I would then land and ask the retreating troops about the situation. The results of my 'scouting trips' clearly indicated that it would not be very long before Holzkirchen too was in the hands of the victors.

My flight that particular morning also had another reason: together with *Oberfeldwebel* Freiburg I wanted to make one last landing on the airfield to check if all our aircraft had been prepared for destruction by explosive charges as planned.

Using our trusty manual pump we filled the fuel tanks of our Storch to the brim. The weather was miserable, and thus ideal for my purpose, and after the usual pre-flight checks we were off once more.

It turned out to be quite a day. Already while banking towards the airfield it seemed rather odd that I could not detect any sign of activity on the ground. That should have warned me, but I soared on towards our parked aircraft and touched down nearby. However, an instinctive precaution made me leave the engine running, and that saved us. Hardly had my *Oberfeldwebel* put his feet on the ground when there was a bang and rattle, and a whole spider's web of tracer appeared over our aircraft. Next instant, I could also hear the first hits slapping into our machine. Fortunately the shooting was wild and wide off the mark, perhaps because of the weather or distance. Be as it may, I immediately made up my mind to get out of the place, shooting or not, and waved to my companion to jump back in. He seemed to hesitate a moment, but then was back in his seat behind my back with one jump.

At the same time I rammed the throttle lever forward and took off.

As the shooting grew in intensity from all directions, I made a steep climbing turn to starboard into the low clouds accompanied by another series of hits rattling into the Storch. After crossing the south-easterly airfield boundary I was over the *Autobahn*, and there I saw the first American troops – a stationary mile-long column of vehicles and tanks with large white stars on their roofs and turrets.

Just as I thought I had managed to get away unscathed from the trigger-happy Americans on the airfield I was greeted by another sudden hail of fire from the *Autobahn*! Fortunately the shooting here was even more desultory and wild. Nevertheless, a light plywood and fabric aircraft has not got much going for it against bullets and I had no interest in finding out how much it could take. However, I resisted the temptation to pull into the clouds and instead tried to sneak away in low-level flight between the gunners on the airfield and their pals on the *Autobahn*.

The shooting stopped just as suddenly as it had started as we made ourselves scarce by literally jumping over the hedges, and finally returned to our meadow by a roundabout route. Forty minutes after take-off we were back on the ground again; our Storch displayed more than two dozen bullet holes.

What had happened was that contrary to their usual habits the Americans had made a big jump forward during the past twelve hours and had just reached the airfield when I unsuspectingly landed right in front of them like a welcome practice target.

We knew then that our hours as German soldiers were numbered. The first batch of men took leave soon afterwards to try to avoid captivity according to previously worked out plans. Our measures for this moment had included the preparation of 'original' discharge papers for Members of the Armed Forces (Luftwaffe), copied on a duplicator according to a pattern document supplied by our office. Furnished with an official *Ersatz-Heimat-Flak Abt.* (Reserve Home Defence AA detachment) stamp, all these discharge papers were signed by me personally. Every man from our detachment was issued with these documents, plus a sack of durable provisions, a final service pay of RM 87, and most of them also with a bicycle.

Each one of them took leave of me personally, and we shook hands for the last time. It was a very touching moment and some men I had least expected to had tears in their eyes.

And that is how Detachment *Olga* of KG 200 was disbanded and how we parted and went our own ways. Some who had a place to go to, to their homes. Others remained with the local farmers, or moved further on.

I had some luck on the way and managed to reach my parents' house as soon as 12 May.

In the meantime *Hptm* Braun and his crew had been dressed up in a kind of fantasy uniform and engaged in ferrying different German aircraft, which the Americans wanted to take back home for more thorough examination, from Germany to various airfields in France. One of these aircraft was his own Ju 290, and at Orly near Paris he also had to instruct an American crew to fly it. After that he was allowed to return home as probably the last active pilot of the Luftwaffe.

As has been mentioned previously, as soon as the war was over the Allies, and particularly the Americans, mounted an extensive and specific search action for former members of this – in their opinion – 'ominous secret *Geschwader*'.

Most probably this was done for two principal reasons: it was hoped to find some war criminals and unearth information about vanished Nazi 'bigwigs' who were assumed to have been taken to 'safety', and gather details about the activities of the German secret service.

These intentions were never fulfilled. There were no war criminals in the *Geschwader*, and not a single KG 200 aircraft had 'vanished' during the last days of hostilities – in fact, the entire KG 200 aircraft park had fallen into Allied hands. And it was also quite impossible to satisfy their curiosity regarding the German secret service – the KG 200 personnel were not privy to intelligence organisations.

The fact that not a single former member of KG 200 has ever been accused of any specific misdeed, never mind prosecuted, speaks for itself.

The results of Allied endeavours to clear up this business of 'Hitler's Spy *Geschwader*' must have been so disappointing that nobody dared to reveal the details publicly. And so the legend lives on and feeds the fantasy of film script writers and novelists.

The author's intention has been to show what really happened, and not necessarily what could have happened. Of course there are bound to be some 'know-alls' who, without having experienced anything themselves, would nevertheless readily point out from the present point of view that the airmen and soldiers at that time should have thought, done, or let things happen differently than they did. As if it was possible to change history!

But what can one do to prevent that?

Epilogue and Acknowledgements

The incentive to start compiling this work was provided by my own reminiscences of experiences while serving with KG 200, notes in diaries, logbooks and other documents. However, it took years of often fruitless research in German and foreign archives and countless conversations with former comrades to enable me to present, with the help of recounted facts and events, an overall impression of this in every way exceptional flying formation.

By selecting the information used in this book I have limited myself to what seemed to be historically established and at the same time typical of what had in fact taken place. Any attempt to present the complete history of KG 200, a unit still exuding the aroma of secrecy, would founder for the simple fact that apparently most of the documentary evidence was carefully destroyed or otherwise lost at the end of hostilities. For that reason the author would be most grateful for any help, and hopes that this book will result in a wide response from readers in the way of criticism, documents, photographs and reminiscences.

I should like to thank the *Herren* Noack and Dr Haupt of the *Bundesarchiv* in Freiburg and Koblenz who have generously made it possible for me to search for, and evaluate documents and photographs from the largely still unsorted material entrusted to their keeping. An especial thanks is due to my friend and comrade Eckard Dittmann for his lively description of his own experiences, likewise to *Oberst* (Rtd) Heinz Braun, who willingly provided extensive and valuable information from his own personal recollections.

From the many people I have met and talked to and exchanged correspondence with in the course of my research I would like to mention in particular the following: Alfred Oppermann, *Oberst* (Rtd) A. Koch, *Oberstleutnant* (Rtd) Wilhelm Kuschke, *Oberstleutnant* von Pechmann, Major Hanno Valtonen in Finland, Theo Prein, Karl Kössler, Oskar Rumler, General Wolfgang Kessler, Egon Blohm and *Oberst* (Rtd) Kurt Randl-Semper.

For some of the pictorial and documentary material used in this book I am indebted to the *Bundesarchiv* in Freiburg and Koblenz; the

Imperial War Museum, London; Egon Blohm; Karl Rauchfuss; Pilot Press Ltd, Bromley, Kent; Terushi Jimbo in Japan; and *Oberst* (Rtd) Franz Kirsch. The rest of the material is from my own personal collection.

Last but not least I would like to thank *Herr* Wolfgang Schilling of Motorbuch-Verlag, Stuttgart, who initiated this book.

Appendices

Der Reichsmarschall des Großdeutschen Reiches
und Oberbefehlshaber der Luftwaffe
(Genst.Gen.Qu.2.Abt.)

Az. 11 b 16.10 Nr. 13 820/44 g.Kdos. (IIB)

H.Qu., den 12.11.44

90 Ausfertigungen
16.Ausfert...

Betr.: Umgliederung von Kampfverbänden auf Jagdflieger-Stärken.

1.) Mit sofortiger Wirkung werden folgende Kampfverbände auf Jagdflieger-Stärken umgerüstet und auf Jagdflieger-Stärken umgegliedert:

Gen.Kdo.IX.Fl.Korps

Stab Kampfgeschwader 6
Ln.Komp.(mot)/K.G.6
I./Kampfgeschwader 6
mit allen unterstellten Einheiten
II./Kampfgeschwader 6
mit allen unterstellten Einheiten
III./Kampfgeschwader 6
mit allen unterstellten Einheiten

Stab Kampfgeschwader 27 "Boelcke"
Ln.Komp.(mot)/K.G.27 "Boelcke"
I./Kampfgeschwader 27 "Boelcke"
mit allen unterstellten Einheiten
II./Kampfgeschwader 27 "Boelcke"
mit allen unterstellten Einheiten
III./Kampfgeschwader 27 "Boelcke"
mit allen unterstellten Einheiten

Stab Kampfgeschwader 30
Ln.Komp.(mot)/K.G.30
I./Kampfgeschwader 30
mit allen unterstellten Einheiten
II./Kampfgeschwader 30
mit allen unterstellten Einheiten

Stab Kampfgeschwader 55
Ln.Komp.(mot)/K.G.55
I./Kampfgeschwader 55
mit allen unterstellten Einheiten
II./Kampfgeschwader 55
mit allen unterstellten Einheiten
III./Kampfgeschwader 55
mit allen unterstellten Einheiten

- 2 -

Die umgerüsteten und umgegliederten Verbände erhalten zusätzlich zu ihrer bisherigen Bezeichnung die Kennzeichnung

"J"

z.B. "Gen.Kdo.IX.(J)Fl.Korps"
"Stab Kampfgeschwader (J) 6"
bzw. "I./Kampfgeschwader (J) 6"

2.) Im Zuge der Umrüstung und Umgliederung werden
a) aufgelöst:
IV./Kampfgeschwader 6 mit allen unterstellten Einheiten
IV./Kampfgeschwader 27 mit allen unterstellten Einheiten
IV./Kampfgeschwader 30 mit allen unterstellten Einheiten
IV./Kampfgeschwader 55 mit allen unterstellten Einheiten

b) aufgestellt:

III./Kampfgeschwader (J) 30
mit F.B.K.(mot)
und 9.-11.Staffel

Erg.-Kampfgruppe (J)
mit F.B.K.(mot)
und 1.-4.Staffel

3.) Die Umgliederung der F.B.K.(mot) der Kampfgruppen auf Stärken der Stabskompanien der Jagdgruppen wird zunächst zurückgestellt. Bis dahin sind die F.B.K.(mot) der Kampfgruppen (J) entsprechend ihrer neuen Aufgabe (Wartung von Jagdflugzeugmustern) umzurüsten. Entsprechender Befehl ergeht durch Chefing.d.Lw. im Benehmen mit Genst.Gen.Qu.2.Abt.

4.) Durchführung durch Lfl.Kdo. Reich im Einvernehmen mit Gen.d. Kampfflieger und Gen.d.Jagdflieger.

5.) Als K.St.N. galten:
für Gen.Kdo.IX.(J)Fl.Korps   K.St.N. gem.OKL.Genst.Gen.Qu. Nr.16195/44 g (2.Abt.) v.25.5.44 (IIA)

Stab eines Kampfgeschwaders(J)	K.St.N. 1131 (L)
Ln.Zug.(mot) eines K.G.(J)	K.St.N. 3561 (L)
Ln.Zug I.-III.Gr. eines K.G. (J)	K.St.N. 1192 a
Stab einer Kampfgruppe (J)	K.St.N. 1132 (L)
F.B.K.(mot) einer K.Gr. (J)	K.St.N. 1336 (L)
Kampfstaffel (J)	K.St.N. 1134 (L)
Stab einer Erg.K.Gr. (J)	K.St.N. 1442 (L)
Erg.Kampfstaffel (J)	K.St.N. 1444 (L)

-3-

188

- 3 -

6.) Personal und Material der gem. unter 1 umgegliederten Einheiten sind - soweit geeignet - in die Kampfeinheiten (J) zu übernehmen.

Personal und Material der gem. Ziffer 2a aufgelöst. Einheiten sind zur Aufstellung der III./K.G.(J) 30 und Erg-Kampfgruppe (J) (eine Erg.-Staffel je K.G.(J)) und zur Deckung von Fehlstellen der gem. Ziffer 1 umgegliederten Einheiten zu verwenden.

Personal und Material der F.B.K.(mot) können auf Planstellen der Kampfstaffeln (J) übernommen werden.
Auffüllung der F.B.K.(mot) erfolgt jedoch nicht.

7.) Neuzuweisung von Personal erfolgt nicht.
Erforderlicher Austausch von Personal ist durch Gen.Kdo.IX.(J) Fl.Korps umgehend zu melden an:

	Genst.Gen.Qu.6.Abt.
	Lr.?
	Wehrmt II
	Gen.d.Jagdflieger.

8.) Besetzung der Planstellen für Material erfolgt

a) für Flugzeuge:	durch Genst.Gen.Qu.6.Abt.
b) für Schulflugzeuge:	im Rahmen des Möglichen durch Gen.d.Jd.
c) für Gerät:	durch Chef d.Nachschubw.d.Lw. nach Weisung Genst.Gen.Qu.6.Abt.

Zuweisung von Kfz. erfolgt nicht.

9.) a) Für Jagdeinsatz ungeeignete Flugzeugführer stehen mit ihren Besatzungen Gen.d.Kampfflieger für verbleibende Kampfverbände zur Verfügung.

b) Nicht benötigtes sonstiges Personal steht LP bzw. Lw. Wehramt zur Verfügung und ist in die Ersatzluftwaffe zu überführen.

10.) Nicht benötigtes Material steht wie folgt zur Verfügung:

a) Flugzeuge:	G.n.t.Gen.Qu.6.Abt.
b) Schulflugzeuge:	Chef d.Kraftfahrw.d.Lw.
c) Gerät:	Chef d.Nachschubw.d.Lw.

11.) Zur Umrüstung und Umschulung verlegt Gen.Kdo.IX.(J)Fl.Korps mit seinen nicht im aktiven Einsatz stehenden Einheiten nach Lfl.Kdo.Reich in den Raum Provinz... - Paderborn.

Vorzusehende Feldplätze sind umgehend durch Lfl.Kdo.Reich nach Festlegung im Benehmen mit Genst.Gen.Qu./Abt.Lw.Bodenorg. an Lw.Führungsstab (Io) zu melden.

12.) Reihenfolge der Umrüstung wird gesondert befohlen. Entsprechender Vorschlag ist umgehend durch Gen.Kdo.IX.(J)Fl.Korps vorzulegen an:

- Lw.Führungsstab (Ia)
- Genst.Gen.Qu.6.Abt.
- Gen.d.Kampfflieger
- Gen.d.Jagdflieger

13.) Lehrpersonal für Umschulung ist durch Gen.d.Jagdfl. im Rahmen des Möglichen auf Anforderung IX.(J)Fl.Korps zu stellen.
Ausbildung der Verbandsführer regelt Gen.d.Jagdflieger.

14.) Flugbetriebsstoffzuteilung für Umschulung erfolgt durch Genst. Gen.Qu.4.Abt.

15.) Es werden unterstellt:

a) Gen.Kdo.IX.(J)Fl.Korps

truppendienstlich:	Lfl.Kdo.Reich
ausbildungsmäßig:	Gen.d.Jagdflieger

b) Verbände gem.Ziffer 1 und III./K.G.(J) 30

in jeder Hinsicht:	Gen.Kdo.IX.(J)Fl.Korps

c) Erg.Kampfgruppe (J)
zunächst unter Gen.Kdo.IX.(J)Fl.Korps.
Endgültige Regelung wird später gesondert befohlen.

16.) An der kriegsgliederungsmäßigen Zugehörigkeit der umgegliederten Einheiten ändert sich nichts.

III./K.G.(J) 30 gehört kriegsgliederungsmäßig zum Lg.Kdo.III
Erg.Kampfgruppe (J) zum Lg.Kdo.VII
Ersatztruppenteile sind durch Lg.Kdo.III bzw. VII festzulegen.

17.) Bezüglich Mobil.Fr., Fp.Nr., Erkennungsmarkenverzeichnis der umgegliederten Einheiten und Abgabe der Akten der aufgelösten Einheiten ist gem. Vfg. OKL.Gen.Qu. Nr.15000/44 geh. (2.Abt. I) vom 11.5.44 zu verfahren.

18.) Stand der Durchführung ist durch Lfl.Kdo.Reich zum 1. und 15.J.M. beginnend am 1.12.44, zu melden an Genst.Gen.Qu.2.Abt.

Verteiler: (nur im Entwurf)

zuständige Dienststellen des OKL
und RdL sowie im beteiligte Lfl.Kdos.
sind kriegsgliederungsmäßig zuständige
Lg.Kdos.

gez. G ö r i n g

F.d.R.

Oberstleutnant i.G.

189

Chef.Sache!
Geheim

Geheime Kommandosache

SSD ROBINSON NR 2161 19.10. (2200) -

GLTD: AN KG 200 - LFL KDO 6 - VO LW 6 CHEF GENST D H

- W FUEST ROEM EINS / KURFUE -

ADJ REICHSMARSCHALL NACHRICHTLICH.
GEHEIME KOMMANDOSACH. CHEFSACHE NUR DURCH OFFIZIER -

BEZUG: LFL KDO 6 ROEM EINS E NR 2412/44 GKDOS=CHEFSACHE
VOM 17.10. - 1.) MIT DURCHFUEHRUNG VERBINDUNGSAUFNAHME
UND-VERSORGUNGSFLUEGE FUER DEUTSCHE KAMPFGRUPPE RAUM
BERESINO WIRD KG 200 BEAUFTRAGT, DAS ENG ZUSAMMENARBE[
MIT LFL 6 UND HEERESGRUPPE MITTE =FLUGZEUGE UND
BETRIEBSSTOFF STELLT LB 200=SONDERZUWEISUNG ERFOLGT NICHT
2.) ZUNAECHST BESTEHEN KAMPFGRUPPE FESTSTELLEN UND
VERBINDUNG LANDEPLAETZE DURCHFUEHREN. DA FUNKSPRUECHE MIT
ERKUNDUNGSOFFIZIERS ERFORDERLICH, BA FUNKSPRUECHE MIT
ALS ABREICHEND SICHERE MELDUNG ANZUSEHEN. -
3.) ABSICHTEN SIND VOR DURCHFUEHRUNG ZU MELDEN=
V- GEZ- K R E I P E, OKL FUEST (ROB IMOGN) NR 1030/44
CHEFSACHE ++
+ 2300UHR FLUK CHEFSACHE OKL FUEST (OB SON) NR 1030/44
GKDOS CHEFS. ERHALTEN WOCH OBLTFLJAG+

Nur durch Offizier
* * * durch * * * *

An   O.K.L - Fl.St. Ia (Robinson)
etwa.:   O-K.L - Fl.St. Io (Rob)
            K.G. 200 Kommodore, Berlin - Gat (nachrichtlich)

Mit Anschriftenübermittlung . . . . .

Bezug: SSD - FS O.K.L.-Fl.St. (Rob.) Nr.6305/44 6.Kdos.

Betr.: Scharnhorn - Aktion

Zum Bezugs- FS meldet LfL Kdo.6 nach Absprache mit
Hstr. Mitte und K.G. 200 Folgendes Bericht

1.) Bei dauager geeigneter erfahrge. Absetzen von 3
    Wehtsche Fühler im Bereich einer leisungs-
    fühige Funkverbindung und als erneute Sicherungs-
    maßnahme

190

Appendices 2 and 3: Action Scherhorn (translations)

Appendix 2

SECRET !

By Officer Only !

One copy

To : O.K.L - Operations Staff Ia (Robinson)*
For consideration : O.K.L. - Operations Staff Ic (Robinson)
K.G 200, Kommodore, Berlin-Gatow (via communication)
Incl transmission of addresses !

Ref : SSD-teleprinter message - Operations Staff (Robinson) No 0303/44 (Secret) of 19 October 1944

Re : Action Scherhorn

In respect of the above teleprinter message Lfl Kdo 6 reports the following intention after consultation with Army Group Centre and KG 200:

1) To set down 3 German (Army) radio operators during the next suitable weather period to establish an efficient radio contact and as a renewed security measure.

2) Two days later to set down a German detachment to reconnoitre a (suitable) landing field (Fähnrich Wild) as well as a Staff Doctor from Army Group Centre for medical care.

3) After successful reported reconnaissance of a suitable landing field by Fähnrich Wild a flight by 4 Ar 232, if possible in the same night, for once-only large-scale supply operation (20 tons) as well as the evacuation of badly wounded and those unable to march.

4) It is intended to supply the returning Combat Group by air on the march back, but no details have been worked out as yet.

5) Lfl Kdo 6 requests permission to carry out the above operation and the requisition of available Ar 232s (minimum 6 a/c) from XIV Fliegerkorps to KG 200.

Luftflottenkommando 6
Chief of the General Staff
(signed) Kless, Oberst (General Matter)
Br.B.No 766/44 Secret Command Matter

* Robinson: cover designation for RM Goring's command train

Appendix 3

Teleprinter message

Stamped: Chef-Sache ! SECRET
Secret Command Matter !
Luftflottenkommando 6

From : + SSD Robinson 012161 of 19.10 (2200 hrs)

To : Luftflottenkommando 6 (Marked recived 19.10.44 2345 hrs)

For consideration : KG 200 - Lfl.Kdo 6 - Liaison Officer Lw B
Chef / General Staff / DH
Luftwaffe Operations Staff Roem One C (Ic)
- Kurfürst
Reichsmarschall's ADC for information

Secret Command Matter - Chefsache - By officer only

Re : Lfl.Kdo Roem One C (Ic) No. 2412/44 Secret Command Matter - Chefsache

1) KG 200 is charged with carrying out (the task of) contacting and supplying (the) German combat group in (the) Berezino area in close collaboration with Lfl Kdo 6 and Army Group Centre. Aircraft and fuel is provided by KG 200. There will be no special allocation.

2) (Before execution) first to establish (the) existence of this battle group and reconnoitre suitable landing places. Return of (the) reconnaissance officer essential because radio messages cannot be considered sufficiently reliable.

3) (All) intended actions to be reported before execution.

Signed for General Kreipe OKL Operations Staff (Robinson) Nr 10303/44 Chefsache +++ 2300 hrs One Chefsache OKL Command Staff (Robinson) Nr 10303/44 Secret Command Matter Chefs. Received (by) Duty Officer Oblt LJAQ +

Handwritten note : According to consultation of 2330 hrs of 21 Oct Gen Kreipe agrees to drop the 'return of recce officer' clause.

Appendix 4

Anlage zu Lfl.Kdo. 6, Führ.Abt. I., Nr. 1865/45 g.Kdos.
Abschrift von Abschrift!

Der Führer   Hauptquartier, den 1. März 1945.
Gr.B.Nr. 301 / 45 g.Kdos.

1.) Ich beauftrage den Oberstleutnant B a u m b a c h , Kommodore des Kampfgeschwaders 200, mit der Bekämpfung aller feindlichen Übergänge über Oder und Neisse.

2.) Oberstleutnant Baumbach hat hierzu sämtliche geeigneten Kampfmittel aller Wehrmachtteile, der Rüstung und Wirtschaft zum Einsatz zu bringen und hinsichtlich der Durchführung aufeinander abzustimmen.

.) Er untersteht dem Oberbefehlshaber der Luftwaffe und wird eingesetzt im Bereich des Luftflottenkommandos 6.

4.) Durchführung bestimmt er im Einvernehmen mit dem Oberbefehlshaber der Luftwaffe im Einvernehmen mit dem Chef des Oberkommandos der Wehrmacht.

Gez. A d o l f H i t l e r

F.d.R.d.A.

gez. v. Below
O b e r s t

Oberstlt.i.Genst.

2313

Appendix 5/1

Geheime Kommandosache

Luftflotte 6   H.Qu., den 6. 3. 45
Der Oberbefehlshaber   17.Ausfertigung
Nr.85/45 g.Kdos.   1904/5

Betr.: Bekämpfung der fdl. Übergänge über Oder und Neisse.

1.) Der Führer hat mit der Ausschöpfung aller Kampfmittel für die Bekämpfung der Übergänge über Oder und Neisse den Oberstlt. Baumbach beauftragt. Er ist zu Forderungen an OKH und OKM und Verbindungsaufnahme mit den erforderlichen örtl. Kdo.-Stellen des Heeres und der Kriegsmarine berechtigt.

Zur Erfassung aller sonstigen Möglichkeiten, insbes. techn.Art, arbeitet Oberstlt. Baumbach mit dem Reichsminister für Rüstung und Kriegsproduktion sowie mit den örtl. Parteidienststellen und Verwaltungsbehörden (Wasserbauämtern usw.) unmittelbar zusammen.

2.) Unterstellungsverhältnis:

Oberstlt. Baumbach untersteht für seine Person dem Oberbefehlshaber d.Lw. unmittelbar. Zum Einsatz aller Mittel der Luftwaffe ist er dem OB der Lfl.6 einsatzmäßig unterstellt und im Stab Lfl.6 eingesetzt.

3.) Kampfauftrag:

a) Brückenschläge über Oder und Neisse sind ausschlaggebende Voraussetzung für jede fdl. Grossangriffsführung gegen Berlin und in das Herz des Reiches. Ihre rechtzeitige laufende Zerstörung durch die Kampfmittel aller Wehrmachtteile ist daher von schlachtentscheidender, möglicherweise kriegsentscheidender Bedeutung.

b) Oberstlt. Baumbach regelt unter Ausschöpfung aller Möglichkeiten den einheitlichen und sich ergänzenden Einsatz aller Kampfmittel der Lw., des Heeres und der Kriegsmarine gegen fdl. Brückenschläge über Neisse und Oder zwischen Görlitz und Stettin derart, dass diese möglichst rasch nach ihrer Herstellung zerstört werden. Besondere Wichtigkeit kommt der unverzüglichen Brückenvernichtung in den vor Angriffsbeginn erkannten Schwerpunktsabschnitten und in den während der

87

1926

Appendix 5/2

Abwehrkämpfe fallweise sich neubildenden Brennpunkten des Kampfes zu.

In Zusammenarbeit mit Heer und Kriegsmarine hat er dafür Sorge zu tragen, dass im Hinblick auf die Betriebstofflage Lw.-Einsatz nur gegen die Brückenschläge durchgeführt wird, gegen die die Kampfkraft des Heeres und der Kriegsmarine auch unter Zurückstellung anderer Aufgaben nicht zum Einsatz gelangen können.

4.) Im einzelnen ist der Einsatz der Lw.-Verbände wie folgt zu handhaben:

a) Einsatz KG 200 mit Spezialteilen (ferngelenkte Bomben, Mistel usw.) durch Oberstlt. Baumbach unmittelbar.

b) Einsatz der Schlachtverbände des II. und VIII. Flg. Korps ergänzend zu a) ist durch Führ.-Abt. zu veranlassen.

c) Einsatz von Nachtschlachtverbänden des II. und VIII.Flg. Korps, ggf. mit Auslenuchtung wie b).

d) Erprobung, Einsatz und Entwicklungsforderungen aller sonstigen techn. Möglichkeiten der Lw., u.a. "Wasserballon" (auch von Hand einsetzbar), Absprühen von Phosphor oder brennendem Öl usw.

e) Ausnützung aller aus der Brückenbekämpfung sich ergebenden günstigen Möglichkeiten für überraschende oder ergänzende Angriffsführung, z.B. gegen Stauungen und Ansammlungen an angegriffenen Brückenköpfen. Versenchung besonders wichtiger Brückenköpfe mit SD 2 mit Störzündern und Langzeitzündern.

5.) Zwecks Zusammenarbeit mit dem Heer bedient sich Oberstlt. Baumbach je nach taktischen Erfordernissen der Flivos der Lfl.6 bei Heeresgruppen, Armeen oder ggf. Generalkommandos, soweit sie nicht seiner persönlichen Verbindungsaufnahme bedarf, zu der er durch Führerbefehl ermächtigt ist.

Die Kdo.-Dienststellen des Heeres werden gebeten, Oberstlt. Baumbach bei der Durchführung seiner entscheidend wichtigen Aufgabe wo nur irgend möglich zu unterstützen und insbes. Anregungen und Anforderungen hinsichtlich beobachtetem Artl.- Einsatz zur Brückenzerstörung (evtl. Balloneinsatz mit Jagd- und Flakschutz) und Stör- oder Vernichtungsfeuer gegen die

Appendix 5/3

durch Luftangriffe hervorgerufenen Stauungen zu entsprechen. Ferner ist in seinem Auftrag die Ausnützung des Einsatzes von Pionierkampfmitteln und sonstigen Sonderkampfmitteln eingeschlossen.

6.) Zwecks Zusammenarbeit mit der Kriegsmarine zum Einsatz der besonderen Kampfmittel (Kleinkampfmittel) ist er berechtigt, neben den entsprechenden Forderungen an das OKM Verbindung mit den örtl. Marinedienststellen aufzunehmen und sich des NVO der Lfl.6 zu bedienen.

7.) Oberstlt. Baumbach bestellt als ständigen Vertreter und Sonderbearbeiter für den Lw.-Einsatz gegen Brückenseile in der Führungsabt. der Lfl.6 den Führer des Gefechtsverbandes Helbig, Oberst H e l b i g.

Verteiler:

```
Gen.Kdo. II.Flg.Korps ..........  1.Ausf.
Gen.Kdo. VIII.Flg.Korps ........  2.  "
G.n.Kdo. I.Flakkorps ...........  3.  "
Gen.Kdo. II. ...................  4.  "
Okdo. H.Gr.Mitte mit NAf.,4.Pz.Armee ... 5.u.6. Ausf.
Okdo. H.Gr. Weichsel mit NAf.
         9. und 3.Pz.-Armee .....  7., 8.u.9.Ausf.
Mar.Okdo. Ostsee ...............  10. Ausf.
Oberstlt. Baumbach .............  11.  "
Adjutantur d.Wehrm. beim Führer
Lfl.Kdo.6/Ia/Io  Oberst v. Below  12.  "
              /WFSt ............  13.  "
              /O.Qu. ...........  14.  "
              /KTB .............  15.  "
           /OB (lw) ............  16.  "
                                  17.  "
```

v. Rei...
Generaloberst

Appendix 6/1

Gefechtsstand, den 1.5.1945.
59

2.Ausfertigung
Ausfertigung

E i n s a t z b e f e h l .

1.) Lage.

Eisenbahnbrücken Warschau, Deblin und Sandomierz für den Nachschub sowjetischer Angriffsfront lebensnotwendig.

Eisenbahnbrücke Warschau:
Beschaffenheit, siehe Zielunterlagen.

Eisenbahnbrücke Deblin:
Unzureichend teilzerstörte Eisenkonstruktion, instandgesetzt.
Länge 450 m, Breite 10 m.

Eisenbahnbrücke Sandomierz:
Kriegsbrücke Holzkonstruktion, Länge 480 m, Breite 2.50 m.
Nähere Einzelheiten siehe Zielunterlagen.
Flak- und Jagdabwehr gemäß Vororientierung.

2.) II./KG 200 bekämpft am 1.5.45 bei geeigneter Wetterlage diese 3 Brücken.

3.) Kräfte:
6 Mistel I, 8 Mistel III, 9 Zielfinder + 3 Reserveflugzeuge
1 Wetteraufklärer.

4.) Bereitschaft:
a) Bereitschaft für Mistel- und Zielfinderflugzeuge gemäß Vorbefehl so, daß der Start ab 9.00 Uhr erfolgen kann.
b) einsatzmäßige Bereitschaft für Wetteraufklärer ab 4.30 Uhr.

5.) Durchführung:
a) Auslösung des Einsatzes gemäß Wetteraufklärung durch KG 200 mit Stichwort "Brock", Datum, Uhrzeit. Uhrzeit = Startzeit.
b) Hierzu Einsatz eines Wetteraufklärers mit Geschwadermeteorologe. Start 5.00 Uhr
Flugweg: Burg - Qu 15 Ost 9239 - 25 Ost 1378 - 25 Ost 1122 -
15 Ost 9239 - Burg.
Meldungen: Einhalbstündlich Streckenwetter, Zielwetter mit Wetterbeurteilung ob Angriffsdurchführung möglich,
halbstündlich Streckenwetter vom Rückflug.

2309

Appendix 6/2

- 2 -
60

Startfreigabe durch Geschwader.

c) **Wettermindestbedingungen:**
aa) Start: 300 - 500 m Wolkenuntergrenze, Sicht über 5 km.
bb) Frontüberflug: Wolkenuntergrenze 1500 m.
cc) Strecke: mindestens 500 m Untergrenze, 8 - 10/10.
dd) Ziel: mindestens 1000 m Untergrenze, 8 - 10/10, Sicht 10 km.
ee) Rücklandehäfen: Untergrenze 300 m, Sicht 3 - 5 km.

d) **Start:**
Zielgruppenweise in Burg frühestens 09.00 Uhr.
Startreihenfolge: Angriffsgruppe Deblin (5 Mi III, 3 Zielfinder)
Angriffsgruppe Sandomierz (3 Mi III, 3 Zielf.)
Angriffsgruppe Warschau (6 Mi I, 3 Zielfinder)

e) **Marschformation:**
Alle 3 Angriffsgruppen geschlossen bis Abflug des Jagdschutzes.

f) **Flugweg:**
Alle 3 Zielgruppen gemeinsam:Burg - Jüterbog-Damm - Qu 15 Ost
9262. Von dort Angriffsgruppenweise direkt zu den einzelnen Zielen.

g) Aufnahme Jagdschutz gem. mündlicher Rücksprache Einsatzleiter
II./KG 200 - Ia II.Fl.Korps (Armade - Riesenthal).

h) **Flughöhe:**
Auf Anflug: Untere Wolkengrenze, sonst bei Jagdangriff in die Wolken gezogen werden kann

i) **Fliegender Verbandsführer:**
Oblt. Pils, II./KG 200.

k) **Zielmarkierung:**
Durch Zielfinder mit Fühlungshal tor-Leuchtzeichen.

l) **Angriffsziel:**
Entsprechend Startzeit.

m) **Angriffshöhe (Absprengentfernung):**
1000 Meter.

n) **Rückmarsch:**
aa) Zielfinder nach Burg
bb) 109 und 190 auf zugeteilte Rücklandehäfen. 2310

o) **Rücklandehäfen:**
Für Zielfinder:Burg
Für Bf 109 stehen zur Verfügung: Stolp-Reitz, Vietzker-Strand,
Kolberg

Appendix 6/3

Für FW 190 stehen zur Verfügung: Kamenz, Finsterwalde, Dresden-
Klotzsche, Grossenhain, Welzow,
Benneschau, Preschen, Oostelt:
Oberlitz-Süd.

6i

6.) **Beladung:**
Sondermunition .

7.) **Verhalten in besonderen Fällen:** Gemäß mündlicher Anweisung an
Einsatzleiter.

8.) **Firkungsbilder:**
Durch Zielfinder (Handkamera und Robot)

9.) **Nachrichtenbefehl:**
Siehe Anlage.

10.) **Melde- und Berichtswesen:**
Wie bei Unternehmen Drachenhöhle.

11.) **Gefechtsstand KG 200:**
Fliegerhorst Stendal

gez. Bambach

Oberstltn. und Geschwaderkommodore

Verteiler: im Entwurf

Für die Richtigkeit

/ Major

Appendix 7

Erfolgsmeldung
(Kampfverbände)

Tag: 8.3.45.
Stunde:
Melder:
Aufgenommen:

177 | 8.3. 1945

1. Wo... "Ser-Verband Kolbig
2. Verband: II./K.G.200
3. Zahl: 4 Mistel, 5 Ju 188,
4. Typ: 2 Ju 88
5. Startzeit: 09.00 - 09.22 Uhr
6. Ldg.-Zeit:
7a. Angr.-Zeit: 10.00 - 10.12 Uhr
7b. " : Höhe See: auf See a.
8. Auftrag: Angriff auf Brücken hat gehört.

9. Erfolg: 1 Mistel 10.06 Uhr auf
südl. Brücke zu kurz abgekommen,
wegen Treffer in Kurssteuerung.
1 Mistel Treffer hart neben
nördl.Brücke(Mittelstück zerstört.)
1 Mistel auf südl.Brücke von
west nach Ost, Treffer hart
neben Brücke, Mittelstück zerstört.
2 Ju 88 4 Ju 188 Horizontalan-
griff auf Plakstellungen im
Zielgebiet mit 48 50C/SD 1.
Plakstellung Westufer der Oder
250 m west,süd.Brücke stell-
te Feuer ein.
Angriff aus 27oo - 33oo m.

10. Abgebrochen:
a) Zahl: 1 Mistel,
b) Ursache: Fehler in Aberrenganlage.
09.32 Uhr abgesprengen bei Belzig.

11. Bomben (Zahl ...):
10 AB 500/SD 1, 22 AB 70/SD 1.
28 mrk L grün, 2 AB 500/B 3?
28 Zünder 55 b.

12. Abschüsse (Zahl + Art):
keine.

13. Verluste (Zahl + Art durch: 1 Ju 188 To-
talverlust durch Flakvolltreffer.
Absturz SW Finsterwalde,Besatzung
mit Fallschirm abgesprungen.

14. Abwehr:
Jagdabwehr keine.
Erdabwehr südliegende Flak aller
Kaliber.

15. Sonstiges Ziel: Brücke,ein zerstört er-
kannt. Schwimmende Brückentrümmer
in Wasser. 10.05 Uhr Aufschlagbrand
einer Mistel zwischen den Brücken
am Westufer.

16. Wetter:

Kreisvollzugsbericht 22.2oo B 4

1815

Appendix 8

KR Blitz-Fernschreiben!   30.3.1945

An F[...] Flg.Korps, vorgesch.Gefechtsstand Schweidnitz,
Gen.Kdo. VIII. Flg.Korps,
II./K.G. 200, Burg   Oberstlt. Köller
                                            4 Ausfertigungen
                                            4. Ausfertigung

Betr.: Jagdschutz für Mistelangriff E-Brücke Steinau am 31.3.45.

1.) Gefechtsverband Helbig veranlaßt Vormarsch (1 Ju 88 S 3 der
    Ju 188 so, daß Eingreifen dies Flugzeug 10 Minuten vor befohlener
    Aufschlagzeit des Jagdschutzes Flg.Horst Schweidnitz in 300 m
    Höhe im Linkskurve umfliegt Dabei Betrieben EKF und Fallschirm-
    leuchtbombe.

2.) Darauf die sofortiger Start Begleitgruppe (6 Schwärme) und An-
    hängen an Ju 88 S 3 (Ju 188) und Abflug nach Versammlungsort
    Waldenburg. Dabei Steigen auf 2000 m.

3.) Über Waldenburg in Linkskurve werden. Mit Eintreffen Mistelver-
    band (6 Ju 88 mit darauffetzster M 109 und 3 Ju 188) in
    2000 m. bei Frühereintreffen Mistel werden diese in Linkskurve
    über Ort in gleicher Höhe.

4.) Übernahm Jagdschutz durch Jagdverband wird gemeldet durch In-
    flug 1. Mistelflugzeug von links unter Nachzeln am Längsachse
    durch Jagdverbandsführer.

5.) Daraufhin geht Mistelverband mit 3 Schwärmen enger Begleitschutz
    und 3 Schwärmen weiten Begleitschutz auf Malburg.

6.) Voraussichtliche der Versammlungszeit wird fernmündlich durch
    Gefechtsverband Helbig voraus gemeldet.

Verteiler:
Gefechtsverband Helbig 1. Ausf.
Oberst Helbig   2.   "
Lfl.Kdo. 6;   Lfl.Kdo. 6, Der Chef d.Genst.
Chef / I / K.   3.   "   I.V. gez.Schmid, Oberst i.Genst.
Ia Flieg (E)   Führ.Abt. (Ia Flieg)
                                                          4044

Appendix 9

Gejeime Kommandojache!   281

KR - Fernschreiben!   17.4.45.

An
Gefechtsverband Helbig über Lw.Kdo.Nordost, Blesenthal
nachr.:
Lw.Kdo. Nordost,   Blesenthal
OKL, Füst. Ia,   Robinson   3 Ausfertigungen
                                               1. Ausfertigung

1.) Lfl.Kdo. 6 bittet um baldmöglichste Zerstörung der eingleisig
    wiederhergestellten E-Brücke Steinau, durch "Rudnpeck"-Einsatz.

2.) Mitteilung des beabsichtigsten Zeitpunktes der Durchführung so-
    wie der Forderungen bzgl. Jagdschutzzustellung an Ia Flieg.

3.) Fernmündlich voraus.

                                   Lfl.Kdo. 6, Der Chef d.Genst.
                                   gez. K.I.   s Oberst i.G.
                                   Führ.Abt.(Ia Flieg)
                                                          3835

Verteiler:
Chef / I / KFB   1. Ausf.
Ic   2.   "
Ia Flieg (E),   3.   "

Ia/Flieg

17. 4. 1945

V o r t r a g s n o t i z

Betr.: Fliegerführer 200.

1.) Stab Fl.Führer 200 und -tab K.G. 200 seit 6 Tagen in v...
    gung, z.Zt. von Oschatz nach Holzkirchen.
    Oberstlt. Baumbach seit 14 Tagen nicht aufzu...

2.) Unterstellte Verbände wie folgt eingesetzt:
    a) I./K.G. 200 für Aufgaben RKM.
       Unterbringung: Stab u. ...(.200 in Süddeutschland,
    b) II./K.G. 200 Burg.
       Klart Flugzeuge (beleuchtet) der 5./K.G. 200) an I./K.
       ...gebne. In Burg befindliche Kisten können nicht ...
       ...zabeitet werden.
       Personal der Gruppe zur Erdverteidigung Burg eingesetzt.
    c) III./K.G. 200 (KT) Blankense... LG. Reich einsatzmässig
       unterstellt.
    d) Einsatzkommando 200 (FK) 9 He 111 und 1 Do 217 in P.rohm.
       Einsatzmässig Gefechtsverband Helbig unterstellt.

3.) Stab Fliegerführer 200 und Stab K.G. 200 haben z.Zt. keine Aufgaben.
    Bi-reeilte Gruppen sind sich durch andere Dienststellen ein-
    gesetzt.
    Oberstlt. Baumbach hat als Bevollmächtigter für Brückenbe-
    kämpfung bisher nichts wesentliches für die Bekämpfung der
    Oder- und Elbebrücken beigetragen. Alles, was bisher geschehen
    ist, wurde durch Oberst Helbig veranlasst.
    Alle zur Brückenbekämpfung eingesetzten Kräfte (Stab und

-2-

II./L.G. 1, K.G. (z) 30, Restteile II./K.G. 200, Einsatz-
kommando 200 (FK), II./K.G. 4, I./K.G. 66) unterstehen den
Gefechtsverband Helbig, der in jeder Hinsicht der Lw.Kdo.
Nordost unterstellt ist.

4.) Vorschläge:
    a) Auflösung Stab Fl.Führer 200 und Stab K.G. 200. Durchführung
       ...Kdo. West. Personal zur Fallschirmarmee.
    b) ...lösung II./K.G. 200.
    Bei I./K.G. 66 befindliche Teile an dieser Gruppe verstreuen.
    Restliches Personal unter Anrechnung auf Heeresabgaben de.
    örtlichen Abschnittskommandeur in Burg zur Verfügung stellen.
    c) Auflösung Einsatzkommanlo 200 unter Angliederung an II./KG 4.
    d) I./K.G. 200 einsatzmässig Lw Art Kom. (wie bisher),
       truppendienstlich Stab u.Iv L.Kdo.West, 2.Kl., Lfl.Kdo.Reich
    e) III./K.G. (KT) in jeder eisher Lfl. Reich unterstellen.
    f) ...sprechende Befehle durch Gen.Qu. erbitten.

    Varianten:
    Gef Ia

(signature)

197

Appendix 10: Translation

Report Memorandum

Re : Fliegerführer 200
----

1) HQ of Fliegerführer 200 and HQ of KG 200 in transfer for 6 days, for the time being from Oschatz to Holzkirchen. Oberstlt. Baumbach cannot be found for the past 14 days.

2) Subordinated formations operational as follows :

a) I/KG 200 on RSHA tasks.
Deployment : HQ and 1./200 in South Germany
3./200 Bug on the Rügen (island)

b) II/KG 200 at Burg (nr Magdeburg)
Operational aircraft (illuminators of 5./KG 200) to be handed over to I/KG 66. The Mistels based at Burg can no longer be flown out.
The personnel of II/KG 200 is to be used for ground defence at Burg.

c) III/KG 200(BT) at Blankensee subordinated operationally to Luftflotte Reich.

d) Operational Detachment 200 (FK) with 9 He 111 and 1 Do 217 at Parchim; subordinated operationally to Task Force Helbig.

3) HQ of Fliegerführer 200 and HQ of KG 200 have no duties at present. The subordinated Gruppen are all controlled operationally by other command posts.
Oberstlt Baumbach as Plenipotentiary for Combatting the Bridges has not contributed anything substantial to that task. Everything that has taken place to date has been instigated by Oberst Helbig.
All forces used to combat the bridges (HQ and

-2-

II/LG 1, KG(J) 30, remaining parts of II/KG 200, Operational Detachment 200 (FK), II/KG 4 and I/KG 66) are subordinated to Task Force Helbig who in turn is subordinated in every way to Luftwaffenkommando Nordost

4) Proposal :
----

a) Disbandment of HQ Fl.Führer 200 and HQ KG 200, carried out by Luftwaffenkommando West. Personnel to be transferred to the Paratroop Army.

b) Disbandment of II/KG 200. Parts of this Gruppe with I/KG 66 to be transferred to that unit; remaining personnel on account of obligations to the Army put at the disposal of the local Transfer Commander at Burg.

c) Disbandment of Operational Detachment 200 by incorporation into II/KG 4.

d) I/KG 200 remains operationally subordinated to Ia Luft RSHA (as before); in service matters HQ and 1.Staffel to Luftflottenkommando West, 2. and 3./200 to Luftflottenkommando Reich.

e) III/KG 200(BT) to be subordinated in every way to the Luftflotte Reich.

f) Corresponding orders issued via Gen.Qu.2.Abteilung.

Distribution :

Chef Ia
Gen.Qu.2.Abt.
Ia Flieg.

....
(signature)

-2-

Appendix 11

Excerpts regarding KG 200 activities from the Luftflottenkommando 6 War Diary 1945

1 January : Führerbefehl : Oberst Baumbach empowered to combat all enemy crossings over Neisse and Oder rivers. To this end, in addition to KG 200 Baumbach has to 'coordinate and use operationally all suitable means of the armed forces, the armament industry and economy'.

27 February: 35 KG 200 aircraft have to evacuate Garz airfield.

28 February: Orders to KG 200, Stendal : Special operation with Mistels (Ju 88/Bf 109) against the Oder bridges. Minimum fighter escort 1 Gruppe of 30 aircraft from Jüterbog-Damm.

1 March: On orders from the Reichsmarschall KG 200 should be the principal user of guided bombs against the Oder bridges.

1 March: II/KG 200 with 6 Mistels Is, 8 Mistel IIIs, 9 pathfinders, 1 weather and 3 reserve aircraft to attack the railway bridges at Warsaw Deblin and Sandomierz. Take-off from Burg near Magdeburg. Formation leader : Oblt Pilz. Mistel release altitude 1000m. Cover name: Querschnitt durch die Operette Operation cancelled due to unfavourable weather conditions at 1050 hrs; take-off postponed.

3 March: Teleprinter message : the airfields at Rostock, Oranienburg and Lärz are to be prepared for the special operation Vistula Bridges (Mistels and Ju 290).

4 March: 2./KG 200 transfers from Stolp-Reitz to Tutow; 1 Ju 290 and 1 Ar 232 to Rahmel.

5 March: Oberst Helbig made responsible for combatting the Oder and Vistula bridges. Task Force Helbig made up of LG 1, parts of KG 200 and K.d.E (Detachment of Test Centres)

6 March: 4 He 111 of KG 200 escorted by 8 Bf 109 of 1./JG 4 attack the Oder bridge at Görlitz with Hs 293 guided bombs; 1 direct hit. 1 He 111 hit by AA.

8 March: II./KG 200 with 4 Mistels, 5 Ju 188 and 2 Ju 88 attack the Oder bridges at Görlitz. One Mistel operation aborted, 2 Mistel hits close to the bridges; Ju 88 and Ju 188 attacks on AA sites. 1 Ju 188 shot down.

8 March: 7 Ju 87 of SG 151 and 16 FW 190 of I/SG 1 achieve direct hits on the Oder bridges at Auritz and Zellin. 4 Mistels of KG 200 miss the target.

13 March: Experimental Detachment of KG 200 with 3 He 111 and 3 Do 217 with Hs 293 guided bombs attack the bridges at Görlitz. 4 hits, 2 misses.

20 March: 3 He 111 and 3 Do 217; 2 hits, 1 defective drop (Hs 293?)

22 March: Same formation; 2 hits (Hs 293?)

23 March: Same formation, 4 failures (Hs 293?)

24 March: II/KG 200 actual strength : 18 Ju 88A and S; 9 Ju 199A and E; 2 Mistel II; 3 Mistel III.

25 March: Attack on bridges at 1325 hrs : 2 He 111 of KG 200 with Hs 293, 1 hit Görlitz-Nord; 2 He 111 of KG 200 with Hs 293; 1 hit Görlitz-Süd

25 March: KGr.Freih. (Freiheit ?) with 20 Ju 88s attached to KG 200

26 March: 4 He 111 and 4 Do 217 of Exp.Detachment KG 200 attack the Görlitz and Lebus bridges with Hs 293. 1 hit, 1 near miss at Görlitz; 1 hit Lebus

28 March: 'Supply of special jettisonable ammunition to combat the Oder bridges(the so-called Wasserballon or Water balloons) expected shortly.'

31 March: Order to carry out a Mistel attack on the railway bridge at Steinau; 6 Mistels, 3 Ju 188, 1 Ju 88S.

Appendix 13

Führungsabteilung I/Ic   Aktennotiz

Betr.: Einsatz Ju 290 nach Spanien.

Nach Rücksprache mit Oberstlt.i.G.Kienitz, Chef/Ic i.V.
wurde festgelegt, daß für Überbringung einer Delegation
nach Spanien 1 aufgerüstete Ju 290 des K.G. 200 eingesetzt
werden soll.

Von einem Umspritzen des Flugzeuges soll irgend einer
Tarnung ist abzusehen.

Besatzung fliegt in Uniform wie zum Feindflug.

Major i.G.

Verteiler:
I/KTB
Ic (zum Akt Abwehr)

Appendix 12

Luftflottenkommando 6
Führungsabteilung I/Ic
Br.B.Nr.1116/45 g.Kdos.

Aktennotiz

Betr.: Flugzeugführg Ju 290, Hptm.Braun Ic/K.G.200
HQrpshing - Barcelona.

Hauptmann Braun wurde als Flugzeugführer und Kommandant
Ju 290 Pj + PS mündlich durch Major i.Genst.Hollmann in
folgenden Auftrag eingewiesen:

Hauptmann Braun mit Besatzung:

Hptm.Braun	1.Flugzeugführer u.Kommandant
Ofw.Aufdemkamp	2."
Oblt. Haseld	Beobachter
Ofw. Thraus	1.Funker
Uffz.Schlegel	2."
Ofw. Burow	1.Mechaniker
Ofw. Mossloch	2."
Uffz.Krippner	Bordschütze
" Schmidt	"
" Eickeldorfer	"
" Titschkus	1.Wart

fliegt sobald als möglich bei höchst geeigneter Wetterlage
eine von OB fest bestimmte Personengruppe nach Barcelona.

Sofern nach Landung Rückflug nicht möglich und Internierung
erfolgt, ist Hauptmann Braun beauftragt, sich bis zum deutschen
Luftattaché in Madrid zu melden und diesem das Flugzeug in
Überführungszustand zum Verkauf an die Spanier zur Verfügung zu
stellen.

Hauptm.Braun wurde belehrt, daß die Besatzung weiterhin
als Soldaten gelten und dahingehend den militärischen Gesetzen
unterstellt bleiben. Auf strengste Verschwiegenheit in allen
militärischen Angelegenheiten und insbesondere in Bezug dieses
Sonderauftrages wurde Hptm.Braun hingewiesen.

Major i.Genst.

zur Kenntnis genommen und
Verpflichtung unterschrieben:

Hauptmann

6.B.:

Verteiler:
I./K.G.200 Kdr. 1.Ausf.
Chef/I/KTB, Ic(z.Akt Abwehr) 3.Ausf.
2.Ausf.

Appendices 12 and 13: Translation

Luftflottenkommando 6
Führungsstab I/Ic
Br.B.No 1136/45 Secret Command Matter

O.U.
30 April 1945
3 copies

2nd copy

File Memorandum

Re Flight order for Ju 290
Hptm Braun I/KG 200
Hörsching-Barcelona

Hauptmann Braun, pilot and captain of Ju 290 PJ + PS has been advised orally by Major (General Staff) Bellman regarding the following task:

Hauptmann Braun with the crew:

Hptm braun	1st pilot and captain
Ofw Aufdemkamp	2nd pilot
Oblt Hasold	Observer
Ofw Throne	1st radio operator
Uffz Schlegel	2nd radio operator
Ofw Burow	1st flight mechanic
Uffz Mosblech	2nd flight mechanic
Uffz Krippner	Gunner
Uffz Schmidt	Gunner
Uffz Etzelsdorfer	Gunner
Uffz Titschkus	1st engineer

will fly a group of persons appointed by the C-in-C as soon as possible, during the first suitable weather conditions, to Barcelona.

If, after landing, a return flight is not possible and an internment takes place, Hptm Braun is instructed to contact the German Air Attache in Madrid and put his aircraft at his disposal for sale to the Spanish.

Hptm Braun has been advised that in these circumstances members of his crew still come under military law. Hptm Braun has also been advised about strict discretion regarding all military matters and particularly this task.

Taken note of and signed
confirming commitment

(Braun)   By order
Hptm   (Bellmann)
                           Major (GenStaff)

Distribution: I/KG 200 Kdr   1st copy
              Chef/I/KTB   2nd copy
              Ic (to Abwehrfile) 3rd copy

Führungsabteilung I/Ic   30 April 1945

File Memorandum

Re Ju 290 flight to Spain

Following consultation with Oberstlt (GenStaff) Kiemitz, acting Chief of Ic (Intelligence) it has been established that one Ju 290 of KG 200 should be used to transport a delegation to Spain.

No attempt should be made to respray or camouflage the aircraft in any way.

The crew will fly in uniform as on an operational flight.

                                    (signed)
                                    ....
                                    Major (GenStaff)

Distribution:
I/KTB (War Diary)
Ic (Intelligence)
(for Abwehr file)

Appendix 14

Lfd. Nr. des Fluges	Führer	Begleiter	Muster	Zulassungs-Nr.	Zweck des Fluges	Abflug Ort
49	Hptm. Za:flehn	Obl. v. Fuhrmann	Ju 290	9V+FH	8. Feindflug	Belgrad - Emilia
50	" " "	" " "	" "	" "	Überführung z. Einsatz	Agen - Belawas
51	" " "	" " "	" "	" "	9. Feindflug	Veliki - Maza
52	" " "	" " "	" "	" "	10. Feindflug	Veliki - Maza
53	" " "	" " "		" "	Rücküberführung	Wien - Agram
54	Ofw. Knappenschneider	" " "	B 17 G	A 3+BB	Überprüfung	Finow
55	" " "	" " "	" "	" "	Überführung z. Einsatz	Finow
56	" " "	" " "	" "	" "	" " "	Großhausen
57	" " "	" " "	" "	" "	11. Feindflug	Helmstedingen
58	" " "	" " "	" "	" "	12. Feindflug	Helmstedingen

Lfd. Nr. des Fluges	Führer	Begleiter	Muster	Zulassungs-Nr.	Zweck des Fluges	Abflug Ort
59	Ofw. Knappenschneider	Obl. v. Fuhrmann	B 17 G	A 3+BB	Rücküberführung	Helmstedingen
60	" " "	" " "	" "	" "	" " "	Finsterwalde
61	Hptm. Zacklehn	" " "	Ju 290	A3+OB	Überführung z. Einsatz	Bolz - Britz
62	" " "	" " "	" "	" "	13. Feindflug	Gurgrugund
63	" " "	" " "	" "	" "	Überführung z. Einsatz	Bolz - Reitz
64	" " "	" " "	" "	" "	14. Feindflug	Gurgrugund
65	" " "	" " "	" "	" "	Rücküberführung	Gurgrugund
66	" " "	" " "	" "	" "	Überführung	Bolz - Britz
67	" " "	" " "	" "	" "	" " "	Gurgrugund
68	" " "	" " "	" "	" "	Überführung z. Einsatz	Fotos - Eud
69	" " "	" " "	" "	" "	15. Feindflug	Berlin - Süd
70	" " "	" " "	" "	" "	Überführung z. Einsatz	Fotos - Eud

202

Flug		Landung			Flugdauer	Kilometer	Bemerkungen
Tag	Tageszeit	Ort	Tag	Tageszeit			
5.10.44	02.28	Ügau–Balauski	5.10.44	05.21	2.53	2..	
6.10.44	05.20	Balauski–Maga	6.10.44	07.00	1.40	25	Luftschiff durch eigene Flak über Jellis
7.10.44	17.38	Balaiski–Maga	8.10.44	16.01	12.23	21–29	Unternehmen Jagdwal (...)
9.10.44	03.40	Minsk–Agram	9.10.44	07.14	3.34		Die Richtigkeit der Flüge v. Nr. 45 b 53 bescheinigt:
9.10.44	12.59	Firueo	9.10.44	15.10	2..		i.V. ...3 Leutnant
8.1.45	13.57	Finono	8.1.45	14.46	0.49		
9.1.45	10.10	Großenhain	9.1.45	11.06	0.56		Luftschiff durch eigene Flak
10.1.45	08.10	Festodingen	10.1.45	09.35	1.25		
12.1.45	20.30	Festodingen	13.1.45	02.40	6.10		Unternehmen Labella Luftschiff durch Feindflak
13.1.45	23.30	Festodingen	14.1.45	06.05	6.35		Unternehmen Fallschirmjäger ...

Flug		Landung			Flugdauer	Kilometer	Bemerkungen
Tag	Tageszeit	Ort	Tag	Tageszeit			
16.1.45	10.10	Finsterwalde	16.1.45	12.05	1.55		
17.1.45	09.45	Finono	17.1.45	10.10	0.25		
3.2.45	15.40	Gaggengrund	3.2.45	16.08	0.28		
4.2.45	22.07	Pölz–Beitz	5.2.45	06.11	8.04		... m. Flak Einsatz Nauoa I, II, IV, ohne Erfolg (...)
18.2.45	15.32	Gaggengrund	18.2.45	16.00	0.28		
18.2.45	18.25	Gaggengrund	19.2.45	02.38	8.13		eigene Flak und Scheinwerfer Einsatz Raumfeuer ohne Erfolg (...)
19.2.45	06.17	Pölz–Beitz	19.2.45	06.41	0.24		
6.3.45	06.20	Gaggengrund	6.3.45	06.53	0.33		
11.3.45	06.47	Litov–Süd	11.3.45	08.23	1.36		Frontflug
18.3.45	15.38	Beslin–Lag	18.3.45	15.58	0.20		
18.3.45	18.14	Litov–Süd	19.3.45	02.46	8.32		Scho. Flak. Einsatz Raumfeuer mit Erfolg
19.3.45	18.08	Beslin–Lag	19.3.45	18.28	0.20		

Appendix 15: Translated excerpt from KG 200 pilot's logbook

Flight No	Pilot	2nd Pilot	A/c type	Markings	Reason	Take-off airfield	Date	Time
59	" "	" "	B-17G	"	Ferry	Echterdingen	16.1.45	1010
60	" "	" "	B-17G	"	Ferry	Finsterwalde	17.1.45	0945
61	Hptm Sachtleben	" "	Ju 290	A3 + OB	Ferry	Stolp-Reitz	3.2.45	1540
62	" "	" "	Ju 290	"	13th op. flight	Hexengrund	4.2.45	2207
63	" "	" "	Ju 290	"	Ferry	Stolp-Reitz	18.2.45	1532
64	" "	" "	Ju 290	"	14th op. flight	Hexengrund	18.2.45	1825
65	" "	" "	Ju 290	"	Ferry	Hexengrund	19.2.45	0617
66	" "	" "	Ju 290	"	Ferry	Stolp-Reitz	6.3.45	0620
67	" "	" "	Ju 290	"	Ferry	Hexengrund	11.3.45	0647
68	" "	" "	Ju 290	"	Ferry	Tutow-Süd	18.3.45	1538
69	" "	" "	Ju 290	"	15th op. flight	Rechlin-Lärz	18.3.45	1814
70	" "	" "	Ju 290	"	Ferry	Tutow-Süd	19.3.45	1808

Flight No	Pilot	2nd Pilot	A/c type	Markings	Reason	Take-off airfield	Date	Time
49	Hptm Sachtleben	Oblt v.Pechmann	Ju 290	9V + FH	8th op. flight	Belgrade-Semlies(?)	5.10.44	0228
50	" "	" "	Ju 290	"	Ferry	Athens-Kalamaki	6.10.44	0520
51	" "	" "	Ju 290	"	9th op. flight	Saloniki-Mega	7.10.44	1738
52	" "	" "	Ju 290	"	10th op flight	Saloniki-Mega	9.10.44	0340
53	" "	" "	Ju 290	"	Ferry	Vienna-Aspern	9.10.44	1259
54	Ofw Knappenschneider	"	B-17G	A3 + BB	Workshop test flight	Finow	8.1.45	1357
55	" "	" "	B-17G	"	Ferry	Finow	9.1.45	1010
56	" "	" "	B-17G	"	Ferry	Grossenhain	10.1.45	0810
57	" "	" "	B-17G	"	11th op. flight	Echterdingen	12.1.45	2030
58	" "	" "	B-17G	"	12th op. flight	Echterdingen	13.1.45	2330

Landing airfield	Date	Time	Duration hrs	Remarks
Finsterwalde	16.1.45	1205	1.55	-
Finow	17.1.45	1010	0.25	-
Hexengrund	3.2.45	1608	0.28	
Stolp-Reitz	5.2.45	0611	8.04	Well laid medium AA. Operation Narva I,II,IV - unsuccessful ; bad weather conditions
Hexengrund	18.2.45	1600	0.28	-
Hexengrund	19.2.45	0238	8.13	Heavy AA fire and searchlights. Operation Rennstrecke, unsuccessful ; bad weather conditions
Stolp-Reitz	19.2.45	0641	0.24	-
Hexengrund	6.3.45	0653	0.33	-
Tutow-Süd	11.3.45	0823	1.36	Operational flight
Rechlin-Lärz	18.3.45	1558	0.20	-
Tutow-Süd	19.3.45	0246	8.32	Heavy AA fire. Operation Rennstrecke, successful
Rechlin-Lärz	19.3.45	1828	0.20	-

Landing airfield	Date	Time	Duration hrs	Remarks
Athens-Kalamaki	5.10.44	0521	2.53	-
Saloniki-Mega	6.10.44	0700	1.40	Fired on by own Flak over Chelois
Saloniki-Mega	8.10.44	0601	12.23	Operation Parsival (Algiers) - unsuccessful
Vienna-Aspern	9.10.44	0714	3.34	-
Finow	9.10.44	1510	2.11	-
Finow	8.1.45	1446	0.49	
Grossenhain	9.1.45	1106	0.56	Fired on by own Flak
Echterdingen	10.1.45	0935	1.25	-
Echterdingen	13.1.45	0240	6.10	Operation Kadella. Fired on by enemy AA
Echterdingen	14.1.45	0605	6.35	Operation Perlenfischer

Appendix 16: Home-made discharge paper from *Olga*

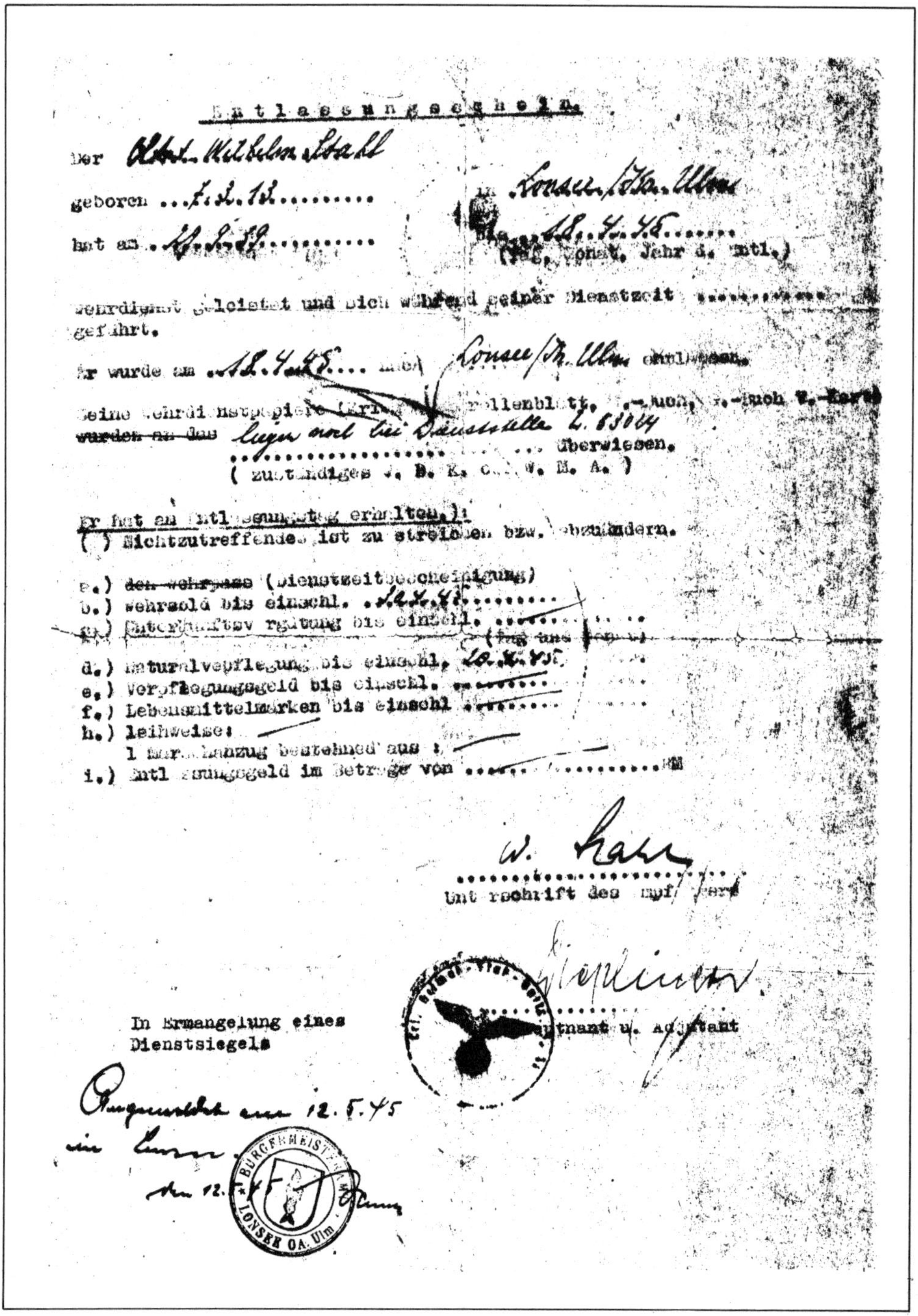

Entlassungsschein.

Der Obgfr. Wilhelm Stahl

geboren ...7.2.13......... in Lonsee/Kr. Ulm

hat am ..26.8.39.......... bis ..18.4.45......
(Tag, Monat, Jahr d. Entl.)

Wehrdienst geleistet und sich während seiner Dienstzeit .... geführt.

Er wurde am ..18.4.45.... nach Lonsee/Kr. Ulm entlassen.

Seine Wehrdienstpapiere (Kriegs... Wehrstammblatt, ...buch, ...buch u. Kart.) ~~wurden an das~~ liegen noch bei Dienststelle L 63064 .... überwiesen.
(zuständiges W. B. K. o. ... W. M. A.)

~~Er hat am Entlassungstag erhalten:~~
( ) Nichtzutreffendes ist zu streichen bzw. abzuändern.

a.) ~~den Wehrpass~~ (Dienstzeitbescheinigung)
b.) Wehrsold bis einschl. ..14.4.45........
c.) Unterkunftsvergütung bis einschl. ....
(Tag des ...)
d.) Naturalverpflegung bis einschl. 20.4.45
e.) Verpflegungsgeld bis einschl. ....
f.) Lebensmittelmarken bis einschl ....
h.) leihweise:
1 Marschanzug bestehend aus :
i.) Entlassungsgeld im Betrage von ....RM

W. Hahn
....
Unterschrift des Empfängers

....
...leutnant u. Adjutant

In Ermangelung eines Dienstsiegels

Angemeldet am 12.5.45 in Lonsee

den 12.5.45

BÜRGERMEISTERAMT LONSEE OA. Ulm